STUDIES IN ENGLISH LITERATURE

Volume 110

CRAFTSMANSHIP IN CONTEXT

The development of Ben Jonson's Poetry

by

JUDITH KEGAN GARDINER

University of Illinois at Chicago Circle

1975

MOUTON

THE HAGUE . PARIS

ISBN 90 279 3191 7

Printed in Belgium, by N.I.C.I., Ghent.

PR
2631
.G3

For my parents, my children, and Richard

With special thanks to Joseph A. Mazzeo,
  P. Jeffrey Ford,
  and the helpful friends who
  read the manuscript

ACKNOWLEDGEMENTS

The editors of *Style* and of *Concerning Poetry* have granted permission to reprint some of the analyses appearing here in Chapter Three.

CONTENTS

CONTENTS

1. INTRODUCTION

A limited figure, Ben Jonson is continually exceeding our notions of his limits. His nondramatic poetry, like his personality, appears simple. On closer study, both reveal surprising diversity and richness. According to his contemporary biographer, William Drummond of Hawthornden, Jonson liked to refer to himself as "the Poet".[1] He called his early epigrams the "ripest" of his "studies"; he referred to his plays as dramatic "poems"; and he appears to have preferred writing nondramatic poetry to writing plays. In the Cary-Morison ode written near the end of his career, Jonson contrasted the tree that grows in bulk for three hundred years with the "Lillie of a Day"[2] and implied that his writing for the popular stage was like the oak, his lyrics like the smaller, more precious flowers. Yet most of the bulky criticism of the past three hundred years has gone to Jonson's great comedies. Long overshadowed by the very different accomplishments of his great

---

[1] "Ben Jonson's Conversations with William Drummond of Hawthornden", 1. 636. Biographical information and documents, Jonson's plays and prose are cited from *Ben Jonson*, ed. by C. H. Herford, Percy Simpson, and Evelyn Simpson, 11 vols. (Oxford: Clarendon, 1925-52), hereafter abbreviated as H & S. Quotations from Jonson's plays, *Conversations*, and *Discoveries* in this essay cite the H & S line number in the text, preceded by identifying abbreviations.

[2] William B. Hunter, Jr., ed., *The Complete Poetry of Ben Jonson* (New York: W. W. Norton, 1968), 3. All quotations from Jonson's poetry are from Hunter's edition. Epigrams are identified in the text in lower case Roman numerals; poems from *The Forrest* are identified by upper case Roman numerals; poems from *Under-wood* are given according to Hunter's numeration in arabic numerals, and poems from the uncollected poetry by Hunter's numbers in arabic numerals preceded by 'Uc'.

coevals Shakespeare and Donne, Jonson's nondramatic poetry is just beginning to receive some of the attention it deserves.

This study discusses Jonson's nondramatic poems in their primary context, the three printed collections of his nondramatic verse. Jonson's nondramatic poetry is not static; it develops from his earlier to his later work. Moreover, developments in his nondramatic poetry are analogous with similar changes in Jonson's plays and masques written over the nearly forty years of his career as an author. Jonson's poetry has rarely been studied chronologically, and it has usually been slighted in treatments of the plays and masques. Before turning to the three collections of Jonson's nondramatic poetry, then, it may be useful to survey some of the current schemes of reference into which Jonson's work has been set, the modern proscenium arches that tend to frame our approaches to Jonson's work.

One of the persistent ironies of Jonson criticism is that where we have liked, we have rarely loved too much. Jonson's critics tend to sound defensive, sometimes even offensive, about his character. All of Ben Jonson's work radiates "an intense sense of personality", as one of his modern readers comments.[3] Jonson is a more "personal" poet than Sidney in that he puts more of his own experience into his literary work, according to another.[4] Whether or not he put more of himself into his poems than others did, his critics have been able to get more of Jonson out. In this sense, Jonson is a more "personal" poet than almost all of his contemporaries. Available information about his life, works, habits, patrons, and friends, about his literary theories and sources probably surpasses that available for any other major figure of the English Renaissance. Yet the apparently solid figure tends to fragment on closer view like the bright colors of an Impressionist painting. The wealth of historical and biographical information about him is accompanied by an even greater plenitude of myth, anecdote, and conjecture.

[3] Jonas A. Barish, "Introduction", *Ben Jonson: A Collection of Critical Essays* (Englewood Cliffs: Prentice-Hall, 1963), 8.
[4] Wesley Trimpi, *Ben Jonson's Poems: A Study of The Plain Style* (Palo Alto: Stanford, 1962), 234.

Jonson's friendships and his enmities were unusually strong and his influence enormous, so that much colorful contemporary description of him has come down to us. The most significant early work about Jonson is Drummond's *Conversations*, possibly transcribed from Jonson's own words in 1618-19. Drummond's report, states Douglas Bush, "has contributed more than anything else to establish in place of the magnanimous Renaissance humanist and poet, the popular picture of a burly, arrogant, swashbuckling toper and scabrous gossip".[5] Most of Jonson's critics since Thomas Dekker have concurred with Drummond's view of Jonson's character. Edmund Wilson translated the usual Renaissance charges against Jonson through the filter of modern psychoanalysis and discovered that Jonson's character and works were those of a disagreeable anal compulsive neurotic.[6] Even a recent partisan like Jonas Barish labels Jonson insecure, envious, and suspicious.[7]

When Jonson's critics discuss his work as separate from the man, they often find that this intrusively personal poet is unoriginal, unspontaneous, mechanical, and impersonal. Algernon Swinburne ranked Jonson highest among the "giants of energy and invention" in English poetry, but found him inferior to creative "gods" like Shakespeare in lyric singing power and imagination.[8] Ralph Walker insists that Jonson's poetry must be "depersonalized" from the bricklayer who wrote it.[9] Many of Jonson's recent

[5] Douglas Bush, *English Literature in the Earlier Seventeenth Century, 1600-1660*, 2d ed. (Oxford: Clarendon, 1962), 231.

[6] Edmund Wilson, "Morose Ben Jonson", *The Triple Thinkers* (New York: Oxford, 1948), 213-32; reprinted in Barish, *Essays*, 60-74. John T. French, "Ben Jonson: His Aesthetic of Relief", *Texas Studies in Literature and Language*, 10 (1968), 161-75, follows in Wilson's tracks. Barish's "Introduction" gives a history of early Jonson criticism, and J. G. Nichols, *The Poetry of Ben Jonson* (London: Routledge & Kegan Paul, 1969), 1-55, extends the review of criticism's negative bias toward Jonson.

[7] Barish, *Ben Jonson and the Language of Prose Comedy* (Cambridge, Mass.: Harvard, 1960), 88. Alvin Kernan's studies of satire show the consistency of the attribution of these characteristics as a result of the contradictions of the *persona* they adopt, *The Cankered Muse: Satire of the English Renaissance* (*Yale Studies in English*, 142) (New Haven: Yale, 1959), 137-40, and *The Plot of Satire* (New Haven: Yale, 1965), 5-6.

[8] Algernon C. Swinburne, *Ben Jonson* (London: Chatto & Windus, 1889), 3.

[9] Ralph Walker, "Ben Jonson's Lyric Poetry", *Criterion*, 13 (1933-34), 430-48.

critics have avoided the pitfalls of prejudice and inconsistency at the expense of breadth of coverage. Typically, they restrict themselves to one *genre* or aspect of Jonson's work, and their restricted views then lead them to draw very different pictures of Jonson's artistic development. Those trying to trace how Jonson's drama develops usually divide his work into three parts: the apprentice works and the four 'humor' comedies written within four years; the four great comic masterpieces written within eight years and flanked by the two tragedies; and the four late plays or "dotages" spread over a sixteen-year period.[10]

To many readers, Jonson's dramatic work seems static. Edward Partridge, concentrating on Jonson's imagery, and Robert Knoll, studying his structures and plots, see Jonson's work as monolithic.[11] To these critics the same central concerns dominate all the plays, including ideas such as authority and its abuses, true and false religion, self-deception and deception of others, and appearance and reality. They see Jonson as a man using the same themes and philosophical ideas throughout his life, whose only growth was in the artistic use of these set themes in his great middle plays. On the other hand, John Enck believes that Jonson's plays are constantly innovative. To him each play is a *genre* in itself.[12]

The pictures of Jonson and his art that emerge from the recent studies of his masques are again different from these images of Jonson as playwright. The writers on Jonson's masques stress his attempts to unify the 'body' of the form, that is, its multiple elements of spectacle, music, and dance, with its 'soul' of poetry through the uses of a symbolic 'hinge'. Like the critics of Jonson's plays, writers on Jonson's masques are divided. Some critics like John Meagher and Todd Furniss concentrate on the uniform

---

[10] The term is from John Dryden's "An Essay of Dramatick Poesie" in *The Works of John Dryden*, ed. by H. T. Swedenberg, Jr., *et. al.*, 17 (Berkeley: U. of California, 1971), 57.
[11] Edward B. Partridge, *The Broken Compass: A Study of the Major Comedies of Ben Jonson* (London: Chatto & Windus, 1958); and Robert E. Knoll, *Ben Jonson's Plays: An Introduction* (Lincoln: U. of Nebraska, 1964).
[12] John J. Enck, *Jonson and the Comic Truth* (Madison: U. of Wisconsin, 1957).

techniques and ideals of the masques, while others trace chronological developments.[13] C. H. Herford and Percy and Evelyn Simpson watch the precarious unity of the early masques disintegrate as comic realism and visual spectacle gain dominance, whereas Stephen Orgel accents Jonson's growing mastery of the various elements of the masque from the period 1605 to 1625 and discusses the changing nature of Jonson's collaboration with Inigo Jones.[14]

The sour but lively satirist of the public stage and the gracefully allegorizing eulogist of the court thus seem to be quite different men and different kinds of artists. Both these sides of Jonson's career may be shown to rest in attitudes common to the moralistic tradition of Christian humanism, though this generalization does not go far toward a specific comprehension of Jonson's work. It is always within the critic's power to abstract an author – or a *genre*, or an age – to some basic common denominator. This approach is particularly easy in the case of Jonson, since his professed critical views and opinions in the *Conversations*, in his prose *Discoveries*, and in the prefaces to his plays are remarkably consistent. Jonson's theory changes much less than does his practice, and even in his practice enough is constant to validate many selective generalizations about the nature of his work. On the other hand, it is easy to knock down half a strawman, so that we find some readers now reasserting the sensual elements in Jonson's writing over the rational, or the comic over the serious, or the moral over the comic, or the static over the dramatic, or the Christian over the classical.

Another way to try to harmonize the apparent differences between Jonson's plays and his masques is to refer them to the varying tastes of their two audiences, the city playgoers and the court masquers. However, these audiences were not totally sep-

---

13 John C. Meagher, *Method and Meaning in Jonson's Masques* (Notre Dame: U. of Notre Dame, 1966); and W. Todd Furniss, *Ben Jonson's Masques*, in *Three Studies in the Renaissance*, ed. by B. C. Nangle (*Yale Studies in English*, 138) (New Haven: Yale, 1958), 97-179.

14 H & S, 2, 247-334; Stephen Orgel, *The Jonsonian Masque* (Cambridge, Mass.: Harvard, 1965); Orgel, ed., *Ben Jonson: The Complete Masques* (New Haven: Yale, 1969), 1-39; Orgel, "To Make Boards Speak: Inigo Jones' Stage and the Jonsonian Masque", *Renaissance Drama*, n.s. 1 (1968), 121-52.

arate. Aristocrats attended public plays, and Jonson's plays were performed at court, at the children's and later adults' 'private' indoor theaters, and at several of the popular outdoor theaters. It is extremely difficult to explain any aspect of Jonson's work simply by a reference to his audience or to contemporary tastes. Neither his public plays nor his court masques were uniformly successful with their audiences.[15] Jonson varied his usual contempt for his audiences with an occasional conciliatory note, but he usually looked past his real viewers to an ideal audience of learned minds committed to poetry. Perhaps the only audience Jonson consistently cared for, and pleased, was himself.

A more satisfactory concept than that of audience for the discrimination of Jonson's work is that of decorum, which includes fitness of manner to matter, not only to the intended audience of a work but also to its speaker, occasion, and *genre*. Jonson indicated his continued devotion to the Horatian model of decorum by his translations of Horace's *Art of Poetry*.[16] The concept of decorum is certainly relevant to all *genres* of Jonson's writing, though the interaction between Jonson's uses of the literary conventions on which decorum is based and his deliberate recasting of them is extremely complex. The third major category of Jonson's writing, his nondramatic poetry, has been given much less attention than his poetry or plays. When it has been studied in its own right, it has been approached chiefly in terms of decorum, and, more particularly, of *genre* study and the history of style.

Several characteristics of Jonson's poetry have contributed to its critical neglect. The nondramatic poetry is uneven in quality, and much of it is occasional and commendatory verse, forms which

---

[15] For criticism of the 'two audiences' idea, see Alfred Harbage, *Shakespeare's Audience* (New York: Columbia, 1941), 139ff.; and Brian Gibbons, *Jacobean City Comedy: A Study of Satiric Plays by Jonson, Marston, and Middleton* (London: Hart-Davis, 1968), 27. Later Harbage discussed the audiences of the public and private theaters, *Shakespeare and the Rival Traditions* (New York: Macmillan, 1952). W. David Kay, "The Shaping of Ben Jonson's Career: A Reexamination of Facts and Problems", *Modern Philology*, 67 (1970), 224-37, discusses the popularity of the plays; Orgel, *Complete Masques*, 22ff., the unpopularity of many of the masques.

[16] H & S, 8, 303-355, print the two versions of *Horace His Art of Poetry*, with Jonson's Latin text, made ca. 1605 and after 1610.

have lost favor since the seventeenth century. Moreover, just as Jonson's dramas suffered from comparisons with Shakespeare, so his lyric poetry for a time was shadowed by incessant comparisons with Donne, who was favored for his passionate intensity and psychological realism. In other words, the current of taste has generally not favored Jonson's kind of poetry, and he has therefore been admired by but a few, and for only a few of his poems.

In addition to this central problem of taste, questions of chronology and originality have long clouded the study of Jonson's verse. Many of his poems are difficult to date; his critics have therefore avoided a chronological approach and turned instead to Jonson's sources and *genres*. Since Jonson was a copious translator and a deliberate adapter of the classic forms into English, the tracing of his sources has been a major preoccupation, and the discovery of close classical originals for many of his poems produced among many of Jonson's earlier critics a distaste for his supposed plagiarism. This complaint against Jonson is an old one. Inigo Jones jibed, "the good's translation, butt the ill's thyne owne", and Herford and Simpson comment that this is a "brilliant hit".[17] By now, the creative viability of Jonson's free adaptations from the classics is clear, though critics still deride his more exact translations as wooden. Dryden's generous view was that Jonson "invades authors like a monarch, and what would be theft in others is victory in him".[18]

The admirers of Jonson's poetry have tended to isolate separate aspects of it for their approval. He appears variously to his modern readers as the pure Elizabethan lyrist, the true neoclassical predecessor of Pope, the vigorous man of wit in the line of Donne, the esthete, the "moralist with no pulpit", the Augustinian Christian, and the one fully serious satirist of the English Renaissance.[19]

---

17 H & S, 11, 385-86.
18 Dryden, "Dramatick Poesie", 57.
19 In order, Willa McClung Evans, *Ben Jonson and Elizabethan Music* (New York: Da Capo, 1965, c. 1929); Felix Schelling, *Ben Jonson and the Classical School* (Baltimore: Modern Language Publications, 1898) and Louis I. Bredvold, "The Rise of English Classicism: A Study in Methodology", *Comparative Literature*, 2 (1950), 235-68; F. R. Leavis, "The Line of Wit", *Revaluation: Tradition and Development in English Poetry* (New York: W. W.

T. S. Eliot described Jonson's poetry as "of the surface", and Earl Miner defines him as a leader of the "social mode" in seventeenth-century poetry.[20] In short, Jonson's poetry is often pronounced good, and good for us, without necessarily seeming warm, interesting, compelling, or deep. Yet Jonson's nondramatic verse is more various and subtle than these views indicate. The first book devoted exclusively to Jonson's poetry, George Johnston's *Ben Jonson: Poet* of 1945, sought to emphasize Jonson's range of abilities.[21]

The most influential book devoted to Jonson's nondramatic poetry is still Wesley Trimpi's *Ben Jonson's Poems: A Study of the Plain Style*, published in 1962. Trimpi follows Yvor Winters' revaluation of sixteenth-century poetry in favor of the authors of "the plain tradition, that is to say, the great tradition".[22] In these articles of 1939 Winters judges Jonson's lyrics superior to those of Sidney and Shakespeare. The qualities of Jonson's verse that Winters and Trimpi admire are its logical disposition, clarity, directness, strength, urbanity, and adjustment of motive to feeling. Winters introduces terms for describing the plain style and criteria for preferring it to the aureate strain of Elizabethan poetry. He also gives suggestive examples of how to discuss poems of simple denotative diction and obvious meaning. Believing Winters' appraisals and using his terms, Trimpi returns to Jonson's classical sources in order to derive Jonson's plain style from them.

Norton, 1963, c. 1947), 10-36; Walker, "Jonson's Lyric"; John Hollander, "Introduction", *Ben Jonson* (New York: Dell, 1961), 9-26; Kay, "The Christian Wisdom of Ben Jonson's 'On My First Sonne'", *Studies in English Literature*, 11 (1971), 125-36; Kernan, *Cankered Muse*, vii.

[20] Eliot is talking about Jonson's dramatic, as well as his nondramatic, poetry, "Ben Jonson", *Essays on Elizabethan Drama* (New York: Harcourt Brace, 1956, c. 1932), 65-82, reprinted in Barish, *Essays*, 14-23; Earl Miner, *The Cavalier Mode from Jonson to Cotton* (Princeton: Princeton, 1971).

[21] George B. Johnston, *Ben Jonson: Poet* (New York: Columbia, 1945).

[22] Yvor Winters, "The Sixteenth-Century Lyric in England: A Critical and Historical Reinterpretation", *Poetry*, 53 (1939), 258-72, 320-35; 54 (1939), 35-51, reprinted in *Elizabethan Poetry: Modern Essays in Criticism*, ed. by Paul J. Alpers (New York: Oxford, 1967), 93-125; and Winters, "Poetic Styles, Old and New" in *Four Poets on Poetry*, ed. by D. C. Allen (Baltimore: Johns Hopkins, 1959), 61.

Virtually all these critics consider Jonson's nondramatic poetry as static over time. J. G. Nichols in 1969 quotes Herford and Simpson's 1925 view of the unchanging nature of Jonson's poetry in order to affirm it.[23] J. B. Bamborough treats the poetry and prose together unchronologically after a developmental survey of the plays.[24] In this essay, I try to reexamine the constant and the changing in Jonson's nondramatic poetry with justice to the full complexity of the subject. Certainly many of Jonson's central preoccupations remain stable throughout his long writing career, and it is on the basis of this constancy that his changes are wrought. Like the monk who sees all the phenomena of this world – from tavern brawls to court coronations – with the steady leveling vision of eternity, Jonson throughout his life sees the world he inhabits in steady contrast with an ideal social order which it is the poet's duty to represent. However, I believe that there are significant changes in Jonson's writing over time. Throughout his life, his work continues to develop, though not necessarily in the post-Renaissance sense of 'to progress'.

Some developments in Jonson's nondramatic poetry can be demonstrated by the solid contrast between Jonson's earlier non-dramatic publications, *Epigrammes* and *The Forrest* of the 1616 folio, and his later poems published in *Under-wood*, 1640. Chapters two, three, and four of this study analyze and discuss each of these three collections separately, attempting to be clear and precise as to what is distinctive and characteristic of Jonson's verse in each collection. No attempt is made to elevate "A Celebration of Charis" over "To Celia", for example, but rather to show the different principles upon which the poems of the different periods were written. Close analyses of several poems in each collection seek to illuminate the opaque clarities of Jonson's 'plain style' and to reveal its variations from one period to the next. In the effort not to discount anything important, I have counted many components of Jonson's poetry. These objective measures of style and content are meant to supplement the explications and other

23   Nichols, *Poetry*, 13, quoting H & S, 1, 120.
24   J. B. Bamborough, *Ben Jonson* (London: Hutchinson, 1970).

traditional methods of criticism used. The figures for these objective counts are presented in tables in the appendix.

After the contrast between Jonson's earlier and later nondramatic poetry has been drawn on the basis of the two folios, chapter five of this study sets up a four-phase division for all of Jonson's work. The two folios divide Jonson's nondramatic poetry into that of the years before and after 1612/13. Dividing each of these periods at the change of reigns gives four periods for Jonson's work: Elizabethan writings, 1597-1603; early Jacobean, 1603-12; later Jacobean 1613-25; and Caroline, 1625-37. These periods correspond approximately to the work of Jonson's twenties, thirties, forties, and fifties. Although there are difficulties in dating many of Jonson's nondramatic poems, I think that the datable poems provide a substantial enough basis for such a division. In particular, I think that this periodization helps to bring into prominence the rather neglected work of Jonson's later Jacobean maturity, that is, of about 1613-25. Because of the paucity of Jonson's play production during this period, the nondramatic works written at this time have often been slighted as well.

The four-period division of Jonson's work proposed in chapter five clarifies the development of Jonson's nondramatic poetry and also corresponds with the development of his masques and plays. When we come to the context of Jonson's work as a whole from the direction of the nondramatic writings, I think that certain patterns and analogies across *genres* become evident in his writing. Chapter five of this study, then, highlights these analogies in Jonson's development rather than assaying a full analysis of the dramatic works. This four-phase division of Jonson's writings, moreover, by being aligned with the reigns through which he lived, reminds us of the greater context beyond the microcosm of one author's work. England from 1597 to 1637 harbored a society in growth, crisis, and transformation. Its literary fashions, its drama, and its audiences all changed fundamentally over this period. Jonson's social attitudes and the objects of his commendation and criticism vary as the years pass, though much in his work remains the same. No attempt is made here to chronicle these changing *milieux*, but only, in the brief concluding chapter six of this study, to anchor the figure of Jonson's development against the varicolored ground of his age.

2. *EPIGRAMMES*

Jonson's first book of *Epigrammes* is a short anthology of brief poems on which the author prided himself. *Epigrammes* illustrate the chief concerns and demonstrate most of the stylistic attributes of Jonson's early maturity. Because their subject matter, scope, and development are limited, they provide clear examples of Jonson's typical devices of style at this period, of his consistent themes and ideals, and of his habitual moral stance.[1]

Jonson was convinced that his epigrams recovered the true classical *genre* of Martial, the "old way, and the true", as he says in Epigram xviii, in contrast to previous English attempts in the *genre*.[2] And, in fact, witty paradox or charming anecdote are with Jonson only a means, not the end of his epigrams, as they are to his English predecessors like Harington. Instead, Jonson's epigrams seek to do 'Platonic justice', to give each man his due. To accomplish this, there are two basic classes of epigrams, those of praise and those of blame.[3] The poems in Jonson's first book of epigrams

[1] Of all Jonson's nondramatic poetry, the epigrams have probably received the most satisfactory treatment, since they are fairly unified in *genre* and in time of composition. Two articles on the epigrams are Rufus D. Putney, "'This So Subtile Sport': Some Aspects of Jonson's Epigrams", *U. of Colorado Studies* (Series in Language and Literature, 10) (1966); and David Wykes, "Ben Jonson's 'Chast Booke' – The *Epigrammes*", *Renaissance and Modern Studies*, 13 (1969), 76-87.

[2] Jonson's patterning of the first four epigrams in his book after Martial's first book corroborates this point, T. K. Whipple, *Martial and the English Epigram from Sir Thomas Wyatt to Ben Jonson* (*U. of California Papers in Modern Philology*, 10) (Berkeley: U. of California, 1925), 387ff.; Hoyt H. Hudson, *The Epigram in the English Renaissance* (Princeton: Princeton, 1947), discusses earlier forms of the English epigram.

[3] O. B. Hardison, Jr., *The Enduring Monument: A Study of the Idea of*

are about equally divided into these classes. Although poems in both groups often appear similar in form, Jonson does not treat the two classes in the same manner. The positive poems rest on the theory that good men have a duty to do praiseworthy things and that the poet has a reciprocal duty to praise them. According to this theory, good men learn from the examples of virtuous individuals who completely fulfill the ideal requisites of their roles. The epigrams cite a number of related reasons why the poet should write poems of praise: he should praise the virtuous in order to teach the nature of virtue, to set an example for others, to reward virtue, to demonstrate the rewards of virtue, to immortalize virtue, and to encourage the virtuous in remaining as they are. Moreover, singing another's praises benefits the praiser by association in the virtue and immortality of the praised and shows the poet's affection for the person praised. Thus the positive epigrams stress ideal roles and reciprocal relationships – for instance, those between friends, patron and poet, king and country. They also often discuss the nature of praise, fame, and poetry. Since ethics are based on choice, these poems abound in fine distinctions. They weigh values, the alternative choices open to good men, and they explore the differences between the inner worth and the outer appearance of things.

However, only the good can learn by example. The ignorant and foolish, Jonson assumes, cannot be taught since they are not willing to learn. Instead, poetry is to "strike ignorance" and make folly its "quarrie" (lxxxv). Somewhat different means are therefore used to hold exemplary portraits of virtue up to the audience for emulation and to expose vice and folly to ridicule. In his censuring epigrams Jonson often relies on puns and tricks of wit, derogatory images and analogies, cutting descriptions or anecdotes, or simple name-calling. Vices need only be called vices to be known for what they are, and the attitude of contempt that Jonson takes toward them is intended to be our attitude, too. Jonson claims he upbraids the typical vice, not the particular sinner, whereas he

---

Praise in Renaissance Literary Theory and Practice (Chapel Hill: U. of North Carolina, 1962), gives the history of the Renaissance rhetoric of praise.

gladly names the specific living exemplars of virtue. But goodness is single while vice is manifold, and, paradoxically, his portraits of virtue therefore tend to be very much alike while his descriptions of the vicious are various and often specifically detailed.

Though the positive and negative poems work by diverse means, their real audience is the same. The poems of praise are written to and for their specific subjects, often as letters or occasional tributes, and for the friends, familiars, and equals of the virtuous addressees. Another class of commendatory poems are those originally used as dedications in the books of others. By reprinting them in his own works, Jonson shows that he wishes to commend these works to his whole elite readership and simultaneously to demonstrate his art and judgment in praise. In contrast, only a few of the satiric poems, those to poet-apes or bad critics perhaps, might be intended to be read by their subjects. Jonson did not expect usurers or alchemists or country clowns to read his poems. Epigram xciv sent to the Countess of Bedford with Donne's satires confirms that Jonson expected his satiric poems to be read only by the good. This poem clearly implies that one's literary taste proves one's morality, a contention which is closely related to the Jonsonian and humanist position that only the good man can be a good poet. "Rare poemes aske rare friends", Jonson states succinctly, intimating a reciprocity of understanding between author and reader similar to the reciprocity of friendship. In the particular case of satire, he invokes the convention of its total efficacy. That is, satire is necessarily so effective in hurting the people whose vice and follies it exposes that anyone unhurt, or, better, amused, must therefore be invulnerable to its barbs. And the people who need the instruction of the satires most, therefore, will be the least likely to be willing to read them.

> Yet, *Satyres,* since the most of mankind bee
> Their un-avoided subject, fewest see:
> For none ere tooke that pleasure in sinnes sense,
> But, when they heard it tax'd, tooke more offence,
> They then, that living where the matter is bred,
> Dare for these poemes, yet, both aske, and read,
> And like them too; must needfully, though few,
> Be of the best: and 'mongst those, best are you.

Epigram lix, "On Spies", indicates the typical attitudes and techniques that Jonson uses in these satiric or censuring epigrams.

> Spies, you are lights in state, but of base stuffe,
> Who, when you'have burnt your selves down to the snuffe,
> Stinke, and are throwne away. End faire enough.

Here Jonson only pretends to address himself directly to the spies. His first image appears to praise them; they are "lights in state", bringing knowledge, but the description is immediately shown to be ironic, through the added qualification, "but of base stuffe", and the remaining two lines of the epigram are a conceit on the similarities between spies, those temporarily-accepted expedients of states, and cheap candles. Jonson hints that the spies' activities are both self-destructive and of decreasing usefulness by blandly assuming, "when you'have burnt your selves. ..." However, no subtlety is wasted in the basic diction of censure: "base stuffe", and "stinke, and are throwne away". The movement of the epigram is conversational, with heavy emphasis on the line-opening words "spies" and "stinke". As in many of the satiric epigrams, the rhythm is a little choppy; there is a pause after the first word in all three lines. The obtrusive alliteration, identified with the sustained tone of scorn, sounds contemptuous: "spies", "state", "stuffe", "selves", "snuffe", "stinke".[4]

Without the last three words, "end faire enough", the poem is one sentence of simple dispraise working through analogy. Then, the last three words add the author's explicit judgment in a tone of brusque contempt. The pun, "end faire enough", indicates in a colloquial phrase of dismissal that the inevitable discarding of the spies is only justice, considering their short usefulness, and that it is also decorously in consonance with the moral ugliness of their activities. That is, their end is "faire", morally and esthetically, but both ironically, in accord with their stinking "end". This crisp dismissal also provides an "end faire enough", that is, not too fair, not too adorned, for a poem that maintains decorum in the agreement between its style and its subject matter.

---

4   George A. E. Parfitt, "The Poetry of Ben Jonson", *Essays in Criticism*, 18 (1968), 27, makes some similar remarks about "On Spies".

Even this very simple poem, then, has its subtleties and proprieties. It works as Jonson's negative epigrams generally do, through tone and image, the common associations of denotative diction, and incisiveness. It does not reason, and it does not try to draw the careful distinctions appropriate to the commendatory epigram which involves moral values and choices.

Despite these variations in approach between the positive and negative epigrams, the basic characteristics of Jonson's style at this period are similar and evident in both classes of epigrams. Yvor Winters speaks of the "fine perception and control of nuances of feeling which are possible only to the stylist who deliberately abandons the obvious graces".[5] There are many poetic devices of which Jonson makes little use in the epigrams and other early poems, and not all of these can be dismissed as the "obvious graces" of the aureate tradition. In the epigrams, for instance, Jonson ignores many of the stylistic possibilities created by variations in rhyme and stanzaic form.

Jonson's rhymes are extremely commonplace. For example, up to ten percent of his rhymes are those in the rhyme group *see*/*me*, *be*/*thee*, etc.[6] Few rhymes are notable, witty, or surprising, except in the burlesque mock epic, "On the Famous Voyage" (cxxxiii), which uses startlingly outrageous rhymes, especially feminine ones, as a principal humorous effect. Typical of that poem are "monster"/ "once stirre", "scar men"/ "Car-men", and "privie"/ "*Livie*". Unlike other epigrams, Jonson's epigrams rarely exploit rhyme to underline striking antithesis or similarity. Sometimes the rhyme is thrown away on a parenthetical word or filler or, often with awkward inversion, on a form of *to be* or an auxiliary verb; Jonson is unusual in often making both the rhymes of a couplet unemphatic. Even when he uses a witty end couplet to sum an epigram, he often puts his antithesis in the middle of the lines: "And, I a *Poet* here,

---

[5] Winters, "16th-Century Lyric", in Alpers, *Essays*, 118.
[6] Out of two hundred fifty pairs of rhymes counted in the epigrams (i-lvi, cxxi-cxxx), sixty-five pairs of rhymes were repeated once or more and twenty-five pairs were in the *be*/*thee* rhyme group. These figures are comparable to counts made of rhymes in Donne's satires; in the first five hundred lines of Dryden's "Absalom and Achitophel", in contrast, forty-two rhyme pairs were repeated, with only eight entries in the *be*/*thee* group.

no *Herald* am" (ix), or "Now, in whose pleasures I have this discerned,/ What would his serious actions me have learned?" (lxxxv). A comparable kind of unemphatic rhyming can be found, for instance, in Donne's third satire, but this satire has fifty percent run-on lines, and its unemphatic rhyming therefore seems part of a general lack of emphasis on the line endings in the interests of a rougher and more colloquial rhythm. In Jonson's epigrams, unemphatic rhyme occurs constantly despite the fact that there are only about twenty percent run-on lines and the lines often deviate from normal speech order. In this respect Jonson's epigrams vary considerably from the norm of the satiric closed couplet developed by Dryden and Pope, despite the similarities in endstopping and caesural placement which have led some scholars to call Jonson's poetry neoclassical. This lack of emphasis on rhyme may be part of a deliberate attempt to imitate the effect of unrhymed classical verse.[7]

Almost all of Jonson's epigrams are in iambic pentameter. Hypo- or hypermetrical lines are extremely rare.[8] Opening inversions are used frequently, but metrical variation never obscures the basic meter; Jonson seemed to feel Donne had passed this proper limit in his satires when he pronounced that "Done for not keeping of accent deserved hanging" (*Cv.* 48-49). Occasionally Jonson uses meter symbolically in conformity with the meaning. Thus the length of time endured in disfavor and the weight of displeasure are represented by the "times long grudge" and "courts ill will" which Jonson wishes on his Muse's next master (lxv).

The structures of Jonson's epigrams are fairly conventional. Sometimes the satiric poems build to a joke or climax in the last couplet, but often they do not. Often the commendatory poems fall into the two parts of the classical epigram as description and

---

[7] Parfitt, "Compromise Classicism: Language and Rhythm in Ben Jonson's Poetry", *Studies in English Literature*, 11 (1971), 109-121, discusses the Latin influence on Jonson's word order and speaks of his unemphatic rhyme as a technique for achieving maximum freedom within the line.

[8] Hubert M. English, Jr., "Prosody and Meaning in Ben Jonson's Poems" (Unpublished Ph. D. dissertation, Yale, 1955), 34, believes hypo- and hypermetrical lines are virtually nonexistent when account is taken of Jonson's elisions, expansions, and alternate pronunciations.

comment or question and answer. Sometimes Jonson seems to be following a logical form, beginning the two parts of the epigram "when" and "then". Epigram xv appears as a syllogism in reverse: "All men are wormes: But this no man. ..." The openings of the epigrams are also conventional with their rhetorical questions, exclamations and apostrophes, and statements of specific time. Particularly Jonsonian are the many oblique openings starting with generalized subordinate clauses or negatives like "not he who". Often the endings are double: one joke is capped by another or one moral by another.

If Jonson's structures are often simple in the epigrams, his syntax is not. Inversions are frequent, and series of clauses become inter-involved, again, perhaps, in imitation of Latin precedent. The epitaph on Jonson's first daughter (xxii), for instance, which Trimpi commends for "its excellence in diction and syntax",[9] is rather complex, as the diagram of the crossed antecedents of lines seven through twelve indicates:

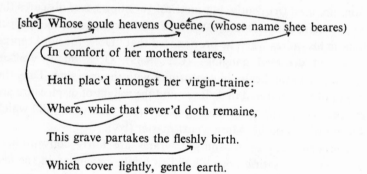

[she] Whose soule heavens Queene, (whose name shee beares)

In comfort of her mothers teares,

Hath plac'd amongst her virgin-traine:

Where, while that sever'd doth remaine,

This grave partakes the fleshly birth.

Which cover lightly, gentle earth.

A very few of the epigrams, particularly the note to Beaumont (lv) and the gnomic Epigram lxxx, are symmetrical, based on parallels in sound, syntax, and meaning. Much more often, how-ever, Jonson avoids or breaks symmetry, as in Epigram xxxii where the parallel series of ideas on Roe's death is not expressed in parallel form. Jonson's uses of rhyme, meter, and epigrammatic structure are low-key; his imagery, too, is quiet.

Edward Partridge, studying the imagery in Jonson's comedies, found commercial, sexual, religious, and animal imagery the most important and the most frequently used.[10] Figures of hyperbole and of ironic understatement are also common in the plays, though the epigrams, in which Jonson can speak out directly, are rather more restrained.[11] The hyperbole of his praise tends to be qualified and quieted into credibility, and the irony of the satiric epigrams is usually obvious and fairly blunt. Animal, commercial, and religious imagery is frequent in the epigrams, as well as in the plays, though the quantity of figurative language in the epigrams altogether is small. Many poems contain no developed analogies or figures of speech. Often Jonson's imagery is at the level of submerged cliché or barely revived dead metaphor. Jonson's images tend to operate, then, not by revealing a surprising similarity or disparity to the reader, but rather by subtly influencing or persuading him into a judgment through the positive or negative connotations of barely perceived images. Thus religious imagery is quite common in the epigrams, though it is often unobtrusive. It sanctifies the moral approbation of the commendatory poems and provides standards against which the censured subjects are judged. Often it provides a sudden unexpected increase in the seriousness of a poem. For example, James' "devout" subjects are concerned for the King's "after-state" (li), and Sir Thomas Over-bury makes the worldly courtiers and the court itself "repent" because of his virtuous example (cxiii).[12]

---

10   Partridge, *Broken Compass*, 70ff., finds these kinds of imagery operative in *Volpone*.
11   Alexander Sackton, *Rhetoric as a Dramatic Language in Ben Jonson* (New York: Columbia, 1948), treats jargon and hyperbole in the plays.
12   The degree to which Jonson's poetry is Christian or classical appears to be recurring as a critical crux. Parfitt, "Ethical Thought in Ben Jonson's Poetry", *Studies in English Literature*, 9 (1969), 123-34, holds a secular view of Jonson, while a more Christian view is taken by Francis Fike, "Ben Jonson's 'On My First Sonne'", *Gordon Review*, 2 (1969), 205-20; Kay, "Christian Wisdom"; and Gayle E. Wilson, "Jonson's Use of the Bible and the Great Chain of Being in 'To Penshurst'", *Studies in English Literature*, 8 (1968), 77-90. I believe that Jonson observed classical decorum in his poems in the

Much of the religious imagery conforms to a larger Jonsonian pattern, that of distinguishing between mere external appearance and the true inner essence of something, between the social or common view and the eternal reality. Thus quarrelsome but cowardly Brayne-Hardie is "valiant" because "he that dares damne himselfe, dare more then fight" (xvi). The terrible impercipience of the sinner to his true good is scored here more deeply than the misunderstanding of the nature of valor. Jonson's Muse has "betray'd" him to a "worthlesse lord", making him commit "idolatrie" to a "great image", that is, making him worship a false appearance rather than a real virtue (lxv).

In contrast with its importance in the later collections of Jonson's poetry, erotic imagery is not very frequent in the epigrams. Here it varies from the simple and conventional allegory on the marriage or "union" of England and Scotland (v) to the equally simple and conventional obscene double meanings of some of the satirical poems, like that on Groyne occupying his land (cxvii). The tenderest images in the epigrams are written for male friends. Thus Jonson bids William Roe farewell hoping that "windes as soft as breath of kissing friends" will accompany him (cxxviii) and Esmé's "timely succours" have "begot" "new life" in Jonson and his Muse (cxxvii).

Although the negative poems more often make their points through imagery than the positive poems do, extended conceits rarely provide the structure even for the satiric epigrams. Similarly, developed similes are rare. Nine animal images are used in the titles of twelve of the satiric epigrams, such as those on Colt, Mungril, Cod, and Hornet. These derogatory analogies are not developed in the texts of the epigrams, though the Court-Worme does develop into a court "butter-flye" (xv). Most of the images in the negative poems are implied by only a word or two. Old-End Gatherer wears "motly" (liii), the Some-thing that Walkes Somewhere is "buried in flesh, and blood" (xi), Surly's whore swims in silk (lxxxii).

---

classical *genres* but adhered to a traditional Christian worldview throughout his work.

Jonson's positive poems use the literary devices of mythological or classical allusions, personification, and rhetorical allegory more often than the negative ones do. The images in these poems of praise are often extremely conventional, even clichés. Mary Wroth is the "crowne" of all her sex (ciii), and William Uvedale's body and soul are respectively "cabinet" and "treasure" (cxxv). Other images, while not as tired as these, still follow Jonson's remarks in *Timber* that figures should be just rather than surprising and that they should be clear and informative. Jonson's allowance of metaphor for "commodity" as well as for "necessity" gives some latitude to his discussion of trope, while most of his figures do fit the more stringent requirements of justness and clarity.[13] Thus Jonson tends to explain or fill out his figures for us. Fame is "breath soon kindled, soone blowne out" (cxxxi), and Margaret Ratcliffe's wit was "like *Nectar* ever flowing" (xl).

Classical references and mythological allusions blend in many commendations. Jonson hopes that Donne will mark one of his poems with the "better stone" of Roman preference (xcvi); Savile's history of England would exceed "*Minervaes* loome" in richness (xcv); and William Roe is to be like an Aeneas in his travels (cxxviii). Jonson may treat the same theme at different times both directly and through classical allusion. Thus Lucy Bedford is praised for "hating that solemne vice of greatnesse, pride" (lxxvi), while Mary Wroth is seen habited as a Juno, but with "no Peacock by" (cv).

Although the imagery and figures of the epigrams are typical of Jonson's early poetry, his diction is perhaps more idiosyncratic and consistent as an attribute of his style. Also distinctive is Jonson's particular use of verbal patterning. In these poems he discriminates moral and esthetic value through the careful placement of negative, comparative, and superlative terms. Jonson's characteristic diction in *Epigrammes* and his use of positive and

---

13   The relevant passage of *Timber* or the *Discoveries* is 11. 1881-1925, H & S, 8, 621-22. The best known comment is "*Metaphors* farfet hinder to be understood, and affected, lose their grace", 1. 1905. Jonson is following Quintillian in this passage, H & S, 11, 266-67.

negative patterning are still recognizable in the more varied style of his later poems.

As has often been noted, Jonson's diction in the nondramatic verse is simple. There is little learned language, slang, or technical jargon, and the selection of words amply fulfills Jonson's declaration in *Timber* that "pure and neat Language I love, yet plaine and customary" (*Disc.* 1870). Many lines are entirely monosyllabic. Certain words are often repeated, giving a sense of consistency to the book of epigrams as a whole. Many of these often-repeated words have a clear moral coloration, and, in the self-consciously literary epigrams, a high proportion of the most common words refer to thinking and writing. Words used twenty times or more in one thousand lines of the epigrams are *good, great, man, name, love, wit, know, make, pay,* and *think.* Some other commonly repeated words in the epigrams are *true, fame, God, life, Muse, time, vertue, world, give, judge, leave, praise, read, see, take,* and *write* (see Table One, Appendix, for the word counts). There are few repeated adjectives, and few adjectives altogether, while a few simple active verbs and abstract nouns are used again and again. Jonson's diction in the epigrams as a whole tends to the general, moral, and intellectual. Few of his common words have sensual or highly emotional connotations. Jonson's positive vocabulary is more repetitious than the satiric, since truth and positive ideals are simple and uniform while folly, vice, and crime take on many particulars of appearance and need to be exposed in all their many variations throughout society. Thus the satiric epigrams use a coarser and more specific diction for their subject matter than do the commendatory epigrams. For example, Sir Voluptuous Beast evokes the words "petticote", "goate", and "cucqueane" (xxv), and the "ripe statesmen" are associated with "projects", "almanacks", "cypher", and the "poulder-plot" (xcii).

Josephine Miles notes that Jonson's style shows "the power of predicates and infrequent epithets".[14] That is, in comparison with

---

[14] Josephine Miles, *The Continuity of Poetic Language: Studies in English Poetry from the 1540's to the 1940's* (Berkeley: U. of California, 1951), 66. The ratio she gives for Jonson for adjectives to nouns to verbs in ten lines of poetry is 6-14-12; for Donne, 7-11-12; for Shakespeare, 10-17-10; for Dryden,

other English poets, Jonson's proportional use of adjectives and adverbs is at a minimum; of verbs, at a maximum. "Who" and "that" clauses continually replace adjectives in his poems, and among adjectives and adverbs, those of quantity bulk large in comparison with those of quality. Words like *first, all, most, no* are extremely common in Jonson's highly moralistic, evaluating style. The poet even uses prepositions for moral discrimination. Pembroke, for instance, is an "*Epigramme*" "of, and to the good" (cii), and all knowing arts must be recognized as "in, if not, from" Jephson (cxvi).

Jonson's diction in the epigrams is seldom very colorful. It varies from sedately dignified to coolly coarse, rarely being decorative or flowery in commendation or wittily racy in censure. Jonson's epigrammatic diction is less various than that of the Elizabethan pamphleteers or of the knaves and gulls of his own city comedies. The main note of Jonson's diction in the epigrams is restraint. Soldiers are referred to periphrastically by the epithet "strength of my Country" (cviii). The word "death" is not mentioned in the elegiac epigrams xxii, xxvii, xxxiii, and xlv.

Particularly in the commendatory poems, adjectives and adverbs are often in the comparative or superlative, since careful weighing and ranking of choices is part of the moral life. Many of Jonson's most famous lines are based on comparisons like "Although to write be lesser then to doo,/ It is the next deed, and a great one too" (xcv). Jonson's Muse is humbly "lighter" than Benjamin Rudyerd's, whose "better studies" Jonson praises (cxxi), as he does Donne's "best life" (xxiii). In a poem that is chiefly a list of

---

10-16-10, Table A, 518. Her list of word counts, using *Under-wood*, is in Table B, 524. Part of it is reproduced for purposes of comparison with the epigrams in my Table One, Appendix. Miles also discusses Jonson's "predicative style" in *Eras and Modes in English Poetry* (Berkeley: U. of California, 1957), 41.

I think such measures can be helpful in describing style. However, caution is necessary in attributing too much to the parts of speech. Parfitt, "Compromise Classicism", 110-11, speaks of the solidity of Jonson's adjectives and the strength of his verbs, whereas Thomas M. Greene sees "centered values" in Jonson's nouns and adjectives and "uncentered activity" in his verbs, "Ben Jonson and the Centered Self", *Studies in English Literature*, 10 (1970), 332.

praised attributes, Jonson yet strives to rank them in proper order of merit. Thus Suffolke is told to "stand high ... in eyes of men,/ High in thy bloud, ... but highest" when his virtues make others recognize his worth (lxvii). Lucy Bedford is "of greatest bloud, and yet more good than great" and each "softest vertue" meets in her "softer bosome" (lxxvi).

Jonson asserts modification, the shadings of moral evaluation, by the use of concessives and conditionals as well as by the use of compared adjectives. He often protects a hyperbole, for instance, with an "almost". Thus, "all great life/ Almost" is exercised in the strife of vice and virtue (cii); Cary's single valor "to upbraid the sloth of this our time,/ Durst valour make, almost, but not a crime" (lxvi); and Jonson could "adore" Uvedale "almost t'idolatrie" (cxxv). Jonson's use of conditionals is similar. Thus he can praise Edward Allen "if Rome" could praise its actors (lxxxix), and Jonson lauds not only Radcliffe's two brothers who fell in battle but also two "that would have falne as great" (xciii). Epigram xxvii on Sir John Roe praises through a series of four "if" clauses which vary in the mood of the verb and the degree of possibility expressed from "if any sword could save from *Fates, Roe's* could" to the climactic near-certainty of "if any pious life ere lifted man/ To Heaven; his hath".

Often the discriminations in Jonson's poems are not between grammatical comparisons, but between two very similar words, so that the reader must dwell on the difference and discover it for himself. The distinction between "love" and "like" in the epitaph on his first son (xlv) is like this, as are "securely"/ "safely" and "built"/ "dwells" of the "Epode" (XI) and "To Penshurst" (II) in *The Forrest*. The differences are a little more obvious in the distinctions "others speake", but only Allen "dost act" (lxxxix); and good men "but see death, the wicked tast it" (lxxx). What has been found most representative of Jonson's epigrammatic style, then, is his clear and morally weighted diction and his use of grammar and syntax to express fine degrees of moral shading.

Epigram ci, "Inviting a Friend to Supper", provides an example of a poem in which Jonson's characteristic style, particularly his use of positive and negative patterning, establishes an ideal of the cultivated life. The poem has been favorably compared with the Martial epigram from which it is derived.[15] Its superiority is generally taken to be its specificity and decorum, the number of English details in the menu and its freedom from superfluous description. I think, however, that the most important contribution to the poem's mastery of tone and vigorously urbane effect comes from its sense of balance. In all but two of its twenty-one couplets, a negative statement or possibility balances an expressed positive or ideal. Thus the entire poem has an underlying pattern of give and take, concession and affirmation. The result of this process of poetic addition and subtraction is a net positive total; the occasion seems to be one whose decorum is an achieved mean among various kinds of opposites – the guest's worth and the host's unworthiness, for example, or excessive license or constraint in the evening's entertainment. This movement toward moderation is carried out in the diction, structure, and rhythmic patterns of the poem, and, most importantly, through negative or concessive statements.

> To night, grave sir, both my *poore* house, and I
> Doe equally desire your companie:
> *Not that we thinke* us worthy such a ghest,
> *But that your worth* will dignifie our feast,
> 5 With those that come; whose grace may make that seeme
> *Something, which, else,* could hope for *no esteeme.*
> It is the faire acceptance, Sir, creates
> The entertaynment perfect: *not the cates.*
> *Yet shall you have,* to rectifie your palate,
> 10 An olive, capers, *or some better* sallade
> Ushring the mutton; with a short-leg'd hen,
> *If we can get her,* full of egs, and then,
> Limons, and wine for sauce: to these, a coney
> *Is not to be despair'd of,* for our money;
> 15 And, *though fowle, now, be scarce, yet there are clarkes,*
> *The skie not falling,* thinke we may have larkes.
> *Ile tell you of more, and lye,* so you will come:
> Of partrich, pheasant, wood-cock, of which some
> *May yet be there*; and godwit, *if we can*:
> 20 Knat, raile, and ruffe too. *How so ere,* my man
> Shall reade a piece of Virgil, Tacitus,

15 H & S, 11, 20-21; Whipple, *Martial*, 389. Trimpi, *Jonson's Poems*, 186-87, compares Epigram ci with Jonson's *Leges Convivales*, H & S, 8, 656.

Livie, *or of some better* booke to us,
Of which wee'll speake our minds, amidst our meate;
And *Ile professe no verses* to repeate:
25 To this, *if ought appear, which I know not of,*
That will the pastrie, *not my paper,* show of.
Digestive cheese, and fruit there sure will bee;
But that, which most doth take my Muse, and mee,
Is a pure cup of rich Canary-wine,
30 Which is the Mermaids, now, *but shall be mine*:
Of which *had Horace, or Anacreon tasted,*
Their lives, as doe their lines, *till now had lasted.*
Tabaco, Nectar, or the Thespian spring,
Are all but Luthers beere, to this I sing.
35 Of this we will sup free, *but moderately,*
And we will have *no Pooly', or Parrot by*;
Nor shall our cups make any guiltie men:
But, at our parting, *we will be, as when*
We innocently met. *No simple word,*
40 That shall be utter'd at our mirthfull boord,
Shall make us sad next morning: *or affright*
The libertie, that wee'll enjoy to night.

The only negative in the first couplet is the speaker's modest "my poore house, and I", set off against the worth of the invited "grave sir". The stress for the couplet, as for the entire poem, is on the word "equally", indicating moderation, moral equanimity, balance, though here at the beginning this balance is yet to be achieved, and the speaker stands humbly before his guest. The positive and negative, give and take movement, is more firmly established in the deferential movement of the next couplet: "Not that we thinke .../ But that your worth ...." The pattern continues throughout the poem, as noted by the negatives and concessives italicized for emphasis.

Only lines twenty-seven and twenty-eight are wholly positive, without negative or conditional statements, following the two negatives in the preceding couplet. Significantly, lines twenty-seven and twenty-eight provide a summary of the physical and poetical aspects of the dinner and put them in their proper places, not this time with a positive and a negative, but with a positive and a superlative.

Of course, this pattern of give and take, plus and minus, is not rigidly imposed; the negatives and conditionals, *but's*, *if's*, *had's*, *no's*, *better's* are varied, and the concession expressed in one couplet may apply to something expressed in another couplet. All in all, the words "no", "not", and "nor" are used eleven times, "yet" and "but" nine times, and there are six conditional or contrary-to-fact clauses.

The structure, tone, and imagery of the poem recapitulate the movement toward balance we have seen exemplified in the first couplet. Although at times the poem seems to be working through opposites, the discriminations expressed in the epigram are not really dichotomies. Virtue is not set against vice or wisdom against folly. Instead, as in very many of the commendatory epigrams, the poem involves distinctions based on balancing, weighing, and ranking several different positive goods. In fact, this separation of positive and negative realms of comparison, springing from a rhetoric of praise and blame, is one of the distinctive characteristics of the epigrams, a characteristic which is modified in Jonson's more comprehensive later poems.

The first eight lines of the poem set its purpose and situation. It is an invitation; one person addresses a second. The tone of these lines is calm, general, abstract. There are no specific images. The merits of the guest are set against the speaker's unworthiness, which is gradually modified to adjust the values of the banquet to those of the guest. The occasion is described as "something" which needs the "grace" of the guest to become anything. This vagueness implies that the guest is needed to create the occasion which the host cannot make specific without his cooperation. After the "faire acceptance" is assumed, then, the host can go on in the rest of the poem to specify the kind of entertainment it will be. A reciprocity of dignified conviviality is described, the worth of each guest gracing the whole occasion and making it more valuable for each other guest.

The next twelve lines, nine to twenty, give a tentative menu; whatever the connotations of this proteinaceous repast, the overt content of the lines is a list of foods, and the direct appeal of the passage is to the appetite. Here Jonson will only claim to "rectify" his guest's "palate", for instance, not his character, and he makes judgments only on the food: "capers, or some better sallade". To every hypothetically-present foodstuff all the ideal accompaniments are added, although the host is willing to admit how all this is really to be obtained: "for our money". This section begins with a very matter-of-fact tone in its listing, but as the possible menu is extended, the host's tone becomes freer and more jocular. He may not actually be able to provide every food the guest might desire, but the host seeks to entice the guest by a deferential though light-hearted show that he understands what is his guest's due on such an occasion. Thus the whole menu seeks to achieve a mean between what the guest deserves and what the host can afford. This spirit of expansiveness concerning the menu reaches a climax in line fourteen where the host says, "Ile tell you of more, and lye, so you will come."

The next six lines, twenty-one to twenty-six, speak of reading the classics at table. The appeal is to the reason, and we expect that these higher things will dominate the occasion. The tone begins as calm and serious, with the sober list of classical authors, though Jonson starts to move toward the freer next section in the pleasantry that only the pastry will show his verses.

The invitation is to a "mirthfull boord", not to a literary meeting, however, and therefore even reading must take second place to the rich Canary wine, which receives the eight lines from twenty-seven to thirty-four. This passage is the most extravagant in the poem in terms of tone and imagery, though of course the whole range of the poem is a decorously limited one. Two hyperboles, one positive and one negative, describe the wine: it could have made the lives of Horace and Anacreon as immortal as their lines, and all other drinks are "*Luthers* beere" in comparison to it. This section appeals primarily to the imagination rather than to the appetite or the reason, though it combines the qualities of the preceding phases of the banquet. Thus wine is a form of food, but it is defined specifically in terms of poetic inspiration. It graces both the private man and the poet, "my *Muse*, and mee", and it overgoes the earlier references to the classics by being the present aid to spontaneous creativity and creative good fellowship.

Finally, there is an eight-line conclusion, lines thirty-five to forty-two, balancing the opening invitation section. It shows the limits of even the supreme Canary and again emphasizes the value of moderation expressed throughout the poem. The emphasis here is ethical, based on the moral will or free choice rather than on the appetite, reason, or imagination. "We will sup free, but moderately", the host states explicitly, giving "free" the wide range of possible meanings it usually held for Jonson: voluntarily, frankly, openly, liberally. The next to last line exorcises two last negative possibilities, the results of verbal intemperance, and the final verse, entirely positive, completes the poem and gives in one line the ideal of moderate merriment built up through the whole: "The libertie, that wee'll enjoy to night". This section returns the poem to a quiet, assured tone. It indicates completion, the circular finishing of the poem and the event. "But, at our parting, we will be, as when/ We innocently met". The poem begins and ends with a reminder of the particular invitation through the repetition of the word "to night". In between, however, the poem has moved from the present request, "I ... desire your companie" to the confident future of "wee'll enjoy to night". The occasion will not change the participants, though its promise is of an enrichment in pleasure in the proper satisfaction of all of the faculties of a literary gentleman.

As always in Jonson's poetry at its best, "figures of sound" are also figures of sense. Thus alliteration and assonance are used to harmonize and balance, to show all sides of the feast. Alliteration draws attention to the balance between the mental and physical in the expression, "wee'll speake our minds, amidst our meate", and it emphasizes the series "*Muse*", "mee", "*Mermaids*". Alliteration joined with assonance gives the two contrasts "pastrie, not my paper" and "lives, as doe their lines", balancing food and poetry, life and art.

In consonance with the movement of the total structure of the poem toward balancing and mediating opposite choices is the movement of the caesura. In the first twenty lines, the medial caesura tends to fall after syllable four, though lines ten through twenty, with their lists of foods, have scattered and frequent pauses. Lines eighteen to twenty-four begin to show a slight preference for a pause after syllable seven. Lines twenty-seven to the end return to a more flowing style, with a tendency for the medial pause to be after syllable six. The pauses in the beginning eight lines tend to indicate the hesitations of polite deference, while the stopping and starting movement of hovering conditions throughout lines twelve to twenty continues the idea that the occasion is being improvised during the poem to match the guest's wishes. The frequent stops and starts here not only list the foods, but they also seem to wait to ask the guest, after each item, is this enough, or this? Thus, though with much flexibility and variation, the poem swings from a normative caesura early in the line, through a passage of scattered frequent and late pauses, to a conclusion characterized by a pause at the middle of the line or slightly beyond.

The moral modulation of the poem that we have been watching works strongly through the diction, particularly the ethically-charged adjectives. The evocative words "pure" and "rich" are saved for the Canary wine, whereas the adverbs and adjectives in the last section describe the occasion, setting "guilty" and "sad" against "free", "moderately", "innocently".

The syntax of the poem is extremely various and highly articulated. The sentences follow the balanced pattern set for the rest of the poem: short sentences follow long, often summarizing the preceding thought; the poem ends with two sentences of mean length and complexity. There are nine sentences in the poem, having a total of seventeen coordinate and twenty-five subordinate clauses in forty-two lines. Again, variety leads to balance. (See Table Two, Appendix.) Of course, these figures do not adequately indicate how the sentences are put together. The tendency throughout the poem and in other works of Jonson's is for the later members of sentences to be longer and more modified, more subdivided than the earlier ones. In the criticism of the prose style of the seventeenth century, this characteristic assymmetry of sentence structure is called "end-linking", and it is asociated with the "loose" Senecan style that attempts to convey the movement of thought.[16] Thus, even though most of the poem is not obviously

---

[16] Barish, *Language*, 55, discusses the rejection of balance in Jonson's prose style. Barish uses the influential terms of Morris Croll, whose essays are

at variance with normal word order, only great skill could cast over its extreme syntactical complexity the illusion that the poem is a transcript of ordinary speech. Devices of asymmetry like "end-linking" help to produce this illusion, but, more importantly, the poem succeeds so well in seeming 'plain', unstrained, moderate, and complete because of the careful construction through which everything in it works out a process of alternate choices, of controlled give and take, reaching an achieved mean.

Thus Jonson's typical device in his early poems of balanced positive and negative statement comes to represent one of his overtly held ideals, that of moderation. Although Jonson extolled moderation and sometimes portrayed it in these epigrams, most of the epigrams tend to fall into the simple categories of praise or blame. Only in his later works are the stylistic devices indicating balance frequently brought to bear on subject matter that also extols balance and moderation in point of view. In the epigrams, Jonson illumines various aspects of his ideals for man and society through the separate windows of positive or negative example. One of his most explicit means for expressing such values in the epigrams is through their titles and the names of the people to and about whom he writes.

The connection between the subject's name and the fame that the poet can give is a crucial one in the epigrams. The word *name* appears in the epigrams forty-three times; *fame*, twenty-five times.[17] The words appear together eleven times, usually as rhymes. Jonson opens his book of epigrams in the dedication to William Herbert, Earl of Pembroke, by setting up one of his typical patterns of reciprocity: "I must expect, at your Lo: hand, the protection of truth, and libertie, ... In thankes whereof, I returne you the honor of leading forth so many good, and great names (as my verses mention on the better part) to their remembrance with posteritie". The main stress in this passage is on the immortality

reprinted in *Style, Rhetoric, and Rhythm: Essays*, ed. by J. Max Patrick, *et. al.* (Princeton: Princeton, 1966).

17 Thomas Dekker, *Satiromastix* in *Dramatic Works*, ed. by Fredson Bowers, 1 (Cambridge: Cambridge, 1953), 299-395, shows "Horace" composing an epithalamic ode, hunting for a rhyme to *name*, I. ii. 1-20.

that the poet can give the good man, simply by preserving his reputation or "name" for succeeding generations.

In contrast, only generalized lessons can be derived from the censuring poems, since evil-doers do not deserve to have their names immortalized and since "riot, ... pride, ... selfe-love" are so prevalent that the barbs against them should be general, without "particulars" as without "names". In Epigram cxv, "On the Townes Honest Man", the lack of a specific name is the clue that the "honest" of the title is ironic. Jonson expects his reader to note the violation of decorum in this respect immediately: "You wonder, who this is! and, why I name/ Him not, aloud, that boasts so good a fame. ..."

With the exception of the "friend" invited to supper and a few positive epigrams about "the Learned Critick" (xvii) and "True Souldiers" (cviii), the individual subjects of all the commendatory epigrams are titled with their own real names. This distinction in itself serves to indicate the generality of vice in contrast to the specific rarity of virtue, even if Jonson devotes his early epigrams equally to bad and to good.

The meaning of the concepts of name and fame in the positive poems is far more complex than in the negative poems. In particular, Jonson often discovers in the good person's name as clear an index to his character as is provided by the invented names of Jonson's dramatic characters or of his negative epigrams. That is, Jonson often sees a person's name as a relevant indication of his character.[18] Jonson praises Sir Horace Vere for the Romanness of both his names (xci), and he sees Susan, Countess of Montgomery as another Biblical Susanna in chastity and beauty (civ). William Herbert, to whom the epigrams are dedicated, has sancti-

---

[18] Wykes, "Chast Booke", 85, stresses the importance and even power of names as "benedictions" or "maledictions". He refers to Robert C. Elliott, *The Power of Satire: Magic, Ritual, Art* (Princeton: Princeton, 1960) on the magic power of naming. I think that Jonson's idea of names as 'real' or 'true' indications of meaning is related to the concept of 'real' etymologies which the Renaissance derived from Plato's *Cratylus*. Martha Craig, "The Secret Wit of Spenser's Language" in Alpers, *Essays*, 447-72, discusses this tradition with relation to the names of the characters in the *Faerie Queene*. She states, "The names of Spenser's characters are clearly philosophic and true, for they reveal the nature of the one named through the etymology", 451.

fied his name through his virtue until it is the epitome of all virtue, an exemplary epigram in itself.

> I doe but name thee *Pembroke*, and I find
> It is an *Epigramme*, on all man-kind;
> Against the bad, but of, and to the good: (cii).

The simplest and most amiable use of names in Jonson is not symbolic. Instead, it shows his affection and respect for male friends. For instance, he addresses "my lov'd Alphonso" (cxxx), "Uv'dale, thou piece of the first times" (cxxv), and "Roe (and my joy to name)" (cxxviii).

Closely related to the concept of name in the epigrams is the rhyme word and sometimes synonym, fame. Fame is double-edged. In every poem Jonson is making and staking his reputation, his own poetical fame, according to the nobleness of the subjects he praises, his accuracy in praise, and his probity of judgment in censure. Errors in praise are matters of grave concern to the poet: Jonson berates his Muse for having once "betray'd" him to a "worthless lord" (lxv).

In Epigram xvii, "To the Learned Critick", Jonson states that he wishes his poems "a legitimate fame", as opposed, clearly, to the "vulgar praise" or the "least selfe fame,/ Made from the hazard of another's shame" (ii). As Jonson tells the learned critic, the fame conferred by a true source is better, because longer lived, than the repute given by a less worthy critic. Truly deserved fame is prolific. While other people "toyle for titles to their tombes", Jonson tells Sir Henry Nevil, "Thy deedes, unto thy name, will prove new wombes" (cix).

The value of praise varies according to the use to which the praise is put and the value of the praiser. Jonson tells "Courtling" that though his "judgment" is unexceptionable, "Thy person only, Courtling is the vice" (lxxii). Worse still is the self-praiser or boaster, like the "Townes Honest Man" who is his "owne fames architect" (cxv). If the praise of the vulgar is to be discounted, it is none the less a special indication of merit for a man's virtues to force the praise of his enemies; Jonson credits Pembroke with this power (cii). The most valuable praise is that of the most virtuous praiser, so that Jonson compares Ned Allen to Roman actors praised by Cicero "whose every breath was fame" (lxxxix), and Vere's Roman virtues deserve a Horace, the poet with whom Ben most often chose to identify himself (xci).

That which gives substance to Jonson's high valuation of name and fame is his notion of ethical example. Of all uses of praise, the most important are those which define the virtuous exemplar and hold him up for the emulation of others. Jonson sums the power of example in telling Benjamin Rudyerd "I need no other arts, but studie thee:/ Who prov'st all these", that is, truth, simplicity, virtue, friendship, "were, and again may bee" (cxxii). This moral idea of the power of example shades easily into the literary doctrine of imitation, as Jonson says, "who affects the state/ Of the best writer, and judge, should emulate" (Rudyerd (cxxiii)).

Related to the concept of the virtuous man as exemplar in Jonson's early poetry is the more general one of ideal role. Jonson has a few such ideals constantly in mind – the ideal writer, the ideal woman, the ideal patron, the ideal friend, or simply the ideal man. His most usual method of praise is to identify the person being praised with the appropriate ideal. Often, in doing this, he contrasts the degenerate present with some nobler past time with which the praised person is associated. Conversely, indications of the violated ideals provide the permanent ethical bite in Jonson's satires.

In accordance with principles of decorum and perhaps also in accordance with the principles of patronage, Jonson did not allocate poems of praise and of blame equally to members of different social classes.[19] He described members of the upper classes as more virtuous than members of the lower classes, although some of Jonson's most caustic censure in his earlier poems is directed at

---

[19]   John F. Danby, "Poets on Fortune's Hill: Literature and Society, 1580-1610", *Cambridge Journal*, 2 (1949), 211, finds Jonson one of the most independent and secure of contemporary poets in his relations with his patrons, as do Patricia Thomson, "The Literature of Patronage, 1580-1630", *Essays in Criticism*, 2 (1952), 267-84, and Hugh MacLean, "Ben Jonson's Poems: Notes on the Ordered Society", in *Essays in English Literature from the Renaissance to the Victorian Age* ..., ed. by M. MacLure and F. W. Watt (Toronto: U. of Toronto, 1964), 43-68.

degenerate or upstart aristocrats. For example, the poet chastises "Fine Lady Would-bee" (lxii), "My Lord Ignorant" (x), the "Court-Worme" (xv), and "Sir Annual Tilter" (xxix), the immoral and vain and affected of the court and the unworthy newcomers to title. Moreover, he slashes brutally at Sir Voluptuous Beast (xxv) where nothing in the content of the epigram requires that Beast be knighted.

The image of what a lord should not be is expressed in the epigram on Don Surly whose form of "greatness" includes not keeping open house, not recognizing people, and not appreciating Jonson's epigrams (xxviii). Even more revealing of Jonson's attitude is the poem "On Something that Walkes Some-where" (xi). This court creature dares do neither good nor ill and is therefore "dead", since life and virtue consist of useful action. The attributes of Jonson's ideal aristocrat can be made up from the qualities he praises in his social superiors and from the opposites of the qualities he censures. The ideal nobleman fulfills his office perfectly and dispenses largesse freely. He is valiant in war or perhaps even "saver of my countrey" (lx). He bears up the honor of his house, like Radcliffe, who stands "like a columne" "to shew the times what you all were" (xciii), where standing is a sign of virtue and stability and where the column as an image of support also connotes a ruin of former, greater times. Public goals should come first to the responsible aristocrat. In all, Jonson writes about twice as many commendatory epigrams to social superiors – defined here as the titled classes, their wives and daughters – as censuring ones, and he writes almost as many about social superiors as the combined number of poems to equals or inferiors. (See Table Three, Appendix.)

The distribution among the three social classes of Jonson's sixteen epigrams to or about women casts an interesting light on Jonson's purported misogyny. (See Table Four, Appendix.) Of these sixteen poems, the only poem written about a social "equal" is the epitaph on Jonson's own daughter. Other epitaphs lament the high-born Margaret Ratcliffe and the anonymous Elizabeth, L. H., leaving nine commendatory poems written to six living women, all aristocratic. The five censuring epigrams on women are divided between Fine Lady Would-Bee and four lower class butts. At this stage in his career, then, Jonson does not portray women as equals in the social and moral world reflected in the epigrams. On the one hand, women may be gracious patrons like Lucy, Countess of Bedford or the three women connected with the Sidney family. On the other hand, women are likely to be worthless, lecherous, and nameless, like Surly's whore (lxxxii) or Hornet's wife (lxxviii). In the tactlessly placed Epigram lxxxiii immediately preceding one of the three poems to Lucy Harington, Jonson implies that the words "woman" and "whore" are synonyms. In other words, in the epigrams Jonson did not think much of women – in quantity of attention or in opinion – except for a few idealized noblewomen with literary connections.

Jonson's ideal noblewoman is explicitly described in Epigram lxxvi, one of the three to the Countess of Bedford. She is "faire, and free, and wise", general attributes suitable for anyone, and also aristocratically "of greatest bloud, and yet more good than great". Though these terms are clearly appropriate to an ideal great lady, they are rather vague and abstract. More specifically, she should be "curteous, facile, sweet", all conventional feminine qualities, though not proud, the typical vice of women and of aristocrats. Her virtue is "softest vertue", and it resides in her "softer bosome". These ideals of feminine aristocratic grace cushion the connotations of a "learned, and a manly soul". She can control her destiny and "spin her owne free houres". Thus she has a 'masculine' mind and self-sufficiency, but it is decorously expressed in terms which remind us that the Fates are women and that to "spin" one's own hours is a higher form of a traditional female occupation.

At this stage in his career, Jonson praised many specific members of the titled classes and vehemently chastised a few examples of upper class vice. He did not identify himself with the upper classes, but he shied even farther from any identification with the London citizenry and the working classes. The son of a gentleman minister and the stepson of a bricklayer, Jonson liked to think of himself as a child of the Muses and an heir of the classical poets. Thus he saw his equals in an idealized class of gentlemen and scholars that included John Donne, William Camden, and Alphonso Ferrabosco. Jonson praised these men highly for their learning, wit, and good poetry, but his highest praises were directed at their virtue and piety, the "best life" he commends in John Donne (xxiii), and their "holiest friendship" (cxxii). Epigram lxxxvi, to Henry Goodyere, discusses the choice of an ideal friend.

> When I would know thee, *Goodyere*, my thought lookes
> Upon thy wel-made choise of friends, and bookes;
> Then doe I love thee, and behold thy ends
> In making thy friends bookes, and thy bookes friends:
> Now, I must give thy life, and deed, the voice
> Attending such a studie, such a choice.
> Where, though't be love, that to thy praise doth move
> It was a knowledge, that begat that love.

Jonson judges people, that is, by their judgments of others. Literary choices are here given equal status with live friends; study parallels life. The chiasmus of "in making thy friends bookes and thy bookes friends" makes a neat reciprocal pattern that implies both that the good man will be on intimate and easy relations with his studies and that his friends will be instructive exemplars of virtue. The poem moves from wishing to know Goodyere to knowing him, from knowing him to loving him, and then from loving him to praising him.

Jonson's fullest exposition in the epigrams of the ideal author is the well-known poem to Sir Henry Savile on his translation of Tacitus (xcv). Jonson discusses the reciprocal relationships between the author and his work and ranks the author's attributes. Savile is especially qualified as a historian by his freedom from the passions of his times and by a knowledge great enough for an active statesman. Jonson's evaluation of writing is always high, although he concedes it is somewhat "lesser" than action. Jonson's other requirements for a good historian include decorum of style and political and psychological insight. Highest of all, since for Jonson the humanist moral qualities must always support intellectual ones, is "faith" or pious integrity and devotion to the truth. In contrast, most of the negative poems about Jonson's social equals are against literary people like Poet-Ape (lvi) and "My

Meere English Critick" (xviii) who have failed to live up to these exacting standards.

As Savile is praised for being "from hope, from feare, from faction free" (xcv) and the Countess of Bedford for spinning "her owne free houres" (lxxvi), so a permanent aspect of Jonson's ideal for both men and women is that of manly self-sufficiency, including making one's "lent life, good against the *Fates*" (cix). Although good men are to be exemplars, Jonson seems at this time to believe that bad men probably will not change and the good need not. Later he was to adopt a more flexible attitude in this as in other respects. Paradoxically, therefore, Jonson in his earlier works often exhorts the virtuous to remain as they are. William Roe is assured that he will return from travel in the best possible way, "untouch'd" (cxxviii), and Sir Thomas Roe is urged to "be alwayes to thy gather'd selfe the same" (xcviii). The imagery of self-sufficiency in this poem combines moral with geometrical stability: "He that is round within himselfe, and streight,/ Need seeke no other strength, no other height."

While Jonson often addresses the titled classes and the learned and literary with praise and friendship, in his early poems he uniformly condemns other 'citizens'. The doctors, lawyers, and merchants in his epigrams are treated as scathingly as the usurers, alchemists, and prostitutes. The only commendatory poem addressed to members of the lower class is the general one to "True Souldiers" (cviii), which admits Jonson's former kinship with that group.

Because he believed his era degenerate, Jonson often relates his idealized man to an idealized time. Frequently, he describes good men as remnants of some former Golden Age. Thus Uvedale is a "piece of the first times" (cxxv), and Rudyerd represents "the aged *Saturne's* age" (cxxii). Susan de Vere Herbert was perhaps named because "our times" need "to behold/ a new *Susanna*, equall to that old" (civ). The fine past age was not always that of the Bible or the Romans, however. Sometimes it was the Elizabethan heyday immediately preceding Jonson's times, with Sidney as its culminating example. More currently, Radcliffe can still "shew the times" what he and his family "all were" (xciii). In contrast to these references to the degenerate present and the glorious past, Jonson wrote only one epigram in the first book employing the opposite literary convention, that of present accomplishments overgoing past precedent, when he commended Edward Allen above the famous Roman actors (lxxxix); later he was to praise Shakespeare in ✓ similar terms.

Throughout the first book of *Epigrammes*, then, Jonson's values and ideals shine clearly and consistently through the poems of praise, while the censuring poems are shadowed by the absence of the same values in their subjects. Out of fifty-eight commendatory epigrams on particular persons, Jonson praises general virtue and piety in about twenty-four poems; mind and learning in seventeen; poetry and literature in twelve; and so on down through public deeds and office, family or "bloud", self-sufficiency, friendship, beauty, and valor. (See Table Five, Appendix, for figures.) The words "example" or "emulate", directly speaking from Jonson's belief in the moral usefulness of the virtuous exemplar, appear in seven of these poems.

Despite Edward Herbert's eight virtuous attributes (cvi) or Lucy Bedford's fifteen (lxxvi), most of these poems of praise are not very specific. Often the words "vertue" or "learning" represent the qualities of the person praised without further specification. Cary's valorous deed in battle (lxvi) is almost the only specific act praised, and it is alluded to rather than described. Epigram cxvi states five times in different words that merit is more important than birth, but it does not develop the idea past neat *sententiae*. Several commendations do not even attempt to define the praised person's character but instead slide off into the easy commonplace that Jonson's praise is insufficient or unnecessary to the subject.[20]

In other words, the commendatory poems rarely detail the nature of the ideal man or of ideal virtue, though they constantly allude to certain fairly conventional ideals. Jonson's most characteristic addition to praise through these conventional humanistic

---

[20] Ernst Curtius, *European Literature and the Latin Middle Ages*, trans, by W. Trask (New York: Harper & Row, 1963), 159, calls this the "inexpressibility" topos. The topos is very widespread.

ideals in his earlier works is his stress on the pattern of reciprocal duties, obligations and pleasures existing between friends and equals or between King and country, patron and poet. Thus James' "manners draw" more than his "powers constraine" his people, and, as he was "preserved" to be England's King, so England was "preserv'd" from plague to be his country (xxxv). Similarly, the false rumor of James' death showed the people the effect of his "losse" and the king, that of the people's "love" (li). In these examples it is not the content of the matters discussed but rather the establishment of a reciprocal pattern in the verse that creates the praise.

Patterns of reciprocity in Jonson are often reinforced by imagery of payment and repayment. In the satiric poems, this takes on a brutal aspect of retaliation. For example, Voluptuous Beast's wife should "leave to be chast" in response to her husband's mental promiscuity (xxv). Shiftless Shift brays "God payes" to all his creditors, until finally he is repaid by the "pockie whore" (xii). Fine Grand literally owes Jonson for some commissioned hack poetical pieces, for which, incidentally, Jonson kept decorum, complaining of the difficulty of writing to fit the vileness of the supposed author (lxxiii). The poem ends not with a joke but a threat: "For which, or pay me quickly', or Ile pay you."

The imagery of debt and payment appears more gracious in the commendatory poems. Thus in the epigram to Esmé, Lord Aubigny, Jonson calls "Posteritie/ Into the debt" and in a progression mildly reminiscent of Donne's St. Lucy's night desolation, he claims that he and his Muse would be "full of want ... swallow'd up ... dead" without Esmé's "timely succours". Therefore, Jonson's "reward" for his poetry, that is, his reputation, will be indirectly "owing" to Aubigny's favor. In return for these debts, Jonson pays with this epigram thanking the lord (cxxvii).

Although the moral as well as financial debtor must "pay", Jonson sees the noblest creditor as the one who need not collect. After the tribute to Cary's bravery, the last six lines of Epigram lxvi go:

> Love honors, which of best example bee,
> When they cost dearest, and are done most free,

Though every fortitude deserves applause,
It may be much, or little in the cause.
Hee's valiant'st, that dares fight, and not for pay;
That vertuous is, when the reward's away.

In these lines several key Jonsonian concepts and terms occur together. "Honors" are not to be loved vainly, but only as they provide an "example" for others. The contrast "when they cost dearest, and are done most free" uses monetary imagery to compare different kinds of value. The dearest "cost" represents personal sacrifice, while the "most free" manner indicates that the deeds are done fearlessly, frankly, voluntarily, with a certain casual grace or *sprezzatura*. The "cost" is then to the individual; the gain in example and in military achievement is to the society. The phrasing, turning the "dearest" cost into something "free", shows the aristocratic magnificence of casually-assumed risk. The discriminations of the next two lines seek to define true valor, a motif that becomes more important in Jonson's later poems and plays, but here the discussion is cut short: "fortitude" must necessarily "deserve applause" since by definition fortitude is virtuous valor, not indiscriminate bravado. The final couplet returns to the monetary image which socially distinguishes the aristocratic chevalier from the mere mercenary soldier; at the same time it enforces the general moral that virtue is, or should be, its own reward.

Since patterns of reciprocity are central to Jonson's conceptions of the nature of things, it is not surprising that he often places himself squarely in his epigrams in one of his roles of moral judge, patronized poet, or loving friend. He refers to himself in the first person in eighty-four of the one hundred and thirty-three epigrams of the first book. Of the poems without a reference to himself, thirty are satiric, mostly short, like the ones on Spies (lix), Sir Cod (xx), Groyne (cxvii) and Gut (cxviii). A few longer derogatory narratives are also entirely in the third person, for example the poems on Shift (xii) and the English Monsieur (lxxxviii). Rather often, even in his satiric epigrams, Jonson includes himself as the personal witness of the folly satirized. For instance, he reports he met the "Some-thing that Walkes Some-where" at court (xi), and he personally knows of "Fine Lady Would-Bee's" hidden fertility (lxii).

By far the largest class of satiric epigrams including a first person reference is that on the unworthy poets, playwrights, and critics. There are eighteen of these, in most of which Jonson portrays himself as a victim needing redress. Usually some insult has occurred to which the epigram is a response: Fine Grand has made off with Jonson's literary wares without paying (lxxiii). Censorious Court-ling praises Jonson's poems "frostily" (lii), or the New Motion no longer greets him on the street (xcvii).

The commendatory poems are even more strongly saturated with Jonson's first person references than are the censuring poems. Only eighteen of the commendatory poems have no reference to himself. Three of these are objective epitaphs, such as could be written on stone; five, commendatory poems on living persons. Several other poems, including three about women, change the *I* into *we* out of politeness and respect. In Epigrams xxxv and li the whole nation is represented as "we" who know God through King James, though Jonson is not too shy to seek James as "my test" in his introductory epigram to the King (iv).

Often, and more emphatically than in the satirical poems, Jonson introduces himself as the authoritative witness of the virtue he praises. Thus he tells Goodyere, "I'm glad, and grateful to report,/ My selfe a witnesse of thy few dayes sport" (lxxxv). Even more intimately, he assures Sir Thomas Roe, "I know nothing more thou has to doe" (xcviii). In Epigram cxxv Jonson claims to be a judge of virtuous character: thus others might love Uvedale's body, "But I, no child, no foole, respect the kinde,/ The full, the flowing graces there enshrin'd."

Closely related to the poems in which Jonson is the witness of virtue are those in which he is a participant in some friendly or reciprocal relation. Thus Epigram lxxxiv to the Countess of Bedford and Epigram cxxvii to Lord Aubigny are thank-you notes. The seventeen poems of friendly gratitude and praise to the learned, friends and poets, are among Jonson's best known. They use the same 'places' of praise as the poems to aristocrats, but their tone is that of an equal speaking to equals, and Jonson is usually more specific when judging literary and learned matters than when he is commending the virtues of the high born.

Among the most interesting of the commendatory poems from the standpoint of Jonson's voice are the ten that make a particular issue of the poet's role as praiser. Epigram xliii to Robert, Earl of Salisbury, makes a fullscale attack on the subject, beginning, "What need hast thou of me? or of my *Muse*?" The question posed in this poem is answered in Epigram lxiii, also to Salisbury, by the further rhetorical question, "Who can consider thy right courses run/ ... /And can to these be silent ...?"

Who, then, is the speaker, the *persona*, in these early epigrams and why do critics so confidently identify him with the author, Ben Jonson? The simplest answer is that the speaker of these poems is a poet, "the poet", in an almost official and certainly in a public sense. The public poet may have private grudges – like those against his plagiarists, his private sorrows – like the death of friends and children, and his private gratitudes – like that to Aubigny, but his tendency is to generalize all these for the benefit of his audience, that is, to set them up in patterns useful for his readers' moral instruction.

The speaker of Jonson's early epigrams is consistent and distinctive. In the other works, there are more speakers; in the later works, more subtle ones. The speaker of these early epigrams is rarely subtle. His main characteristic is his self-assurance. He is confident that he is virtuous, learned, a good man and a good poet, and that he can distinguish among others who is, and who is not a like character. In Epigram xcv, he speaks for the learned community. He knows its character and its needs and can authoritatively, if admiringly, instruct Savile in how and where to use his talents: "We need a man that knowes the severall graces/ Of historie ...." In Epigram lxx, Jonson's 'To the Virtuous, to Make Much of Time', the poet confidently places himself and William Roe among the good: "since we (more then many) these truths know:/ Though life be short, let us not make it so."

Jonson at times represents himself as the voice of all men, even when the poem concerns a private matter. Thus Jonson asks Aubigny, "Is there a hope, that Man would thankefull bee,/ If I should faile, in gratitude, to thee ...?" (cxxvii). Jonson is most explicitly the pure, impersonal voice of virtuous poetry in Epigram cix where he tells Nevil, "Who now calls on thee, *Nevil*, is a *Muse*,/ That serves nor fame, nor titles; but doth chuse/ Where virtue makes them both ...."

Jonson's tone in the epigrams varies from deference through familiarity to scathing contempt. It is always decorous in terms of its subject. Jonson maintains one consistent attitude for poems of praise, another for poems of blame. In these early poems there is no sign of doubt or conciliation or ambivalence. The poet knows where he stands: he is on the side of all that is virtuous, manly, and right. His own role is clearly established, and he maintains it as consistently as his ideals for the roles of aristocrat, friend, or author.

Jonson's tone is perhaps most varied in his epitaphs on children. These poems show an interesting range of degrees of poetic involvement through the handling of the person speaking. In the poem on his first daughter, Jonson achieves a sense of detachment and formal pathos by referring simply to "the father" in his bereavement and his solace (xxii). In contrast, the "me" in "weepe with me all you that read" in the epitaph on S. P. (cxx) is a generalized one, the voice of any mourner. The voice is not very different from that of the speaker commanding "marble weepe" for Margaret Ratcliffe (xl). On the other hand, the epitaph of Elizabeth, L. H. (cxxiv) connotes a certain amount of artistic pride in the apparently impersonal "Would'st thou heare, what man can say/ In a little?" where Jonson, the "man" saying in little, seems to be openly challenging comparison with classical elegists. The most personal and moving of these epitaphs is the poem on Jonson's first son, Epigram xlv.[21] This poem combines Jonson's very personal use of the first person speaker with many of the most typical poetic techniques of his early poems, including strong patterns of reciprocity enforced by the imagery of payment. Although it is in

---

[21] Fike, "First sonne", and Kay, "Christian Wisdom", emphasize Jonson's acceptance of Christian consolation in the poem, and both critics give pertinent contemporary theological background. Fike attributes to the poem the sentiments of other Jonson epitaphs.

many ways representative of Jonson's style and his typical themes at this time, it is a unique poem in the Jonson canon. In this single poem the objective public voice of the poet which is so consistently represented in all the other early epigrams is overwhelmed by the private voice of the author, Ben Jonson, even as it tries to come to terms with this moving and dissenting second voice.

> Farewell, thou child of my right hand, and joy;
> My sinne was too much hope of thee, lov'd boy,
> Seven yeeres tho'wert lent to me, and I thee pay,
> Exacted by thy fate, on the just day.
> 5 O, could I loose all father now. For why
> Will man lament the state he should envie?
> To have so soone scap'd worlds, and fleshes rage
> And, if no other miserie, yet age?
> Rest in soft peace, and, ask'd, say here doth lye
> 10 *Ben. Jonson* his best piece of *poetrie*.
> For whose sake, hence-forth, all his vowes be such,
> As what he loves may never like too much.

This epitaph is one of the most powerful poems on death in the English Renaissance. The restraint of the language in comparison to the depth of the emotion has been indicated as one source of its power.[22] More specifically, the poem gains its force from its redefinition of the father's role during the poem and from its avoidance of most traditional formulae for Christian consolation or triumph. Like many of Jonson's most effective poems, the epitaph is bound together by an extensive pattern of repeated sounds, and it achieves a sense of dignity and weight through its handling of sound and rhythmic effects.

The sound effects provide one indication of the mastery and control found in all aspects of the poem and characteristic of Jonson's best early work. Probably the most important assonance linking key words in the poem is that which connects the words "child", "my", "right", "why", "envie", "lye", and "poetrie". This extensive echoing emphasizes the crucial word "like" in the last line, helping to raise it to distinctness against the usually stronger word "love".

[22] Lester A. Beaurline, "The Selective Principle in Jonson's Shorter Poems", *Criticism*, 8 (1966), 66.

The pattern of pauses in the poem works together with the repetition of sounds for the total effect. The more emotional words in the first part of the poem are placed at the ends of the lines, after the caesurae so that they have an effect of correction, restatement, surprise. Thus "Farewell, thou child of my right hand" has dignity and weight in its Englished periphrasis of the Hebrew name Benjamin. The more charged words "and joy" come to this statement as correction, the tardily admitted parental emotion. In the second line, "my sinne was too much hope of thee" is again followed by the emotional words, "lov'd boy", the sequent address to the more formal "child of my right hand". Of his epitaphs on children Jonson uses the full pentameter line only in this poem. In the first two lines, however, he appears to be setting up tetrameters, each time to add the remaining foot after the late caesura.

Along with these effects, the diction of the opening lines establishes the tone of the poem. The meanings and connotations of the rather abstract words begin the process of definition and redefinition that gives the poem its distinctive character. For instance, the statement "my sinne was too much hope of thee" raises several questions and forebodes the distinction of the last line in its own surprising redefinition. Hope is one of the three primary Christian virtues, not a sin, and proper Christian hope is of heaven, which the son has presumably achieved. Clearly, then, the "too much hope" of which Jonson speaks was not only excessive in degree but different in kind from this Christian hope, and we are probably to deduce from this compressed statement that Jonson in his fatherly pride had too many, too fond, earthly expectations for his young son. The destruction of the father's hopes gains added poignancy from comparison between his child and the Biblical Benjamin, the most beloved child of an old father, the father's hope for a long posterity, and the pledge for his father's life. Thus the redefinition here, as at the end of the poem, refers to one father's emotional investment in his son. Hope is not normally a sin, and is in fact so far from it that the personal application which makes it such seems wry and pathetic, the result of unusually unhappy circumstances. The poem is not obscure, but it is so compressed that the reader must fill in much of its meaning for himself.[23] Thus the reader becomes a participant in the poem's moving play of emotions. Despite the finished quality of the verse, therefore, the poem must be read as a series of emotions in process.

Lines three and four at first seem to express the idea that life is a loan, a commonplace in Jonson and throughout Renaissance literature: "Seven yeeres tho'wert lent to me, ..." However, the lines here have a tougher and more personal application than in Epigram cix, for instance, where Nevil is praised for having made his "lent life, good against the *Fates*". After the caesura in line three of the epitaph, the metaphor "tho'wert lent" is turned into actuality by the unconventional addition "I thee pay", with its three strong stresses and compressed inversion of syntax. The clause has several peculiarities. First, "thee" would normally be the indirect object of the clause, followed by the object paid, whatever it was, but here the boy is himself the loan paid back. Second, the verb is in the present tense, as though the speaker is still feeling the press of the exactions upon him. Third, who is paid? Absent is the easy reciprocity of acceptance in Jonson's poem on the death of his first daughter: "All heavens gifts, being heavens due,/ It makes the father, lesse, to rue" (xxii). In the epitaph on his son Jonson does not see God taking the boy to Him. There is not even the consolation of the epitaph on S. P. who was "too good for earth" so that "Heaven vowes to keepe him" (cxx). Instead, God is not mentioned, and the focus is firmly on the father who is forced to "pay" back the precious son. Some irony here springs from the disproportion between the cliché of life as a loan and the terrible application of the image when made concrete, of the idea of the child as recallable flesh. The fact that Jonson addresses the boy here, not God or fate, makes his control more admirable and the force of the situation more clear; it is as though he has been asked to give the child up and is voluntarily, if reluctantly, taking leave of him.

These ideas are confirmed by the fourth line of the poem, "Exacted by thy fate, on the just day". The word "exacted" is a

---

[23]   Trimpi, *Jonson's Poems*, 189, speaks of "a type of obscurity peculiar to the plain style", the result of the reader's lack of the proper context to adjust and restrict his associations to the poem's denotation.

harsh one, connoting heartless creditors, and "by thy fate" almost seems to be a periphrasis – a true statement, but one that does not clarify the difficult question of the necessity for the boy's repayment. The force at work seems inscrutable rather than benevolent. The metaphor of the loan is not carried out, as it so easily could have been, to the idea of redemption, and the Fate here is far different from the tame classical Parcae musing over S. P.'s disposition. The phrase "on the just day" seems to balance Christian ideas against these implied doubts and questions. The "just day" seems to indicate Jonson's acceptance of the boy's fate, the idea of debt recognized, yet the "just day" automatically invokes a comparison with the more merciful possibility. "Just" also implies "exact" in the sense that no extensions of the loan are allowed. The phrase shows a confidence at least that the boy has received divine justice, but its connotations of the day of judgment are not elaborated, and there is no hint of ultimate reunion. Much of the force of this poem, then, is that while it provides a Christian context it does not portray a complete Christian consolation but keeps hinting at the possibilities, so that we know precisely the solace Jonson the father does not feel and therefore the desolation of his expressed state – one of acceptance of an inscrutably "just" fate but not of thanks to a merciful God.

In the next four lines, the middle third of the twelve-line poem, Jonson releases himself from the untenable emotional and tonal constraint of the first quatrain into the despairing exclamation, "O, could I loose all father now". And he does lose enough "father" in the rest of the poem to refer to himself as "man", generalizing his situation, and to speak of himself only in the third person. The compressed phrase "all father" here states what Jonson has already lost and what he wishes yet to lose. He has lost his child, and he is therefore less of a father, but, as the grievous wish indicates, he has not automatically upon the death of his child lost all of his fatherly hope and love. Thus this released lament shows the basic falsity of the financial metaphor of the first four lines with its rigid glossing over of human realities. His apparent acceptance based on this metaphor of the child as a debt is now seen as untenable, and Jonson lets his questioning of the harsh realities of man's fate become general: "For why/ Will man lament the state he should envie?" The echo "man", "lament" seems to indicate the usual state of man, while the generalization asks if any man could rejoice and not lament at Jonson's fate. In contrast, Jonson invokes with calm assurance the reward of Christian consolation and the friend's proper response to the death of John Roe: "O happy state! wherein/ Wee, sad for him, may glorie, and not sinne" (xxvii).

The nature of the "state" that man should envy but actually laments is defined only negatively, as "to have so soone scap'd worlds, and fleshes rage,/ And, if no other miserie, yet age". Jonson does not mention heaven in this poem, and these lines sound as though the enviable state is death, not heaven. Ironically, such sorrows as a son's death make a man's own life seem not worth having. Far different is Jonson's poem on his first daughter with its assurance that the Virgin Mary, to comfort little Mary Jonson's mother, has placed the girl's soul in Heaven "amongst her virgin-traine" (xxii).

The word "envie" in the epitaph's question "For why/ Will man lament the state he should envie?" is striking; a more usual word in this context would be "hope". But Jonson's hopes for the boy have been shattered. Moreover, to ask why man laments the state he should rejoice over would belie the implication of the poem that for the father all his joy, love, and hope were placed in his boy, and it is for this sin that he is now visited with a numbing fate. Thus he describes the boy's enviable state only by its freedom from the world's evils and miseries. The force of the lines comes from the implied contrast between the bright innocence of a young child and the evils remote from a boy's experience that he has escaped by dying – ambition, lust, old age. This is a description of adult evil in a sour world, ungraced, deserted by such innocence and joy as contrastingly Jonson found in his young son. Now the bereft father sees only this gloomy set of possibilities as his own world.

After four lines of tightly controlled resignation and four more lines of loosed lamentation, then, the poem receives a kind of resolution in the last four lines. Line nine begins, "Rest in soft peace", where the child's peace reasonably seems "soft" in contrast with the hissing rages and miseries of the father's living world. That is, by showing his own misery and lamentation in lines five to eight, the father has demonstrated to himself the sorrows of life and therefore the boy's relatively better state in death. It is almost implied that the misery the child missed by dying young was living long enough to have his child die before him. As in the rest of the poem, the father's emotions dominate, but the emphasis in these last four lines is on redefining the father's role in a more humanly acceptable way than through the debtor image in lines one to four. Thus after the brief conventional quietus of "rest in soft peace" with its hushed *s*'s (in contrast to the more obvious alliteration of "so soone scap'd") Jonson tells his child the answer that he has at last worked out to his own question, the question, that is, of what a son is and what part a father has in him. "Rest in soft peace" makes a new start with its inverted first foot, and the three pauses after syllables four, five, and six set up the answer as deliberately thought out: "and, ask'd, say here doth lye/ *Ben. Jonson* his best piece of *poetrie*". If Jonson here implies that this epitaph is his best piece of poetry, he is not illustrating pride of authorship but the fact that the son is the best part of himself and hence evokes his best poetry. Moreover, there may be an implied recognition here that all poetry of words is pale and superficial in contrast to the human creation, even if lines of verse will outlive their authors, according to the easy Renaissance commonplace of the immortality of poetry.

Beaurline claims that the "neat trick" here is the pun on the word "maker", a word not used in the poem, as poet and as creator in general.[24] This pun on "maker" raises a wider ambiguity, that between the earthly and the heavenly father as maker. The poem then reassesses which has what rights in the son. Moreover, the statement "here doth lye/ *Ben. Jonson*" has several possible meanings that are not altogether cancelled out by the full reading. First, simply, here lies dead little Ben. Second, here lies the father, dead in the death of his son, in his hopes and ambitions for him,

---

[24] Beaurline, "Selective Principle", 67. Trimpi, *Jonson's Poems*, 182-83, says that "poetrie", meaning "that which is made or created", is the pun.

and in his craving for the immortality of his name and lineage through a long posterity. The image of the child as a "piece of poetrie" revises the unfeeling earlier definition of the child as a repaid debt. Thus if God is the maker of all with final rights of recall on all of his earthly creation, Jonson still has some valid claims in the son, whom he too has truly made. The child, then, if not in the fulfillment of earthly hopes, is in this sense as immortal, as individual, as uniquely valuable as poetry.

The poem ends with this muted and indirect consolation contrasted with the present reality of the father's desire never again to be visited with such pain. "For whose sake, henceforth", he says, implying that it cannot be helped this time, and the future now does not seem to matter so much, "all his vowes be such,/ As what he loves may never like too much". The explanation that "like" means "pleases", following the distinction in Martial, gives the basic meaning here,[25] but the paltriness of the distinction between "loves" and "like" in the usual sense of the word "like" seems to be intended. Jonson is vowing not only to be less self-engrossed, less hopeful for private and prideful ends in those he loves – an admirable and Christian vow, but he is also wishing to be saved from the 'too much' of human passion, affection, and hence affliction. Thus the poem ends, with acceptance of the boy's fate and with a definition of fatherhood that does justice to the father's role in his son, but also with recognition of the inconsolable in the father's sorrow and thus with a covert prayer for the peace of mind of the bereft father, poet, 'maker'.

Jonson's epigram on his first son, then, is the most moving and emotionally charged of the one hundred thirty-three epigrams of the first book. As we have seen, these early epigrams divide into the two categories of praise and blame, according as their subject is virtue or vice. The audience for both kinds of epigrams is the same, the learned and the virtuous, often members of the upper classes, like those people to whom the commendatory epigrams are

---

[25] H & S, 11, 9. Hunter's reading of *thrive* for "like", *Complete Poetry*, 20, gives a very bitter interpretation to the poem; I doubt it can be the dominant meaning in this context. The additional *OED* meaning for *like* as 'liken, create an image' may also be mentioned.

addressed. The two classes of epigrams are treated somewhat differently in terms of the author's style and tone. Derogatory analogies and direct, harsh diction occur in the satiric epigrams, while the commendatory poems abound in the finer discriminations and qualifications applicable to the moral choices of the virtuous. None the less, Jonson's 'plain style' throughout the epigrams is fairly consistent, with its frequent use of abstract diction, unobtrusive imagery, functional figures of sound and rhythm, simple rhetorical structures, and highly articulated syntax. One of the most distinctive characteristics of Jonson's style in these early epigrams is his consistent use of negative, indirect, and conditional statements which often, as in Epigram ci, "Inviting a Friend to Supper", establish a balance among various alternative possibilities. A very similar kind of patterning stresses reciprocal relations in Jonson's verse. Thus Jonson's distinctive traits of style in the epigrams serve to demonstrate his main themes, like the values of moderation and of the proper reciprocal relations between people, which are often underscored by the imagery of payment. Jonson tries to point out in the epigrams not only how men should act toward one another but also what they should be in themselves – as ideal aristocrats, women, authors, or friends. He believes men should be self-sufficient and stand firm in virtue to the credit of their names and the increase of their fames. In his four most common words, his message in the epigrams is often, 'great men, make good'.

The concepts of name and fame indicate the reciprocal duties of the poet to praise the virtuous and the virtuous to be praiseworthy, and the epigrams are as much about the nature and function of the poet as they are about virtues and vices. The poet in the epigrams is always firmly didactic as he exposes vice and displays examples of virtue for emulation. His aim, in another arrangement of Jonson's four favorite words, is to 'make man great, good'. Jonson's style in the epigrams follows this didactic aim in its restraint and concentration, its emphasis on clear and useful effects. The speaker of these poems is the 'Muse', the public voice of moral poetry. Jonson's epitaph on his first son is unique in the epigrams in the force with which the personal voice of Jonson as father interacts with the public voice of Jonson as poet. The epitaph is also unique in that it exploits some of the tensions and conflicts hidden under Jonson's conventional moral theme. It discards the imagery of payment as inappropriate for some human relations, and it probes the emotional implications of the ideals of self-sufficiency and of the immortality of poetry. Jonson's epitaph on his first son transcends the categories of praise and blame into which the other epigrams are divided. While it stands as the finest example of Jonson's early plain style, in this respect, it looks forward to Jonson's more mature verse.

3. THE FORREST

Jonson's *The Forrest* is a sophisticated group of fifteen poems that was published along with the *Epigrammes* in the 1616 folio of the *Workes*. It represents Jonson's poetry in other *genres* for the same chronological period. No single literary work forms an organizing model for *The Forrest* as Martial's books of epigrams do for Jonson's *Epigrammes*, and *The Forrest* therefore complements the *Epigrammes* as a demonstration of Jonson's earlier poetry, as he wished it to be known, showing Jonson ranging in new fields and attacking new poetic problems.[1] *The Forrest* divides into two main groups of poems. The first group is primarily made up of songs. The poems in this group are short, concise, and well-crafted like the epigrams. Unlike the epigrams, which are written almost entirely in pentameter couplets, the songs are usually in tetrameter. Sometimes, too, they use more elaborate stanzaic forms than the couplet. The songs restrict their content chiefly to the conventional Elizabethan lyric topics of women and love, and their tone is often humorous and gay. The first person is used in all of these poems, but, in contrast to the more striking lyrics of Jonson's later verse, the speaker's voice in these earlier songs is usually not represented as the author's. Instead, it is the voice of the suave or cynical man about town, the witty cavalier. Poems in this group include Forrest I, "Why I Write Not of Love"; Forrest V, VI, and IX, "Come My Celia", "Kisse Me Sweet", and the famous "Drinke to Me, Onely", all addressed "To Celia";

---

[1] Kay, "Shaping", 224-37, reminds us of the extent to which the folio of 1616 was a conscious selection of Jonson's work designed to establish him as a poet worthy of respect.

and Forrest VII and VIII, two songs about women, "That Women Are But Mens Shaddowes" and "To Sicknesse". (See Table Six, Appendix, which gives the dimensions of the poems in *The Forrest*.)

The songs are like the epigrams in compression and craftsmanship, but they differ from the epigrams in subject matter, speaker, and tone. The other group of poems in *The Forrest* resembles the epigrams in subject matter, speaker, and tone, but varies from them in length and construction. Like the epigrams, these poems are moral and serious. Four of them are epistles, with a strong vein of compliment, as in the commendatory epigrams. As in the epigrams, the pentameter couplet is the most usual meter in this group of poems, and their rhythms are closer to speech than to song. Forrest II, "To Penshurst", is the most famous of this class of poems, followed by III, "To Sir Robert Wroth". There are two epistles to noblewomen: Forrest XII to Elizabeth, Countess of Rutland and XIII, to Katherine, Lady Aubigny. Similar to these epistles in length, theme, and structure is Forrest XI, the "Epode". The humorous prelude preceding the "Epode" serves as its introduction. The "Ode" to Sir William Sidney, Forrest XIV, is written in complex lyric stanzas rather than in couplets, but it gives advice to a member of the aristocracy in the manner of the epigrams and epistles. The literary sources for these epistles are the satires, epistles, and odes of the Latin poets, especially Martial and Horace. The "Epode" has roots in Renaissance neoplatonism and Christian allegory.

There are also two religious poems in this group of serious poems. Uniquely in Jonson's earlier nondramatic poetry, the speaker of Forrest IV, "To the World, A Farewell for a Gentlewoman, Vertuous and Noble" is a woman. The other religious poem, "To Heaven" (XV), is the shortest of the serious poems; its tradition is rather that of the personal meditative religious lyric than that of didactic religious allegory found in "To the World".

In contrast to the moral epigrams and epistles, Jonson's songs tend to be amorous and even immoral. In the broad sense, they are often still based on praise or dispraise, like the epigrams, but the focus has shifted to praise of woman, dispraise of love or the envious or disease. This emphasis connects the songs of *The Forrest* with many of the poems in *Under-Wood*, though the earlier poems tend to be simpler.

The phrasing in the songs is shorter and evener than in the epigrams and epistles. Phrase groups in the songs tend to be about three or four words long and the sense is easy to grasp.[2] Most lines are endstopped, and couplets tend to be closed. Many critics' favorite examples of Jonson's sleeked diction can be found in these songs. This spareness of word and particularly of adjective is a trait of the epigrams continued in both Jonson's dramatic and purely lyric songs.

Volpone's seduction poem (V) is typical of Jonson's dramatic song-writing; it is the only song from his plays that he chose specifically to include in his nondramatic works, perhaps because of its origin as an adaptation of Catullus V. Like Clerimont's song in *Epicene* or Wittipol's in *The Devil is an Ass*, it advances the dramatic action of its play. Alone, the poem stands as a seduction piece by a corrupt speaker who is exposed by what he says, not by the poet's moralizing. For instance, Volpone asks, "Why should we deferre our joyes" with a bland assumption of eventual success, and his dismissal of fame as a toy shows him to be untrustworthy. Several of the rhyme words, including "spyes", "beguile", "wile", and "steale" have sinister or criminal connotations, while the line, "Tis no sinne, loves fruit to steale" recalls Eve's apple and primal sin. The entire non-Catullan ending of the song emphasizes the illicit nature of the proposed "sports", exposes the speaker's reliance on external standards like exposure, and leaves the strong word "crimes" as the judgment on the whole seduction. Forrest V is thus an effective poem of indirect censure using a dramatic speaker in contrast to the direct condemnation of the satiric epigrams and epistles.

"Drinke to me, onely" (IX), is often considered Jonson's most accomplished poem, a perfect lyric and even the quintessence of pure lyric poetry.[3] Unquestionably it is an example of Jonson's

---

[2]   Evans, *Music*, 15, relates these characteristics of the verse to the requirements of singing.

[3]   C. V. Wedgwood, *Seventeenth-Century English Literature* (Home University

peculiar devices of style applied most successfully to erotic praise
rather than to the commendation of an aristocrat.

> Drinke to me, onely, with thine eyes,
> And I will pledge with mine;
> Or leave a kisse but in the cup,
> And Ile not looke for wine.
> 5 The thirst, that from the soule doth rise,
> Doth aske a drinke divine:
> But might I of *Jove's Nectar* sup,
> I would not change for thine,
>
> I sent thee, late, a rosie wreath,
> 10 Not so much honoring thee,
> As giving it a hope, that there
> It could not withered bee.
> But thou thereon did'st onely breath,
> And sent'st it back to mee:
> 15 Since when it growes, and smells, I sweare,
> Not of it selfe, but thee.

One reason for the poem's popularity is undoubtedly its idealism,
that is, its romantically worshipful tone in contrast, for instance,
to the seducing cynicism of Forrest V.

"Drinke to me, onely" is in iambic meter, forming two eight-
line stanzas of alternating line length on a rhyme scheme with
three rhymes per stanza: $a^4b^3c^4b^3a^4b^3c^4b^3$. The intertwining effect
of the rhyming short lines is especially appropriate to the wreath
motif in the second stanza.

An article has been written to explicate the single word "but"
in line seven of the poem,[4] and the line's seeming transparency,
which turns to opaqueness and ambiguity upon close inspection,
indicates something about the nature of the poem. In the first
stanza in particular, the longer lines tend to be slightly ambiguous
or metaphorical, while the shorter lines are emphatic and unequi-
vocal. The resulting sense carried by the reader, then, tends to be

---

Library) (London: Oxford, 1950), 64.
4   Marshall Van Deusen, "Criticism and Ben Jonson's 'To Celia'", *Essays
in Criticism*, 7 (1957), 95-103. A brief exchange on this *but* occurred between
Gerald Bullett, "Drinke to Me Only", *Times Literary Supplement*, June 1,
1956, 329; and E. A. Horsman, *Times Literary Supplement*, June 8, 1956, 345.

that of the shorter lines, which are felt as clarifications. They achieve a kind of bright resolution, even if only by juxtaposition with the longer lines. It is the placement of the adverbs and the elliptical terseness of the metaphors that causes most of the difficulty. Thus in the first line the word "onely" can apply either to "drinke to me" or to "with thine eyes", and ends by meaning both drink to no one except me and use nothing but your eyes in drinking to me. The action the lover requests of the lady is thus left to her discretion. It is clear that he is tentatively presenting the adored mistress with a set of alternatives, any of which would make him happy, would, indeed, be beyond his expectation. His ambiguity is thus almost gallant and very respectful. Whatever she likes to do, he will be unchanged. His promised reciprocal pledge is appropriate to any of the preceding possibilities.

"Or leave a kisse but in the cup" follows the same pattern. Again, the speaker's responsive promise is clear and forceful: "And Ile not looke for wine". The parallel with the first two lines sounds exact, partly from the impact of the steady iambs. However, in lines one and two the speaker promises a positive act in response to a positive action of hers – pledging her with his eyes in return for her gaze; in lines three and four, instead, he is giving an indirect indication of respect – not desiring wine – in response to an action of hers which may not be related to him at all – drinking from a cup. Only his adoration converts her everyday action into the equivalent of a kiss. Already the poem is moving to a less physical and more metaphorical plane. Thus the step in the next four lines to a spiritual "thirst" and "drinke" is not precipitous.

As is true throughout Jonson's earlier work, his best poems often owe their success to their controlled manipulation of a set of alternatives or choices that are actually quite close together. In Forrest IX, the range is from polite and polished gallantry to equally polished, but more diffident, adoration. All other possible attitudes to a beloved lady, all the more traditional moods of desire, reproach, gaiety, exaltation, and, especially, familiarity, are carefully ruled out.

"The thirst, that from the soule doth rise", starting with three *th*'s in a neat iambic line, is unclear just insofar as the meaning of the soul's thirst is unclear. Its predicate in the short line, "doth aske a drinke divine", completes the metaphor, using three *d*'s, but without explaining it at all. Whatever a soul's thirst may be, its gratification is naturally a divine drink. The postposition of the adjective indicates its climactic emphasis. The language sounds like that of Christian mysticism, though the fact that the stanza began with real wine somewhat insulates this new phase from transubstantial blasphemy. Clearly, the metaphor is a compliment one step more refined than the preceding one, but not of an utterly different kind. Moreover, if the speaker has successively raised the pitch of adoration in each line of the poem, and hence raised the implied hyperbole to his mistress, he has also correspondingly elevated his own responsive character. It is his *soul* that thirsts. When he returns to the balancing reciprocities of his adoration, he uses the myth of Jove's nectar, the immortalizing fluid, as an analogue of the "drinke divine" that his beloved may provide, a superior token to wine or even kisses and glances.

"But might I of Jove's Nectar sup/ I would not change for thine" are the most controversial lines in the poem. The critical "but", according to the *O.E.D.* and various critical partisans, may mean either "even if" or "only if".[5] "I would not change for thine" parallels "and Ile not looke for wine" and sounds clear and confident. The sense that stays with the reader, then, despite possible vagaries of syntax, is that the lover compares his beloved's powers over him favorably to Jove's nectar. The first four lines of the stanza are in the simple future: although all the conditions are hypothetical, the tone is firmly one of you do this and I will do that. In contrast, the proposition of the second four lines is in the subjunctive and clearly indicates an impossible condition. It is therefore almost irrelevant whether the speaker would or would not put Jove's nectar, a poetic fiction, ahead of the "drink divine" which his beloved might provide. It can hardly matter which is the slightly superior of these two fictive liquids. The point, of course,

---

5 William Empson, *Seven Types of Ambiguity*, 3rd ed. (Norfolk, Conn.: New Directions, 1953), 242, rather surprisingly prides himself on finding this *but* a mistake rather than a genuine ambiguity.

is that the lover has thought to make the comparison, a hyperbolic one in either case, between his beloved and the glorious Olympians who have been sung through centuries. The reference to Jove also limits the possible Christian suggestiveness of the "drinke divine", showing that it is to be taken metaphorically, and not as the literal truth it would be if applied to the true God. The sense of the comparison, then, is that the beloved has some kind of power that may be called rejuvenating or immortalizing, analogous to the power imputed by old poetic traditions to Jove's nectar. The very poetic reference possibly even implies that while the beloved makes the speaker immortal in some sense, the poet makes the beloved immortal by writing the poem as a monument to her power.

Instead of the three hypothetical parallel and reciprocal situations, two physical and one spiritual, of the first stanza, in the second stanza there is only one situation. It consists of the speaker's action and the beloved's response with the speaker's interpretation of both. The pattern thus shifts from "if you do this, I will do that" to "I have done this, and you did do that". The second stanza is linked with the first through the even tone and the steady iambics. More subtly, the whole conceit of the second stanza can be seen as a proof of the beloved's immortalizing power honored in the first stanza. The poem moves into the past to detail the lover's action in a factual tone: "I sent thee, late, a rosie wreath". The balancing Jonsonian negative is now brought forward at the beginning of the next line, "Not so much honoring thee". The slight uncertainty of accent on "not so" contributes to a diffident, moderate tone, leading from the pure statement of fact which precedes it to the compliment which follows it. As in the first stanza, the negative indicates a condition insufficient, not improper, for praise of the beloved, though the order is here varied to give the negative first. The positive then is a tentative one. It starts with a light tone and a quickened pace in the longer line, "as giving it a hope, that there" and becomes more assertive and emphatic in stating the expected miracle in the short line, "it could not withered bee".

Her response, opening the second quatrain of the stanza, is

narrated as a past event: "But thou thereon did'st onely breath,/ And sent'st it back to mee". The adverb "onely" is here attached rather more firmly than usual to the verb, and the rebuff to the lover is saved from harshness by the intimacy of "onely breath". The lover's response is a further compliment, this time stated as a fact. "Since" then "it growes, and smells, I sweare", he marvels in a long, slowed line with two pauses, the parenthetical "I sweare" added in a tone of naive conviction, "not of it selfe, but thee". The final hyperbole is emphatic yet again negative and indirect in expression. "Not of it selfe" opens strongly with an inverted foot, but the negative does not apply to the whole line, as in the other short lines, only to the first half. It is offset after the only caesura in the poem's short lines by the positive assertion, using "but" for the fourth time, "but thee". The tendency to negative statement and indirection is thus cut off, and the poem ends on a clearly complimentary note.

Different as it may seem in tone and content, "Drinke to me, onely" shares many stylistic qualities with Jonson's best epigrams like "Inviting a Friend to Supper", including the sparse but effective use of connotative adjectives. The only adjectives in this pared-down poem are "divine" and "rosie", plus the past participle "withered". The rhetorical parallels in the poem give a sense of neatness and concision though the sentence structure is considerably varied. The larger pattern of respectful negatives and overgoing positives unifies the poem.

While the first stanza was arranged climactically in terms of its compliments, each higher on a scale of value from the sensual to the spiritual, the second is organized about a single reciprocal action that is interpreted by powerful but understated hyperbole. Much of the poem's power comes from this lack of explanation. Jonson does not describe the "drinke divine" or explain how the beloved will keep the flowers fresh. Instead, he states these hyperboles as simple facts so that the listener either accepts them unquestioningly or must work out the possible grounds for these praises by himself.

Jonson is variably successful in these early short lyrics. "To Sicknesse" (VIII) gets out of hand and becomes a shapeless hybrid between song and satire, polish and spit. In those poems based upon a discrete, unified situation or set of analogies, however, Jonson achieves an enviable purity of diction and an apparent clarity by using many of the same techniques he employs so successfully in the epigrams and particularly the short epitaphs.

All but one of these short lyrics vary from the epigrams and longer moral poems in having dramatic speakers. The speaker of Forrest V is a seducer like Volpone. An ardent lover speaks in song VI, a devoted one in IX, a playfully teasing male in VII. The use of a *persona* in each case strengthens the unity of tone in the lyric, and part of the problem of "To Sicknesse" is that the speaker changes from gallant to railer without apparent reason. The only short love lyric in *The Forrest* in which the speaker can be identified with Jonson is "Why I Write Not of Love" (I). This poem dramatizes the interplay between Jonson's roles of man and of 'Muse', or public poet, and so looks forward to many of the poems in *Under-Wood*.

As an introduction to a group of poems, Forrest I presents its author in a curious manner. As an excuse, "Why I Write Not of Love" would seem to indicate that no love poems are included in the collection. Though this is true of the *Epigrammes*, it is false for *The Forrest*, though Jonson's love poems in *The Forrest* are of a very limited range. Like Charis I, "His excuse for loving", Forrest I is an apology, although the earlier poem takes the less conventional theme of apologizing for not loving.

> Some act of *Love's* bound to reherse,
> I thought to binde him, in my verse:
> Which when he felt, Away (quoth hee)
> Can Poets hope to fetter mee?
> 5   It is enough, they once did get
> *Mars*, and my *Mother*, in their net:
> I weare not these my wings in vaine.
> With which he fled me: and againe,
> Into my ri'mes could ne're be got
> 10   By any arte. Then wonder not,
> That since, my numbers are so cold,
> When *Love* is fled, and I grow old.

The situation recounted in this poem seems to be that the poet, by wishing to confine love in verse, frightens away love and subsequently cannot write about it. This seems as senseless as Love's question, "Can poets hope to fetter mee?" Certainly love has always been a favorite topic of poets, and Cupid and Venus may be the inventions of poets. However, poets cannot "fetter" love in the sense that they cannot utterly explicate or define it; its true essence may always escape full expression in poetry. Moreover, they may not be able to moderate or control it. Thus despite Jonson's denials, "Why I Write Not of Love" can be seen as a serious poem on love and poetry. Like centuries of poets before him, Jonson gives love a physical form, wings, and voice; then he indicates that this Cupid is meaningless unless it is related to the human realities of love. However, to discuss love meaningfully in verse is a difficult thing, one not possible for every author, even this honest poet who can call up the traditional Cupid but cannot control him once he appears.

The poet as love lyrist claims that in writing of love he is hampered by the poet as man – old, cold and stodgy. Despite these defects, the poet-speaker is honest and hearty. He apologizes for his failings but he does not try to go beyond his capacities, as he implies love poets usually do. Jonson's silly and affected Cupid thus represents the conventional voice of love poetry that Jonson cannot and will not write. Instead, he remains the cool craftsman, writing a poem that dramatizes his incapacity to write another, lesser kind of poem.

In this poem Jonson thus portrays himself as the speaker instead of using an assumed dramatic speaker as in the other songs. However, his self-portrait here is very different than in the epigrams. There he is the scourge of the age's defects and the rewarder of its virtues, the perfect public poet and urbanely civilized private man, maintaining a high and decorous tone of public intercourse with his friends, his patrons, his King, and his art. There, except when mourning his children, the voice of Jonson the man is submerged under that of Jonson the poet. His speaker in Forrest I is still Ben Jonson, still a poet, but he reveals in addition some personal characteristics. The interplay between Jonson's roles of man and of poet is treated lightly in this poem; in *Under-wood* it recurs often as a fully developed motif. In the serious moral poems of *The Forrest*, the speaker is usually again the public poet of the *Epigrammes*.

The serious poems in *The Forrest*, particularly the four epistles, show many similarities with Jonson's epigrams. The importance of name and fame, the superiority of virtue over gifts of fortune, the exemplary role of the virtuous aristocrat and his connection with a golden age, the power of poetry to immortalize virtue, and the proper and natural connection between the muse-loving aristocratic patron and the poet: all are treated at length, though often without any more significant development than that found in the epigrams. Repeatedly in the epistles these themes are varied by contrasting censures of nameless others who differ from the acts and values of the persons praised. These negative, censuring passages in the epistles have much in common with the satiric epigrams. They stress the vice and folly of court and city, of loose women and of ambitious men. Thus the epistles are made up of alternate passages of praise and dispraise, such as are found separately in the positive and negative epigrams. The structures of these epistles are then often filled out according to standard rhetorical formulae.

Difficulty arises in these moral poems when Jonson does not shift smoothly or clearly from praise to censure. Often the tone of vituperation, stronger than that of modest admiration, spreads over the whole poem, and the negative examples often outweigh the positive in length of treatment, force, and vigor. One reason for this imbalance is the varying decorum which governs the treatment of praise and dispraise. The satiric material is treated with low vigorous diction and rough speech rhythms. The praise is handled more smoothly, with more abstract diction and more attention to balance and euphony. The positive sections thus may sound pallid in comparison to the satiric. Moreover, as in the epistle to Elizabeth, Countess of Rutland (XII), Jonson's negative examples are not always very pertinent to the positive.[6] This switching of tone and subject often seems to leave the poet grasping for some

---

[6] This looseness is part of the Horatian precedent, and the question then becomes one of judging unity of tone or of the 'world' the satirist presents.

unifying principle, and he sometimes tries to fill this need through the rather uncongenial doctrine of the divine inspiration of the platonic poet, "rapt with rage divine" (XII).

The epistles "To Penshurst" (II) and "To Sir Robert Wroth" (III) deal more directly with the depiction of the ideal aristocrat in relation to the rest of the world and less with the relationship between poet and patron than do Epistles XII and XIII. Despite this omission of one area of difficulty, the poem to Sir Robert Wroth is still haunted by some of the disunifying factors of Epistles XII and XIII.

After its opening complimentary couplet, lines three to twelve of the epistle to Wroth indicate some of the evils, the court and city's expensive "vice" and "sport" which Wroth disdains and because of which he has withdrawn to enjoy the innocence of the country. In contrast, lines thirteen to sixty-six picture Wroth "at home" "free from proud porches", enjoying "securer rest" where sleep is "softer then it is". Whereas the court was masked with false art, the country is truly artful and courtly. Nature is "painted" and "curled"; the shade is "courteous" and the stag makes the estate his "court". As at Penshurst, the farm provides plenty, though on the lower economic scale of hogs and apples and grains "humble in their height". As in "To Penshurst", Jonson uses mythological references to connect Wroth's estate with the golden age and to show the interpenetrative harmony between nature and the estate. The poem parallels the structure of "To Penshurst" by moving from the natural beauty to the social hierarchy represented on the estate, from Wroth's "noblest spouse" and her heroic relatives to the "rout of rurall folke". The free old reciprocity among all classes of society is symbolized by the festivities when "freedome doth with degree dispense". This idyllic descriptive passage, lines thirteen to sixty-six, has a relaxed regularity of rhythm. It uses Popean adjectives and easy alliterations and assonances to describe "flowrie fields, of cop'ces greene,/ The mowed meddowes, with the fleeced sheepe". There are no awkward consonant clusters, wrestings of meter, or difficult junctures.

After describing these country pleasures, Jonson instructs

Wroth, "Since thou canst make thine own content,/ Strive, *Wroth*, to live long innocent". Jonson's vigorous bias here is perhaps evident in the idea that country contentment must be made, not merely felt, and even innocence fought for. Throughout the poem, the poet seems to be a dweller of court or city writing to a country friend. Thus from lines sixty-seven to ninety he plunges off into a set of negative examples of the evils of the world. The evils of others include fighting in unjust wars and litigiously and greedily grabbing money; they have no specific opposites or parallels in Wroth's idyllic pastoral life. Jonson's diction in this satiric passage is vigorous, packed, and harsh, and the meter is not always regular.

From line ninety to the end of the poem, the poet returns to the positive, but instead of continuing to praise Wroth for his country self-sufficiency, he now exhorts him to Christian trust. The meter, rhythm, and diction change for the third time. Here the style is sententious; the diction is abstract; and the rhythm is a crisp, even staccato; but the concepts are unclear. Jonson urges Wroth, "doe thy countrey service, thy selfe right". If arms, law, the court are all hopelessly riddled with corruption from which he must flee, how can he do his country service? The poem ends on the Jonsonian and Renaissance commonplace: "But when thy latest sand is spent,/ Thou maist thinke life, a thing but lent." The latent image of the hour glass is appropriate, and the sentiment is emphasized by the parallels "think"/"thing" and "life"/"lent".

In contrast to the epistles addressed to specific persons, Jonson's "To Penshurst" does not describe the Sidney family directly. Instead it works inductively, describing the estate first. The poem has a unity of structure and a perfection of finish unique among Jonson's epistles, though many of the means used to achieve that perfection are the best traits of Jonson's earlier style familiar to us from the epigrams and songs.

Description of the physical estate at Penshurst structures the poem as it moves from the perimeter of the grounds to the house at the center, listing all the estate's inhabitants from mythological deities to creatures of all the elements. Time provides another principle of structure, and the poet follows the orderly succession of fruit and harvest through the seasons. The social scale from peasants through poet to king provides the major ordering of the second half of the poem.[7]

"To Penshurst" starts with a six-line rejection of the elaborate houses of the *nouveaux riches* that imply the opposite of the values reflected in the Sidney estate. The diction is morally weighted to show the evil of these new houses. They are proud, envious, boastful, "grudg'd at". Critics sometimes speak of the attention to specific English detail in Jonson's poem, in comparison to Martial's epigram on the Baian villa which is generally regarded as a source for "To Penshurst".[8] However, these proud buildings are described with more physical detail than Penshurst itself, which is merely an "ancient", "reverenc'd" "pile". G. R. Hibbard finds this rather vague term apt for the actual Penshurst.[9]

The first descriptive passage of "To Penshurst", lines seven to twenty-one, deals with the environs of the estate and their permeation with natural mythology. The adjectives in this passage tend to be in the comparative, often with no clear reason in the context. By referring to "better markes, of soyle, of ayre", to the "taller tree" dedicated to Sidney, to the "lighter *Faunes*" dancing about, Jonson continues the idea of comparison developed in the opening section but in a muted and moderate manner. The next section of the poem, lines twenty-two to forty-four, describes the grounds and edible produce, animal and vegetable. To make clear that he is painting an idealized portrait, Jonson uses the translated Latin "painted partrich", the conventionally artful "purpled pheasant", and the hyperbolically flattering fish running to be caught. Jonson lists a set of alternative choices to show the ideal relation between

---

[7] The structure of "To Penshurst" is discussed by G. R. Hibbard, "The Country House Poem of the Seventeenth Century", *Journal of the Warburg and Courtauld Institutes*, 19 (1956), 159-74; Paul Cubeta, "A Jonsonian Ideal: 'To Penshurst'", *Philological Quarterly*, 42 (1963), 14-24; Jeffrey Hart, "Ben Jonson's Good Society", *Modern Age*, 7 (1962-63), 61-68.

[8] Cubeta, "Jonsonian Ideal", 17; Hardison, *Enduring Monument*, 112.

[9] Hibbard, "Country House", and Cubeta, "Jonsonian Ideal", compare Martial's epigram with "To Penshurst". Hibbard, "Country House", 163, notes the resemblance to Kalendar's house in Sidney's *Arcadia*. Gayle Wilson, "Bible", 79, finds distant echoes of Solomon's Temple in the description of the proud buildings.

nature and the household. Any would be typical of Penshurst. Eels "leape on land,/ Before the fisher, or into his hand" – either will do. Similarly, one may choose among the seasonal profusion of the orchard. It is the order, the sequence, not the particular crops which are important.

Establishing Penshurst's role in the social hierarchy of England takes most of the rest of the poem: relations with its tenant-peasants (45-56); the house's hospitality to equals, including the poet (57-75); finally the house's ability to entertain the King, at the pinnacle of the social scale (76-88). As the King is unique, his surprise visit to Penshurst is the one specific event in the history of the estate detailed in the poem. The transition between the first half of the poem, dealing with the physical description of the estate and this second half, with its social emphasis, is effected through a brief set of negative contrasts (45-50) that recall the opening of the poem. Penshurst's walls are "rear'd with no man's ruine. .../ There's none, that dwell about them, wish them downe". As the poem began with a physical description of the odious mansions which connoted the moral degradation of their owners, this section begins with an implied contrast between Penshurst's innocent walls and those other walls whose owners have had to squeeze the tenants to pay for their own extravagance. These contrasted negatives set the stage for the recital of Penshurst's good social relations, and the poem rapidly returns to recounting the idyllic, yet typical, reciprocity of edibles up and down the social scale. No peasant brings any one thing in particular: "Some bring a capon, some a rurall cake". All these proferred dainties, like sacrifices to a god, are unnecessary except as signs of the worshipers' devotion. The real "flow" of beneficence as symbolized by food comes from the house's "liberall boord".[10]

The passage on the poet's treatment at Penshurst (61-74) is also framed in terms of unobtrusive negative contrast: There "comes no guest, but is allow'd to eate". Unlike the customs at other

---

[10] Raymond Williams, "Pastoral and Counter-pastoral", *Critical Quarterly*, 10 (1968), 185-88, discusses the idealistic, aristocratic, and conservative bias of this ideal with its "ethic of consuming"; the "curse" of labor that actually produced the bounty is ignored.

"great mens tables" from antiquity to the present, the poet does not dine far away from his host on inferior food while the waiter portions out his wine. The total excellence of Penshurst's hospitality is expressed by the hypothetical reciprocity "all is there;/ As if thou, then, wert mine, or I raign'd here". After this conditional expression, the description of James' entertainment at Penshurst seems more forcefully positive, though even here Jonson maintains balance and moderation in praise. The King receives "(great, I will not say, but) sodayne cheare". Jonson will not presume that the honor of the King's visit was expected, but only that everyone in the house was ready "as if it had expected such a guest!"

Lines eighty-nine to ninety-eight sum the excellence of the house by praising the owners, as a more conventional poem would have begun by doing. Everything in the preceding description is now justified as an emanation of the fruitful chastity of its lady, the regular and quiet piety pervading the household, and the total perfections of the virtuous Sidneys' "noble parts". The last four lines of the poem (99-102), set up a final "proportion" between Penshurst and "other edifices", which are "proud, ambitious heaps". Presumably the word "heaps", connoting moral and physical disarray, refers to the *nouveaux riches* mansions at the beginning of the poem and the inhospitable houses mentioned within the poem. The climactic distinction "their lords have built, but thy lord dwells" exposes the other lords as passers-through the countryside who build more for their own pride than to govern and care for their estates. In this context the word "dwells" sets up an analogy between Penshurst's owners and God in benevolent immanence. Like His, the Sidneys' influence permeates, characterizes, and controls the ordered harmony of their estate. This climactic contrast is created not only by the differences between the words "build" and "dwell", but also by the difference between the simple past "have built", indicating a single historical action, and "dwells", the present of apparently permanent ideal continuance used throughout the poem for descriptions of all the activities of the estate.

Though the picture of Penshurst is moral, schematic, and ideal rather than pictorial and specific, it none the less provides a viable scheme for inductive praise. The results of the Sidneys' character, care, and governance are described through the order and fecundity of their estate and the esteem in which they are held. The final praise of them thus seems logically justified by the prior description. The negative contrasts beginning and ending the poem and heightening the major passages are merely hints. Only about one-eighth of the poem contains elements of negative contrast, whereas positive description accounts for a full three-quarters of the poem. The negative elements provide a context to demonstrate Penshurst's real difference and superiority, and also its perilous uniqueness.

In contrast to the epistle "To Sir Robert Wroth", the very structure of "To Penshurst" incorporates the symmetry and harmony that the poem praises. (See Table Seven, Appendix.) The Wroth poem is weighted much more heavily to the negative than is "To Penshurst". Over one-third of "To Sir Robert Wroth" contains negative contrast; only a little over half is positive description. Moreover, the Wroth poem lumps together the natural and social descriptions, following them with a long satiric passage just prior to the conclusion. There is no apparent numerical pattern in the line structure of "To Sir Robert Wroth". In "To Penshurst" the two positive passages, natural and social, are separated by a short transitional passage of negative contrast. The positive social description then leads smoothly into the positive moral and religious conclusion. Moreover, the line count shows a symmetrical pattern structuring the poem: six negative lines, thirty-eight positive, six negative, thirty-eight positive, and then fourteen lines of positive conclusion.

Similarly, the texture of "To Penshurst" is much more uniform than that of "To Sir Robert Wroth", just as the structure of "To Penshurst" is more balanced and symmetrical. The impression of greater consistency in "To Penshurst" is corroborated by part-of-speech counts for three parallel passages in the two poems. (See Table Eight, Appendix, for figures.) In "To Penshurst" the ratio of adjectives to nouns to verbs remains fairly constant throughout the three passages. The number of verbs is about one per line; the number of nouns about two; and there are fewer adjectives than verbs. The idyllic passage adds more specific nouns than usual, but it does not lose verbal vigor. The number of adjectives is not increased, nor of verbs, decreased. In the epistle to Wroth, the number of nouns similarly remains constant, but the ratio of verbs to adjectives and the absolute number of each varies widely. In the passage of idealized description there are two-thirds as many verbs as adjectives and less than one verb per line, corroborating the impression of slack verbal texture. In contrast, the satiric passage has only two adjectives and many more verbs. Of course there is nothing intrinsically good or bad about any of these proportions, but those of "To Penshurst" are more typically Jonsonian and help to indicate one of the sources of the vigor, symmetry, and balance which readers uniformly find in the poem. In contrast, the very different styles in the passages of the epistle to Wroth underscore the poem's uncertainty, its variations in tone and subject matter.

"To Sir Robert Wroth" has virtually all the elements of "To Penshurst", but in a different order, with different focus and a more various range of styles. In addition, the attempted portrayal of country innocence and stoic self-sufficiency clashes awkwardly in the epistle to Wroth with an undercurrent ideal of civic duty. "To Penshurst", which does not imply that the Sidneys have no duties other than those on the estate, avoids this conflict between action and withdrawal. Forrest IV, "To the World", solves this conflict in the other direction by taking a traditional religious stance from which withdrawal is the only possibility in a completely corrupt world; furthermore, the gentlewoman's withdrawal there, like Lady Aubigny's in Epistle XIII, is less controversial than a man's.

The themes of virtuous self-sufficiency, the nature of the evil world, and the desire to withdraw recur in *The Forrest* outside the epistles in the neoplatonic "Epode" and the two religious poems, "To the World: A Farewell for a Gentle-woman, Vertuous and Noble" and "To Heaven". The "Epode" is preceded by a prelude, a short humorous poem that, like Forrest I, banishes false inspiration and tired mythology in the name of true poetry. The Epode then distinguishes false turbulent "blinde Desire" from the "pure, perfect, nay divine" true love, treating love as a special case of moderate and self-sufficient virtue.

"To the World" uniquely has a woman speaker whose virtue is indirectly praised and portrayed as she speaks. She easily rejects the "toyes, and trifles, traps, and snares" of the world and concludes, instead:

> Nor for my peace will I goe farre,
> As wandrers doe, that still doe rome,
> But make my strengths, such as they are,
> Here in my bosome, and at home.

The final line of the poem gains considerable irrational force from the fact that it is particularly appropriate to a woman, whose 'place' is in the home and who is assumed to have a soft heart in her bosom. Thus "home" and "bosome" are identified dramatically as the same place, and it is the place that the virtuous self always and alone occupies. Part of the strength and surprise of the poem's ending is that after what seems to be a conventional religious poem rejecting the world, the woman elects to stay in the world as we understand it and does not make any overt plea to, or even mention of, God or heaven. Furthermore, the mode of her withdrawal from the world is unclear. She does not appear to be entering a convent; she is not even covertly wishing for death like the speaker of "To Heaven". Her final resolution is a declaration of moral independence, of stoic self-sufficiency as well as of Christian trust.

"To Heaven", the last poem in *The Forrest*, is not an opposite to "To the World", as their contrasting titles might imply. In fact, the two poems have much of their theme in common: the sorrows and snares of earthly life. Somewhat surprisingly, it is the more medieval-sounding "To the World" that achieves a stoic resolution in the person of its anonymous feminine speaker, while "To Heaven" is more emotional and less clearly resolved. It is a more complex and interesting poem than "To the World", particularly in terms of its speaker, who is a man more nearly like the grief-stricken father of the epitaph "On My First Sonne" than like the assured didactic moralist of the other serious poems of *The Forrest*.

Good, and great *God*, can I not thinke of thee,
But it must, straight, my melancholy bee?
Is it interpreted in me disease,
That, laden with my sinnes, I seeke for ease?
5   O, be thou witnesse, that the reynes dost know,
And hearts of all, if I be sad for show,
And judge me after: if I dare pretend
To ought but grace, or ayme at other end.
As thou art all, so be thou all to mee,
10 First, midst, and last, converted one, and three;
My faith, my hope, my love: and in this state,
My judge, my witnesse, and my advocate.
Where have I beene this while exil'd from thee?
And whither rap'd, now thou but stoup'st to mee?
15 Dwell, dwell here still: O, being every-where,
How can I doubt to finde thee ever, here?
I know my state, both full of shame, and scorne,
Conceiv'd in sinne, and unto labour borne,
Standing with feare, and must with horror fall,
20 And destin'd unto judgement, after all.
I feele my griefes too, and there scarce is ground,
Upon my flesh t'inflict another wound.
Yet dare I not complaine, or wish for death
With holy *Paul*, lest it be thought the breath
25 Of discontent; or that these prayers bee
For wearinesse of life, not love of thee.

The alliteration and three heavy stresses of "Good, and great *God*" start the poem forcefully, followed by the question, "can I not thinke of thee,/ But it must, straight, my melancholy bee?" After fifteen monosyllables, the four-syllable "melancholy" casts its aura over the entire poem, establishing its subject and setting much of its tone. The opening question makes clear that this is meditative personal prayer, not formal liturgical praise. The rest of the poem has as its subject the answer to this question, a serious matter of religious psychology. The question probes the connection between genuine religious feeling and mere personal moodiness or despair. False religion and the falsely religious are targets of some of Jonson's fiercest satirical zeal in both the plays and the epigrams, and it is not only the knowing hypocrite he condemns but also the deluded enthusiast who mistakes his own self-will for divine inspiration.

"To Heaven" hinges on the question of how one can know true from false religious feeling in oneself. To judge this personally pressing but not finally answerable question, the poet calls in as witnesses his own feelings, others' observations of him, and God. Thus the third and fourth lines of the poem are not a repetition of the second line, but a recasting which emphasizes the external view.[11] "Disease" is a stronger word than "melancholy", which denotes a wide range of possible feelings from almost pleasurable gravity to dangerous illness or madness.[12] The central position of the words "in me" in the question "Is it interpreted in me disease ...?" highlights the speaker's self-concern, the internal nature of his spiritual dilemma and debate. The religion that seems so easy to others is not so to him; he pictures himself "laden with my sinnes". By describing himself as laden with sins, the speaker appears to be in the first stage of conversion, recognition of sin with accompanying expressions of contrition and sorrow.[13] The first four lines, with their double question, end with the emphasis on "seek for ease", that is, on a quest needing fulfillment but having an ambiguous goal.

The next four lines, a petition to God rather than a question, and almost a demand rather than a petition, at first appear to be a sufficient answer to the questions posed by the first four lines.

[11] Swinburne, *Jonson*, 71, comments, "The opening couplet of the striking address 'To Heaven' has been ... misunderstood by Gifford; its meaning is not 'Can I not think of God without it making me melancholy' but 'Can I not think of God without its being imputed or set down by others to a fit of dejection'". William Kerrigan, "Ben Jonson Full of Shame and Scorn", *Studies in the Literary Imagination,* 6(1913), 206, believes "the lines mean, 'Can I not think of you, Lord, without the world, and certainly you, judging my thoughts as melancholy ...?'" Kerrigan reads "To Heaven" as an expression of the "abiding melancholy of Jonson", p. 199.

[12] As defined by Lawrence Babb, *The Elizabethan Malady: A Study of Melancholia in English Literature from 1580 to 1640* (East Lansing: Michigan State, 1951).

[13] Louis L. Martz, *The Poetry of Meditation* (Yale Studies in English, 125) (New Haven: Yale, 1954), 132, speaks of Donne combating his sins of "feare" and intellectual pride through the seventeenth-century tradition of self-examination: "The way to deal with these [sins], as we have seen, is to face them squarely, arouse the sinful impulses deliberately, and then repel them by examining all situations in the light of one's ultimate goal: conformity with the will of God."

In these lines the speaker says that he is religious in appearance, and that his single genuine aim is "grace". H up all claims to merit for his contrition or sufferings as well his works. However, some elements in the four lines imply unsettledness in this assertion and indicate why the poem is not yet complete. First the speaker calls on God to witness his sincerity. In line six the false position of which the speaker is accused is expressed as being "sad for show". Phrased in this way, the accusation against the speaker seems momentarily to be the simple one of religious affectation or hypocrisy. From this accusation, of course, he can easily exonerate himself. The eye-alliteration "sad"/"show" and the rhyme "know"/"show" both stress the underlying difficulty of discriminating appearance from reality.

In parallel with the earlier statement "O be thou witnesse", Jonson's petition to God continues, "and judge me after". Like calling upon God as a witness, asking him to judge one is un- necessary, the request of a man flaunting his willingness to be brought to account. God will judge us all "after", and the isolation of the adverb makes the indefiniteness of the condition clear. To keep parallel with the preceding clause, the verb "judge me" would apply only to the following clause, "if I dare pretend". However, by order, punctuation, and proximity, "judge me" also appears to apply to the preceding clause, "if I be sad for show". Whereas the first "if" clause disposes of the accusation of religious affecta- tion and hypocrisy, the second "if" clause puts the more serious question. The word "pretend" may simply mean 'fake' and thus enforce the idea of hypocrisy in the phrase, "sad for show", but the basic denotation of the word is 'to claim' or 'to aspire'. Thus the speaker is trying to assert the purity of his religious intentions, to say that his "end" is the only proper one, grace. Thus he em- phasizes his recognition that he has no merit in himself and there- fore can only be saved through grace. The rhyme "pretend"/"end", like the preceding rhyme, highlights the contrast between real and false aims. The phrasing "ought but grace" is negative, tentative, and indirect. This hesitant and indirect phrasing undercuts the basic denotation of the statement so that the clause is not simply

'. Instead, Jonson asks to be judged if he
ise, and the word "dare" implies wavering
:tion and doubt. Thus lines five to eight
f lines one to four unsolved; they do not
uish between false religious feeling and

, nine to twelve, the speaker appears to
about the nature of his religion and the
lge of it by turning to and resting in God,
)utes he now appears to understand. By
shifting emphasis from himself to God's power and love, he shows
that he is what he seeks to be, genuinely religious. His petition is
powerful, incantatory, liturgical, using many repeated sounds and
balanced phrases: it begins, "As thou art all, so be thou all to
mee" where "all" represents God in his total unity and power.
This splendid appeal is followed by an abbreviated summary
of God's power and trinity: "First, midst, and last, converted one,
and three". These invocations are appositives amplifying "thou".
Because of the loose syntax, they seem freely offered worship,
ritual adoration by one who knows God rather than an attempt
to define Him. The four medial pauses in line ten and the three *st*
endings of "first, midst, and last" slow the speaker into respectful
lingering. Line eleven goes on to another trinity, again using formal
and conventional terms, "My faith, my hope, my love". This
series is different from the preceding two, however, in that it
indicates the speaker's absorption in God's attributes; God
has indeed become "all to mee" for the poet. This moving series
uses the compression of the simple abstract nouns to indicate that
God has now become the sole source and object of the speaker's
faith, hope, and, most important, love. He is the absolute definition
of these qualities, and He may be called "mine" because He is
each man's as all men's. The speaker here thus claims a warmer
relationship with his God than mere doctrinal knowledge provides.
Climactically, the final trinity invoked is "and in this state,/
My judge, my witnesse, and my advocate". In lines five and seven
the poet called on God to be his witness and judge in order that
the speaker might justify his religious seriousness to others and to

himself or perhaps that he might relieve his own burden of judgment by relying on God's. Here in line twelve he states that God is
already and inescapably his judge and his witness. Even more
important, he realizes that besides these two stern roles, God is
also his "advocate". Christ will mediate between the imperfections
which the Witness to man's deeds sees and the final judgment that
the Judge will pass on him. Thus, in his love of God and his
realization of God's love for him, the poet now has faith in the
trinity's role in calling him to his salvation.

Throughout lines nine to twelve, sound patterns are repeated,
balanced but varied, giving the Jonsonian finish and perfect control
of tone to a passage of abstract definition. Each list of God's
attributes is slightly longer than the last. In line nine the single
word "all" is enough. The unadorned monosyllables of "first,
midst, and last" take up four syllables; "converted one, and three"
takes six syllables, like the series "my faith, my hope, my love",
which parallels "first, midst, and last" in opening a line but which
fills out its monosyllables with the triple use of the possessive.
In parallel with both of these series is the climactic, full ten syllables of "my judge, my witness, and my advocate". In this last
series the sense of climax is augmented by the increase from one to
two to three syllables in "judge", "witness", and "advocate". This
careful patterning and rhetorical balance and climax contrasts
with the confused, hesitant movement of the preceding four lines
and helps establish the change in tone from over-protesting
uncertainty to rapt conviction. Appropriately for lines praising
Him whose least distorted designation is 'I am', two forms of
to be are the only verbs in the quatrain.

Thus by the end of line twelve, the poem seems to form a complete progression from the sinner's self-regarding doubts to his
over-assertion of religiousness and then to a worshipper's genuinely humble petition which implies the achievement of the
faith petitioned for. Emphasis has shifted from the worries of the
self to the power and love of God, which the speaker now understands. None the less, the poem continues.

Although lines thirteen to sixteen seem still to issue from the
speaker's state of religious certainty, they return to questioning

and to an emphasis on the slippery emotional state of the sinner. From a position of conviction, the speaker asks both God and his former self, "where have I been this while exil'd from Thee?" The internal rhyme "while"/"exil'd" calls attention to the indefinitely long and distant period of alienation from God. His second question confirms this connotation of distance in space and time: "And whither rap'd, now thou but stoup'st to mee?" Here classical legend perhaps introduces its associations of the god's beloved carried off to Olympus, while erotic imagery is conventional in the language of Christian mysticism to express the Christian rapture at union with God. However, the speaker has not been carried to heaven; God has momentarily stooped to him. The word "now" emphasizes the freshness, perhaps the fragility of this new religious moment.

The rhyme in lines nine and ten was "mee"/"three" showing the poem's change in emphasis there from the worries of the subjective "mee" to praise of the heavenly "three". Here in lines thirteen and fourteen the emphasis, with the rhyme, shifts back from "thee" to "mee". Line fifteen confirms this change as questioning again turns to petition: "Dwell, dwell here still ...." The music is urgent and insistent with its tolling of back *l*'s, and its three emphatic stresses. "Dwell" is an often-repeated word in Jonson's poetry, standing for fruitful permanence, as in the final distinction of "To Penshurst", and the request thus has a special poignancy. Lines fifteen and sixteen of "To Heaven" then cast what earlier in the poem seemed to be a solved problem back as a hypothesis: "O, being every-where,/ How can I doubt to finde thee ever, here?" The moment of enraptured near-certainty has passed, and though the speaker's reason knows that God is "being everywhere" — a participle stressing God's continuing and active presence – the negative and indirect question, "How can I doubt to finde thee ever, here?" indicates that he does doubt, though he knows he should not. In doubting that God's "every-where" includes its rhyme word "here", or, perhaps, the place of Jonson's "exil'd" spirit, he doubts that God is "all" to him as he felt it earlier in the poem.

Once this doubt enters the speaker's consciousness, the moment

of self-effacing religious conviction has passed. The tone of the
poem changes. Lines seventeen to twenty begin in a tone of tough-
minded religious pessimism, emphatically expressed. From the
first indication of doubt, the speaker has moved to a state of
knowledge, but what he now knows is not, as before, God's love
for him, but instead his own sin and unworthiness. Thus he says,
"I know my state, both full of shame, and scorne." This woeful
and melancholy "state" contrasts with the rapt "state" in which
God appeared to be "my faith, my hope, my love ...,/ My judge,
my witnesse, and my advocate." "Shame, and scorne" imply both
a subjective and an objective view of sin. The speaker's "shame"
indicates a sense of others – including God – looking on at his
guilt or of his reason's being forced to be ashamed of his will's
weakness, his return to doubting and melancholy. The word
"scorne" normally connotes an external and hostile attitude, that
of a satirist to a fop or vicious person, for instance. By seeing
himself and his relapsed condition as full of both shame and
scorn, then, the poet shows his own critical and rational disapproval
of himself, perhaps a return to the religious melancholy indicated
at the opening of the poem. Thus his new pessimistic self-knowledge may be true, but it is not here clearly balanced with the
appropriate sense of the soul's saving relationship to a loving
God.

In lines eighteen to twenty, the speaker continues to explicate his
condition in a conventional, almost ritualistic way. These neat,
gnomic patterns in the English 'plain style' express a grim traditional view of the state of fallen man, and they balance the statements of God's nature and power in lines ten to twelve of the
poem.[14] In this view, man's whole life is summed as "conceiv'd in
sinne, and unto labour borne", with the emphasis on man's
depravity and God's curse on fallen mankind. Perhaps the rhymes
of lines seventeen and eighteen also add the idea "borne" to
"scorne" to Jonson's picture of the human condition.

---

[14]   Given our ignorance of the nature of Jonson's religious convictions and
doubts, I do not think we can tell whether this poem was written while Jonson
was an Anglican.

This bleak picture continues in lines nineteen and twenty, "Standing with feare, and must with horror fall,/ And destin'd unto judgement, after all." The sentence proceeds from the active "standing" to "must fall" to the passive "destin'd unto judgement" as the poet grammatically and spiritually gives in to resignation and malaise. Jonson's usual association of firm virtue with the word "stand" is here undercut by the modification "with feare", reminding us that the speaker did not "dare pretend to ought but grace". That fallen man "must fall" repeatedly may be doctrinally true in the abstract, but it is especially likely to be true in a particular case when the contrasted "standing" in virtue or grace has been so precarious; the alliteration of "feare" and "fall" stresses this connection. The phrase "with horror" wedges between the auxiliary "must" and the verb "fall", showing the division in the poet between the rational, religiously-knowing onlooker in himself and the helpless backslider whose very fears precipitate the calamity he dreads. The speaker who asked God to "judge me after" now awaits the destined judgment with a horrified acquiescence which is far from the assurance that knew that God was not only his judge but also his advocate.

The tone of this passage has thus descended from tough-minded religious dogmatism toward individual despondency. The speaker does not yield to religious despair, but he is now vulnerable to it since he loses sight of the proper knowledge of himself, man's state, and God. In lines twenty-one and twenty-two, the speaker turns from his guilt to his sufferings. Even after submitting to the will and power of God, he finds that doubts arising from the claims of the flesh persist. "I feele my griefes too, and there scarce is ground/ Upon my flesh t'inflict another wound." In combination with "upon my flesh" the word "ground" recalls the connection of flesh with earth, death, and the return to dust. This foreboding note foreshadows the speaker's suppressed wish for the peace of death, and the alliteration "flesh"/"inflict" underlines the carnal self's susceptibility to do and receive harm. In the face of these persistent claims of the flesh, the speaker seems to doubt whether he is appealing genuinely for grace or only for a release from suffering. Thus he seems to have fallen into a mood approaching self-pity that is riddled with the melancholy doubts with which the poem opened.

The final four lines of "To Heaven", like the end of Jonson's epitaph on his first son, imply a sentiment divergent from their declared meaning. Superficially, the poet closes by saying that he will not discontentedly yearn for death and that his prayers spring solely from love of God. Under the surface, however, this final quatrain deepens the preceding mood of religious doubt, melancholy and yearning for death.

Thus after complaining about his griefs, the poet says, "Yet dare I not complaine, or wish for death/ With holy *Paul*, lest it be thought the breath/ Of discontent ...." In fact, he is complaining, though it is true that he dares not do what he does, recalling the doubts and fears that helped keep him aspiring for grace and the fear with which he stands in precarious virtue. Paul's exclamation in Romans VII: 24, "O wretched man that I am, who should deliver me from the body of this death?" follows the recognition that life in the flesh is sin and therefore death, but it in turn is corrected by the fuller realization that the "law of the Spirit of life in Christ Jesus hath made me free from the law of sin and death" (VIII: 2), so that Paul's wish is not simply for death, but for the death of the old man, the flesh, and for the new life of the spirit. This affirmative aspect of Paul's paradox is omitted from Jonson's allusion. The negative phrasing does not alter his basic desire: one need not be restrained from expressing a desire one does not have.

The last line and a half of "To Heaven" make up a clause beginning "or that" which is not paralleled by an earlier 'that' clause. Presumably this clause is an object of "lest it be thought" along with "the breath of discontent". However, as it is written, the clause stands rather alone at the conclusion of the poem: "or that these prayers bee/ For wearinesse of life, not love of thee." This isolation plus the typical Jonsonian indirection of the statement make the speaker appear to mean the contrary of what he wishes to say. The pause after "life" stresses the "not" which follows it, and the apparent contrast "life"/"love of thee" thus seems to separate this life, with its attendant sorrows, sins, and inability to remain religious, from the love of God which the speaker wishes to realize in death.[15]

Elements of a penitential poem are present in "To Heaven": recognition and confession of sin, contrition, acknowledgment of God's power, trust in God and submission to his will. However, these states are not presented in a simple progression. Instead, halfway through the poem the speaker expresses trust in God and confident, self-forgetful knowledge of God's power. But when he again thinks of his own sinful state, his melancholy and doubts return plagued by new scruples about his purity of motive. The poem is, I think, successful precisely because of this emotionally convincing ordering of its conventional material. The problems and emotions with which it is charged are not wholly resolved by the troubled spirit, by the "infected will", to use Sidney's terms, though Jonson's "erected wit" shows clearly that it understands the proper course and would follow it if it could. Thus at the end of the poem the speaker rationally asserts the purity of his religious motivation, but his tone none the less whispers of the weariness of life that has not been wholly expunged and of the difficulty of maintaining the purity of the wish.

The poem examines the knowledge possible about one's religious condition. In it the poet gives the correct answer, that God knows all, but he also touches upon the false answers of the self and the superficial opinions of others. The poem examines the differences between overt hypocrisy, covert self-delusion, and genuine religious feeling, between true and false self-knowledge and therefore humility and between a pure and a less pure love of God. At the same time, and persistently, "To Heaven" is an expression and portrait of religious melancholy.

This double portrait is achieved largely through the typical Jonsonian techniques of abstract diction and a profusion of indirect, passive, and negative statements and questions. The poem begins and ends with indirect negative statements that seem to mean the opposite of what they say. These negatives are

---

[15]   Winters, "Poetic Styles", 68, agrees that the temptation this poem presents is weariness of life, a temptation that the poet overcomes "with a semi-suppressed despair".

not immediately cancelled and balanced by the appropriate positives, as in Epigram ci. The wholly positive lines nine to twelve, with their rapt and certain tone, stand as the touchstone in the poem of a true, self-forgetful religious state. They show what the speaker can achieve, and has achieved, but they contrast with the sadder mood with which the poem begins and ends. As in the poem on Jonson's first son, this dissonant mood is a quiet one, an undercurrent of possible doubt and discouragement, not an open Donnean despair. Typically in Jonson's successful early poems, the emotions represented vary within a narrow range; he chooses between close poles. These choices gain force from the sense of honesty, depth, and sincerity with which the emotions are depicted and the clarity with which the reason sees them, whether the emotions are ultimately resolved in a balance harmonious to the reason, as in "To Penshurst" or Epigram ci, or remain restless under the veil of reason as in the epitaph "On My First Sonne" and "To Heaven."

In the short anthology of *The Forrest*, Jonson presents a varied group of poems that sometimes succeed by using the best stylistic traits of the epigrams in varying *genres* and that sometimes fail through disunity or the lack of resolution of conflicting elements. In the short amorous songs Jonson uses dramatic *personae* as speakers. Through these dramatic speakers his songs can achieve temporary detachment from the impurities of this world that the satires rail about. That is, since Jonson the didactic poet is not speaking in them, he need not point out moral lessons to his readers, as he does in the epistles and epigrams, although the attitudes expressed by these dramatic speakers may indirectly produce a moral response. "Drinke to Me, Onely" (IX), the best of these songs, like the best epigrams limits the range of tone and emotion that it presents, and the poem asserts its discrimination and control through a carefully-ordered set of alternatives within this narrow range. Forrest I, the only one of these poems about love in *The Forrest* to keep Jonson as its speaker, touches on the conflict between man and poet and defends the integrity of the man against the conventionalities of most love poetry. The prelude (X) to the "Epode" (XI) also takes up the question of true and false

poetic inspiration and decides in favor of "my owne true fire",
while the "Epode" distinguishes between true calm love and
false desire in a more conventional manner. An appeal to the
sources of poetic inspiration again appears in Epistle XII, but there
Jonson uncharacteristically and unsuccessfully tries to claim the
position of the divinely-inspired neoplatonic poet-priest. The
epistles are also troubled by other inconsistencies. Instead of the
division of praise and blame into separate poems, as in the epigrams,
the epistles alternate between praise and blame in single poems,
and their unity of tone and content often suffers. "To Penshurst"
solves this dilemma in the manner of the epigrams and "To Celia"
by restricting its range, subordinating the satiric, and inductively
leading to the praise of the Sidneys through the artfully arranged
series of ideal details of life on their estate. The poet's sense of
wonder and satisfaction, even exaltation, at the apparent congruence of real and ideal in the affairs of the estate and the character of its owners gives the emotional force to this much-admired
poem. Another conflict vexing some of the epistles which "To
Penshurst" avoids is that between the attraction of withdrawal
from a corrupt world and the necessity of virtuous action in it.
These conflicts are latent in the undeveloped ideals praised in the
epigrams, but they emerge somewhat more clearly in the wider
scope of the epistles of *The Forrest*. "To the World" (IV), based on
a medieval tradition of religious allegory, comes out strongly and
simply for withdrawal. In "To Heaven" (XV) the urge for withdrawal becomes a wish for death that is part of the temptation
of religious melancholy.

   Compared to the two categories of epigrams, then, the range of
the fifteen poems of *The Forrest* is wide, and its range of problems
and accomplishments is also wide. The chief successes are still
predominantly in the modes of praise, as in "To Penshurst" and
"To Celia", and of censure of the world in "To the World". The
collection begins and ends with poems where the double role of the
author as man and as poet raises pertinent questions. In Forrest I,
as in all Jonson's early poems on the relations between men and
on the nature of poetry, the poet is basically confident and in
control. His attitudes and moral stance remain static. Only in

Forrest XV, as in the epitaph on his first son, does the speaker's attempt to cope with the mystery of death produce an effective unsettledness in his attitude.

Thus the *Epigrammes* are often finely-crafted achievements within a limited form, marked by a fixed and uncomplicated moral stance. *The Forrest* is a collection of fifteen poems experimenting with other forms and showing some complexities and inconsistencies in outlook which Jonson has not yet been able to resolve satisfactorily. Only in the more mature *Under-wood* are form and *persona* in the nondramatic poems adapted to meet the demands of Jonson's expanded interests.

4. *UNDER-WOOD*

Under-wood, containing Jonson's later lyric work, is the most heterogenous collection of the three, and its poems represent many *genres* and traditions. In contrast to the *Epigrammes* and *The Forrest*, Under-wood was not culled or corrected by the poet himself but by his friend, Sir Kenelm Digby, after Jonson's death.[1] The opening poems of the collection appear to have been arranged by the poet to follow *The Forrest*, but after these first few poems, it is hard to tell what Jonson intended to include in the collection or in what order. Digby's order groups the poems loosely, sometimes by subject matter, sometimes by approximate date.

In *Under-wood* new themes, such as love and valor, the poet's poverty and his person, appear in conjunction with new techniques and forms. In these later poems Jonson adapted to new uses his tried and often perfected techniques for achieving stylistic balance, concision, and purity of diction, and he also developed new stylistic devices to embody his new concerns. In many of these later poems Jonson sets himself up as a character. This device and the attitude it entails color many of the poems of *Under-wood*, giving them a compassionate yet ironic tone, inviting the reader's participation in more than one point of view. Unlike the earlier poems, many of those in *Under-wood* can no longer be understood solely in terms of a rhetoric of praise and blame. Jonson's earlier rhetorical pattern of contrasted positive and negative extremes tends to be altered toward a pattern of various extremes gradually explored in the search for a mean. The *Under-wood* collection represents a

---

[1] H & S, 2, 337; 11, 47-48; and Hunter, *Complete Poetry*, 113, discuss the circumstances of the publication of *Under-wood*.

maturing and development of Jonson's poetic interests and insight, if not necessarily an improvement in the quality of specific later poems over specific earlier poems.

The poems in *Under-wood* that are most similar to Jonson's earlier types of poems often show signs of disinterest or fatigue; others are expanded into fuller variations on the earlier forms. For example, the many scattered later epigrams do not serve quite the same simple didactic purposes as those of the first book. There are only a few genuine satirical epigrams in the new collection, like "A Little Shrub Growing By" (23),[2] which is a piece of pure invective that does not define the type of person reviled. Instead, most of the epigrams in *Under-wood* are public, politic, commendatory, and occasional. Often their flattery seems directed to a particular and personal end: there are poems to be inscribed on tribute plates and poems to influence judges.

Longer poems related to these public epigrams are Jonson's public odes and miscellaneous poems for persons and occasions of the court, like the birthday ode for the Queen (69). These poems, too, often seem more servile than those addressed to aristocratic patrons in the earlier works. In contrast to this stiff court verse, other poems addressed to the court and high officials are light, sometimes even flippant in tone like the dedication of the King's cellar to Bacchus (50).

Several other kinds of poems related to the epigrams make fitful appearances in the later works. Many dedicatory epigrams and longer dedicating poems in the uncollected poems combine eulogy and criticism as in the mature poems on Drayton (Uc. 48) and Shakespeare (Uc. 41, 42). A very few epitaphs in *Under-wood* resemble those in the first book of epigrams, like those on Vincent Corbet (14) and Phillip Gray (18). In consonance with the general movement toward longer forms in the later work, *Under-wood* contains several formal funeral elegies, a genre not represented earlier. This very popular 'metaphysical' form of elegy combined the eulogy of the aristocratic exemplar, a mainstay of Jonson's

---

[2] Since Hunter numbers "Poems of Devotion" as three separate poems, all his numbers thereafter are two higher than the numbers in H & S. Hunter's numbers are used here.

earlier work, with religious and philosophical doctrine and meditation.[3]

In the tradition of aging poets, Jonson seems to want to highlight his religious poetry in *Under-wood* while linking it with his
former work. *The Forrest* ends with the serious personal religious
poem "To Heaven" (XV). *Under-wood* begins with three less personal religious poems collectively headed "Poems of Devotion, the
Sinners Sacrifice" (1-3) and presents the Christian elegies on
Venetia Digby (86) among its final and longest poems. However,
Under-wood includes only a few religious poems. In *Under-wood*,
as in his earlier work, Jonson's concerns remain predominantly
moral and esthetic rather than doctrinal.

Among these poems in *Under-wood* are several epistles addressed
to friends and social superiors which resemble those in *The Forrest*
in style and themes, in their mixture of satire directed against a
corrupt society and commendation of the virtuous addressee,
and in their frequent lack of unity. As in the earlier collections,
there are poems distinguished for their fine reciprocity of friendship, like the epistles to Arthur Squib (47, 56) and "Answering to
One That Asked to be Sealed of the Tribe of Ben" (49). These
poems carry over from the earlier collections such ideas as the
exemplary nature of the virtuous man, the free beauties of equal
friendship, and the contrast between the decadent present and a
vanished great age, though their emphasis is somewhat different
from that of the earlier epistles. There are only a few full, essay-like
epistles in the *Under-wood*, including the thank-you letter to
Sir Edward Sacvile (15), the dedicatory poem to John Selden (16),
and the epistle persuading a friend to the wars (17). The poems
to Sacvile and the friend Colby (17) are relaxed in structure
and about fifty lines longer than the epistles in *The Forrest*, while
the "Epistle to a Friend" (19) is an eighteen-line epigram. Another

---

[3] Hardison, *Enduring Monument*, 142-45, 164-84, provides an excellent discussion of the funeral elegy in terms of the conventions of praise. In particular,
he analyzes the elegies for Jane Pawlet and Venetia Digby and compares the
latter with Donne's *Anniversaries*. The 'metaphysical' aspects of the tradition
are treated by Ruth Wallerstein, "The Laureate Hearse: The Funeral Elegy
and Seventeenth-Century Aesthetic", *Studies in Seventeenth-Century Poetic*
(Madison: U. of Wisconsin, 1950), 1-150.

"Epistle to a Friend" (39), written in triplets, is a short poem closely related to the love elegies that follow it. In other words, Jonson seems less concerned to follow a strict classical form for the epistle here than in *The Forrest*. At any rate, the new interests shown in *Under-wood* are more often presented in the lyric forms of elegy and ode. Corresponding to this shift in dominant form from the moral epistle to the amorous elegy and lyric is a shift in attention from men and manly virtue to women and love.

Several love lyrics near the beginning of *Under-wood* recall the songs in *The Forrest* and in Jonson's plays and masques. In the same way that *Under-wood* expands the epitaph into the funeral elegy, the collection includes a few brief amorous songs or paradoxical lyrics like "The Dreame" (13) and "Against Jealousy" (12) and several long erotic elegies based on classical and metaphysical models. Elegies 20, 21, 24 form one series of such poems on the theme of love and beauty. Elegies 40, 42, 43, 44 form another series.[4] Similarly, though several of the separate poems in "A Celebration of Charis in Ten Lyrick Peeces" (4) resemble the earlier songs, the composite poem as a whole considers the themes of love and beauty and poetry in the manner of the elegies. In these longer poems on love Jonson retains the best craftsmanship of his earlier dramatic songs while deepening the point of view. At the same time, he usually solves in these poems the problems of artistic unity and glibness of thought that often flawed his earlier moral and philosophical poems.

Related to many of the amorous lyrics in tone and to the public odes in form are some of the most appealing and original poems in *Under-wood*, Jonson's odes to himself and other personal lyrics. In these poems the author becomes his own subject for a variety of light and serious purposes. Poems like the "Execration on Vulcan" (45) and the diatribes against Inigo Jones (Uc. 56-58) are also autobiographical in content.

Despite many lines of connection with the earlier groups of poems, then, it is clear that *Under-wood* as a collection differs

---

4 Evelyn Simpson, H & S, 11, 66-68, argues persuasively for the attribution of "The Expostulation" (Hunter 41) to Donne and the other elegies of the series to Jonson. However, the issue is still being debated.

significantly from the *Epigrammes* and *The Forrest*. The latinate
'plain style' genres of epigram and epistle are less dominant than
in the earlier two works, and many more poems in *Under-wood*
than in the earlier collections are based on native English traditions and seventeenth-century experimentation. In line with his
freer use of sources and models in *Under-wood*, Jonson experiments
with new meters and forms, including many elaborate stanzaic
patterns, though his standard for the epistles, funeral and love
elegies and invectives is still iambic pentameter couplets. This basic
meter takes on a looser and more dramatic form in *Under-wood*
than in the earlier collections. Run-on lines in the iambic pentameter poems of *Under-wood*, for instance, often run to thirty
or forty per cent of the poem, instead of the usual twenty per
cent in *Epigrammes* and *The Forrest*. (See Table Nine, Appendix.)

As in the earlier collections, Jonson repeats topics and images
from poem to poem. Beauty is persistently "pure and perfect".
The old encomiastic tropes are used again and again; for instance,
social position is repeatedly held less important than inner worth.
Satirical imagery tends to cluster even more frequently than in the
earlier poems on certain images and figures, for example on
metaphors based on garbage, disease, and clothing. Jonson's
concentrated diction in *Under-wood* is essentially like that in
Epigrammes, though it reflects its changes through the greater use
of such words as *sweet, eye, face, fire,* and *love*. (See Table One,
Appendix.)

The three main new themes of the *Under-wood* collection are
valor, love, and the poet himself. The poems dealing with the
theme of valor are mainly epistles and epigrams similar to the
didactic poems of the earlier collections, while most of the poems
on love are in the form of elegy or lyric. Unlike the static love
songs in *The Forrest*, these love poems explore their material
in a new manner, cleverly and often ironically manipulating
the poet's point of view in interaction with his projected *persona*
as a character in the poem. Finally, Jonson's new attitudes and
approaches show most clearly in the poems on himself, in which
he is both speaker and subject. Thus, the best poems in *Under-*
wood show gains over those in *The Forrest* and the *Epigrammes* in

subtlety of tone, breadth of concern, and ability to handle moral and esthetic matters flexibly.

To investigate his new concern with the nature of valor, Jonson uses forms and methods familiar from his earlier work. The epigram on Sir Henry Cary (lxvi) touched on the subject of valor, and the bragging cowards in the comedies provide stereotyped butts and obvious contrasts for ideals of courage themselves not developed in the early and middle comedies. However, in *The Devil is an Ass*, *The New Inn*, *The Magnetic Lady* and in several of the poems of *Under-wood*, the question of the nature of valor becomes a dominant concern, the subject of conscious rather than incidental investigation. There are many possible reasons for this concern. According to one view, the court of Charles was experiencing a vogue of false chivalry, a reemphasis on honor and the duel, which Jonson thought pernicious.[5] Another explanation is more literary. According to Renaissance psychology, love and valor were respectively the highest manifestations of the concupiscent and irascible passions of man, standing just below reason and above the appetites in the hierarchy of man's nature.[6] Lust and ire were the lowlier versions of love and valor. Because of this belief, love and valor were considered the most appropriate themes for heroic poetry and drama in the Restoration, according to tenets codified from earlier French, English, and Italian sources. Love and valor are among the main new concerns in *Under-wood* and Jonson thus appears to be on the advance wave of a coming literary trend. From the standpoint of his own work, an interest in valor seems to be an avenue for exploring the nature of the virtuous and manly action which Jonson presented as an unexamined ideal throughout the epigrams and moral poems of *The Forrest*. In the epistle to Sir Robert Wroth (III), for example, an

---

[5]   Larry S. Champion, "The Comic Intention of Jonson's *The New Inn*", *Western Humanities Review*, 18 (1964), 67, believes that *The New Inn* parodies "Senecan valor" and the neoplatonic love cult at the court of Charles and Henrietta Maria.
[6]   Sir William Davenant, "Preface to Gondibert (1650)", in *Critical Essays of the Seventeenth Century*, ed. by Joel E. Spingarn (Oxford: Clarendon, 1908), 12-14, speaks of "Love and Ambition" as "The raging Feavers of great minds". He finds models for both in the "Schools of Morality" of "Courts and Camps".

ideal of virtuous withdrawal from an evil society clashes with
another ideal of public service. Jonson's concern with valor, then,
appears to try to grapple with the complex interactions between
a man's passions and motives and those of other people in terms
that are relevant to the contemporary society. Another possible,
more personal, explanation for the new interest in valor is that
Jonson in his old age felt he had much to suffer and was interested
in defining a virtue that might range in its manifestations from
the furious activity of youth to the passive endurance of illness,
poverty, and hardship. It is probable that the concurrence of false
standards of honor and valor around him with a predisposition
in himself to present what he felt to be true valor led to Jonson's
interest in this theme at this time in his career.

   Jonson presents several different views of valor in *Under-wood*.
The simplest identifies valor with physical bravery. In his ode to
the "High spirited friend" (28), Jonson says that "True valour doth
her own renowne command/ In one full Action." Since the friend
is young and wounded, "happy in that faire honour", it seems
likely that he was hurt in a duel or other affair of honor. Jonson
does not chastise the friend for this action, but warns him against
being over-bold. The epigram to William, Earl of Newcastle (61),
similarly appears to commend dazzling bravery in arms: "I hate
such measur'd, give me mettall'd fire/ ... A sight to draw/ Wonder
to Valour!" However, he shortly turns on this intemperate idea
and redefines valor in ethical, not passionate or pictorial, terms.

> ... No, it is the Law
> Of daring, not to do a Wrong, is true
> Valour! to sleight it, being done to you!
> To know ... where 'tis fit
> To bend, to breake, provoke, or suffer it!

His concluding paradox drives home the point that good men
are valiant "with or without their hands".

   "An Epistle to a Friend, to Perswade Him to the Warres" (17),
too, appears in its opening to support a conventional view of valor
as martial bravery: "The Drum/Beates brave, and loude in *Europe*
and bids come/ All that dare rowse ...", he tells his friend Colby,

who must be waked from "vitious ease" to revive "Mans buried honour". In contrast to the deeds of war, "All other Acts of Worldlings, are but toyle/ In dreames, begun in hope, and end in spoile". To prove this point the poet enumerates the false and meretricious activities of the world; that is, he swings into a satire on the false ambition and lust and vanity of the times in the manner typical of his earlier poems. Because of this world of peace-induced vice and surfeit, diseases of the pampered state, Jonson repeatedly tells his friend, "O times,/ Friend flie from hence" "from hell on earth". Despite the poem's opening, then, war is not seen chiefly as a field for honorable and daring exploits of bravery in the flamboyant martial sense. Instead, going to war is an escape, a withdrawal from the evils of contemporary society rather than a positive good in itself. In fact, Jonson sees martial action too as potentially dangerous to the soul. While warning against these dangers, he holds out instead the contrasting opportunities for the exercise of stoic virtue. He hopes Colby's desires will be "just, and honest, that thy Deeds/ Not wound thy conscience". He instructs him not to swear, not to shrink from fate, to think of "truth" before "glory", and to command himself before commanding others. Only the last line of the poem, "Who falls for love of God, shall rise a Starre", raises the possibility that the war is itself a holy war and a positive sphere of action. However, since this idea is not mentioned in the rest of the poem, it appears to be a conventional notion useful for a striking close rather than one to which the poet gives full endorsement and attention. Thus during the epistle the current topic of the nature of valor has been modified from its conventional meaning of martial bravery to something almost identical with stoic self-reliance and virtue – ideals consistently upheld by Jonson in the earlier commendatory epigrams and epistles.

Another epistle treats the subject of valor much more didactically and generally. The epistle to Sir Edward Sacvile (15) begins as a letter of gratitude expanded into a treatise on the proper giving and receiving of gifts. As usual, Jonson sets up the positive ideal by using many negative examples, and his satire moves from false borrowers and the ingrateful to another kind of extremists, the swaggerers or falsely valorous. Typically, he rails first and then resumes the tone of teacher.

> Cannot a man be reck'ned in the State
> Of Valour, but at this Idolatrous rate?
105 I thought that Fortitude had been a meane
> 'Twixt feare and rashnesse: not a lust obscene,
> Or appetite of offending, but a skill
> Or Science of discerning Good and Ill.
> . . . .
> Her ends are honestie, and publike good!

He does not relate the issue to his patron's character or deeds except to affirm that "you Sir, know it well to whom I write". But despite the formality and impersonality of the discussion, he does admit "I have the lyst of mine owne faults to know,/ Looke too and cure", and thus he implies a breath of tolerance of actual human experience in his textbook definition of valor. The poet remains constant to this Aristotelian summary of Fortitude in Lovel's discourse on valor in *The New Inn* and in several other poems. The emphasis here as in many of the later poems is on the end of an action rather than on its motive and on a mean that must be sought between negative extremes rather than on an already-known good starkly contrasted with an already-known evil.

If valorous action should be only for the public good, action of some kind is none the less necessary to every good man. "We must more than move still, or goe on/ We must accomplish", Jonson tells Sacvile (15). This stress on the need for active virtue is a commonplace throughout Jonson's work. In the epigram to William Roe (lxx), the Sidney birthday ode (XIV), the Cary-Morison ode (72), for instance, he repeats the idea that standing still, even in virtue, is a kind of death. The virtuous must be ever active. The poet uses the same line of reasoning to reprimand himself in his first ode to himself for being "buried" in sloth (25) since knowledge dies when not exercised. In "An Epistle Answering to One That Asked to Be Sealed of the Tribe of Ben" (49), the poet even seems to find it necessary to assert his own willingness to "draw the Sword" for the honor of king and country if necessary.

There remains in Jonson's treatment of valor or fortitude, then, some ambivalence. A source of disunity in several of the poems of *The Forrest*, especially in the epistle to Wroth, was a confusion about the respective values of activity in society and withdrawal from it. In *Under-wood* the comparable problem is that of active or passive valor. It is possible that this ambivalence led Jonson to consider the problem repeatedly. In some of his latest poems, Jonson implies that fortitude is truly defined as the endurance of evils. In the Epistle Mendicant of 1631 (73), he compares himself, the "Bed-Rid Wit", with a town besieged by "disease" and "want", unable to throw off these oppressors without some outside aid. Similarly, in the long funeral poems written late in his own life, Jonson emphasizes the patient endurance of sickness and death of Lady Jane Ogle (Uc. 45) and Lady Jane Pawlet (85). These feminine forms of fortitude are consonant with the increased emphasis in *Under-wood* on the importance of women and their virtues in comparison with the earlier collections.

Poems that seriously consider the nature of women and of love are considerably more common in *Under-wood* than poems that treat valor, and the large number of poems in *Under-wood* on these themes indicates a significant change in emphasis from Jonson's earlier works. As we have seen, the epigrams include a very few positive poems to or about women, chiefly learned literary patronesses. Two epistles in *The Forrest* praised aristocratic ladies similarly, and the gentlewoman of "To the World" (IV) is shown as stoically self-sufficient and confident in Christian trust. In contrast, the satires, satiric epistles and epigrams include numerous vigorous passages on women's lechery and vanity. Although these passages spring from a very old tradition,[7] they are so emotionally charged and so similar in their repeated imagery of disgust that a tirade against women seems to make up one of Jonson's private setpieces.

Equally traditional, though from different sources, are the amorous lyrics in *The Forrest*. They translate conventional attitudes and poses of love relationship into beautifully-finished Jonsonian verse, but without examining these attitudes and

---

[7]   Cited by Johnston, *Jonson: Poet*, 73ff.

postures. The early "Epode" defines true love in comparison with false desire, but this comparison is treated as part of a larger, quite conventional allegory on virtue having little to do with the complex varieties of human emotions. The only poem in the *Epigrammes* or *The Forrest* that seems even to begin an investigation of the nature of love is Forrest 1. However, this slight lyric implies more than it produces. It is hung on a meagre fable about Cupid and only begins to develop a projected *persona* of Jonson the poet as potential lover.

In marked contrast to this minor strain in the earlier works, Jonson seems to be conducting a concerted effort in *Under-wood* to investigate the nature of women and of love outside the frameworks of static satire or rapt praise. Over one-third of the poems of *Under-wood* are to or about women, and several poems treat love in the abstract. In contrast to those in the earlier collections, the women in *Under-wood* are not exclusively defined as sluts or patrons. Charis and the women of the elegies are addressed as equals, and even the titled Ladies Covell and Digby are treated familiarly, with a playful raillery mixed with the reverence due to their rank.

One of the central questions that these poems raise is the real place and worth of women. Is she ever the pure idol, the goddess of much conventional love poetry, and if not, is she then always the tainted creature of the satires? Even if imperfect, can she spur men to greater heights than they could have reached alone? Another major concern of this group of poems is the role of beauty in producing and sustaining love. Other matters raised peripherally concern knowledge, self-knowledge, and the relationships between poetry, language, persuasion, and love. Can the lover have true self-knowledge? Will he find himself ennobled or made ridiculous? Another debated point is the role of words in love. The lover may use poetry as a means to persuade, to enamour or to seduce his lady, or to relive his own sufferings and joys. Or he may take a cooler, more objective stance and expose his own and the woman's follies. He may even deliberately idealize, creating perfect exemplars of beauty and virtue to which love can and should be directed, idealizations more worthy than the actual women or experiences on which they are based. Finally, he may record his experiences and his impressions of them and so immortalize the objects of his attention – for good and ill. These matters are not treated didactically, as in the earlier collections of poems, nor even consistently. Jonson's attitude and approach in these later poems is altogether more flexible and exploratory than in the earlier work, and, though these poems are informed by the same ethical serious- ness and persistence as the earlier ones, they display a lighter touch and a more realistic assessment of human nature.

"A Celebration of Charis in Ten Lyrick Peeces" (4) with its evidence of rearrangement and slow compilation,[8] presents many insights about Jonson's attitudes on all these matters, but it also presents many problems. Jonson seems to intend the ten numbered and labeled pieces to form a deliberate whole as finally arranged, and there are many links from poem to poem in the group. There are also some close links between the Charis poems and other lyrics, especially elegy 21, and there are connections between Charis, a speech for a masque, and two of the later plays. Moreover, the ten Charis poems display a wide variety of attitudes to love, not all of which are consistent with each other, though the disparate parts tempt critics to hypothesize narrative or psychological consistency.[9] If he was responsible for the arrangement, Jonson may have placed this series after the opening religious poems of *Under-wood* as an introduction to the topics of love, beauty, and poetry that are dominant in the collection.

Charis 1, "His excuse for loving", is often anthologized separately

---

[8] H & S, 11, 49, give 1623 as the date of Charis 1 and 1612-16 as the range of probable dates for Charis 2-10. Paul Cubeta, "'A Celebration of Charis': An Evaluation of Jonsonian Poetic Strategy", *ELH*, 25 (1958), 163-80, believes that Charis 2-3 and 5-10 are probably later than 1612-16.

[9] Cubeta, "Charis", 164-67, sees the whole series, including Charis 1, as parody; he thinks the poet's "revenge" is to seduce Charis. Arthur F. Marotti, "All About Jonson's Poetry", *ELH*, 39 (1972), 234-35, thinks the "revenge" is the exposure of Charis as a "shallow-brained, and aging, coquette". Trimpi, *Jonson's Poems*, 210-27, provides the indispensable context for the series in his discussion of its relation to neoplatonic discussions of love and partic- ularly to the question of the old lover in the fourth book of Castiglione's *Courtier*. Horace's persona of an old lover is also relevant, especially Ode IV.i.

and referred to as one of Jonson's few genuine love poems. With its controlled verse and apparent detachment, it sets the mood for the series, providing both a strong standard against which the reader measures the other poems and a promise that certain implications of a whole will be fulfilled, so that the reader waits patiently for the parts to unfold. Many of the terms of Charis 1 recur in ironic modifications and variations in the later nine poems of the series. Charis 1 provides an example of Jonson's craftsmanship at its most artful. Unobtrusive balances, symmetries, and contrasts build the poem into as tight a structure as the lyric to Celia (IX). However, Charis 1 surpasses "To Celia" and the encomia of the epigrams and epistles in depth, for it supports its integrity of artistic finish with supple and various attitudes to its subject.

Like several of the other poems in the group, Charis 1 is written in headless iambic tetrameter. The tendency of this verse form to canter along aimlessly or to sound sing-songish is carefully controlled here by one-hundred-percent end-stopping, short sentences, and a flexible caesura.

> Let it not your wonder move,
> Lesse your laughter; that I love.
> Though I now write fiftie yeares,
> I have had, and have my Peeres;
> 5   Poets, though devine are men:
> Some have lov'd as old agen.

The opening sentence of the poem is a negative exhortation addressed not to Charis but to the reader. In fact, the person "that I love" is not presented in the text until line eighteen, and the whole opening discussion is thus the lover's "excuse" to himself and to his reader, a matter of self-definition and self-justification. The opening is typically Jonsonian in its negative, indirect statement and its simple, abstract words. The word "wonder" seems to promise marvels, but the alliterated modification "lesse your laughter" undercuts the opening grandeur. In fact, the series shows the lover and his love as both grand and ridiculous.

The sources for both these contradictory states are slightly hinted in the next four lines (3-6). The old lover is more than an old man; he is a poet. He implies that he is a long-time viewer of human affairs and of the folly of loving. The alliteration on "Peeres" and "Poet" stresses the equation of these two groups: only poets are the speaker's equals. Here the author's grammar and word order establish that his prime role is as poet, a special kind of person who casually balances a "devine" office against his inevitable but secondary qualities as man. However, if the first suggestion of the lines is that the poet's humanity makes him susceptible to the folly of loving, the second is that the man's divine role of poet provides his excuse for continuing to love past the usual age. Throughout the series Jonson thus exaggerates the ridiculous aspects of his love without compromising the seriousness of its ideal possibilities or of its actual effect on him, and he plays repeatedly on the complex interaction between his two roles of man and of poet. These first six lines of Charis 1 are thus set up in pseudo-logical form, as though a proof of the necessity of loving, and the negative connotations of something needing to be excused are balanced by the commanding and authoritative tone of the speaker.

If the controlled sentences of lines one to six show the speaker as a poet, lines seven to twelve pick up a cumulative urgency and a quickened pace that begin to show him as a man and lover. While the first six lines of the poem take the defensive about poets being lovers, the next six, comprising one sentence, spring to the offensive to demonstrate that "the Language, and the Truth", that is, the tools of the practice of poetry, can provide the poet with advantages to outweigh the more external and obvious attractions of the usual young lover.

> And it is not alwayes face,
> Clothes, or Fortune gives the grace;
> Or the feature, or the youth:
> 10   But the Language, and the Truth,
> With the Ardor, and the Passion,
> Gives the Lover weight, and fashion.

Through the poem, as in so many of his poems, early and late, Jonson establishes a rhetorical pattern of evenly balanced positive and negative units. "Not your wonder" is set against "lesse your laughter", and both are completed by "that I love". Line four corrects line three, while line five maintains its own contrast between divine and human poets. Moreover, line six answers line three; line five explains line four. In this extremely artful structure, the addition of the unexpected and assymmetrical line nine with its two negative alternatives after the preceding three gives a strong sense of tumultuous and passionate expression. As in "To Heaven" (XV), small stylistic variations produce significant shifts in tone because of the controlled context within which they operate.

In place of the five superficial attributes which he does not have, the speaker lists four he does: language, truth, ardor, passion. Lines nine to twelve are again in careful rhetorical and metrical balance. Lines nine and ten both break after the fourth syllable; each line includes a two-syllable noun before the caesura and a one-syllable noun after it, though the balance is offset by the fact that line nine belongs grammatically with the list of unnecessary attributes beginning with line seven. Line eleven also divides after the fourth syllable, and it parallels the two abstract nouns of lines nine and ten with two more abstract nouns, breaking monotony by adding a second syllable to the second noun and thus creating a feminine rhyme. Line twelve completes the predicate with "gives" parallel to "gives the grace" of line eight and the object "love", and then two abstract noun objects, "weight, and fashion" with reversed order of one and two syllables and with delayed caesura. The meter throughout the passage is relentlessly regular, like a fast pulse. Thus the impression of excitement in the passage is augmented by the change in grammatical structure from the balanced clauses of lines one to six to the paratactic series through lines seven to eleven. The language, truth, ardor, and passion are listed in series as though all are possible together. The argument concludes abruptly that these attributes give the lover "weight, and fashion" – though Jonson's own immense and renowned bulk, he slyly implies, may not be a result only of his ardor, and it may not be a great incentive to hers. Moreover, the very word "fashion" undercuts the distinction the poet has been trying to draw between unnecessary superficial characteristics and these deeper qualities he claims are his.

After focusing on himself in his roles as lover and poet in the first half of the poem, the speaker turns in the second half to describe the object of his love, to introduce his "storie" and to give some evidence of his language, truth, ardor, and passion. This half is still part of his "excuse for loving", since the more desirable the woman he describes, the more clearly he cannot help loving her.

> If you will then read the Storie,
> First, prepare you to be sorie,
> 15   That you never knew till now,
> Either whom to love, or how:
> But be glad, as soone with me,
> When you know that this is she,
> Of whose Beautie it was sung,
> 20   She shall make the old man young.

The introduction to the "storie" is elaborate, mannered, suspenseful, and playful. It is not a tale to be listened to without adequate preparation. "Whom to love" is "she" and "how" is shown by the example of Jonson's poetry and the wooing described in it – a subtle, various, and wryly ironic "how". The expected contrast to lines thirteen to sixteen comes in lines seventeen to nineteen. Like the first few lines of the poem, lines thirteen to nineteen are carefully balanced and interinvolved. The idea of conscious poetry in "if you will then read the Storie" is complemented by "of whose beauty it was sung". "Be Sorie" (1.14) is reversed by "be glad" (1.17), and "you never knew" (1.15) by "when you know" (1.18). Line thirteen emphasizes the reader's will; lines fifteen and eighteen, his knowledge; lines sixteen and seventeen, his emotions. Lines seventeen and eighteen condense the persons of the poem: "with me"/"you know"/"that this is she". The triumphant pronoun at the end of line eighteen hints that the beloved is the only "she" that counts.

This passage shifts back and forth among all the tenses. "If you will then read"/"you never knew"/"be glad ... you know". This shifting pulls the reader into the action, and it continues with "this is she" and "of whose beautie it was sung", arriving at the climactic prediction, "she shall make the old man young". This use of all three tenses supports the implication that the subject of the poem represents a permanent force in the universe as well as a specific woman, and it also underlines the basic contrast between the old lover and his young beloved.

As in the first half of the poem, so in the second a balanced positive and negative set of lines is followed by a cumulative series which by contrast seems passionately emotional in tone. Thus the poet sings that his beloved's beauty will do many things:

20   She shall make the old man young.
     Keepe the middle age at stay,
     And let nothing high decay.
     Till she be the reason why
     All the world for love may die.

As in lines one to twelve, so in lines thirteen to twenty-four, the rhythms of speech in the cooler first portion of each passage shade into more emphatic iambic meters in the second half. Lines nineteen to twenty-four have no internal pauses to chop up the incantatory rhythm of the lines. As befoie, the apparently parallel series is not exactly parallel as the results of her actions become more general. First she operates on "the old man," then on "the middle age", then on everything "high", and finally on "all the world", which, ambiguously in a favorite contemporary pun, "may die" for her love. She may rejuvenate old men or she may make fifty-year olds into doting fools in their second childhood. According to these predictions, the power of Charis' beauty seems to be to reverse and arrest the course of nature and to fix everyone of any age in an eternal attitude of admiration for her. Thus she is represented as acting like the elixir of life or like Celia whose presence made the flowers grow in Forrest IX.

Trimpi speaks of the beauty that "transcends the physical world and leads the lover to the realm of permanent values" while causing the world to lose its own identity to unite with her.[10] Like the poet, Charis is in some sense "devine", and, conversely,

---

[10]   Trimpi, *Jonson's Poems*, 216.

his "excuse" for loving is double: he is only human, and, besides, she will "make the old man young". As the series progresses, the effects her beauty actually produces in the poet are set against the potentialities, and thus both lover and lady are revalued.

In marked contrast to the suavely ironic yet convincing poetic passion of Charis 1, Charis 2 and 3 have a light, flippant tone conveyed through a sing-song use of meter. Charis 2, "How he saw her" appears to begin the story that Jonson promised his reader in Charis 1. The conditionals and balancing negatives of Charis 1 and most of Jonson's other serious poems are missing from these two light poems. The extreme absolutes of praise in them, combined with feminine rhyme and rapid, pattering meter indicate a foolish abandonment. The poet-lover has responded to Charis' pretty face and clothes by trying foolishly to "Ape" a young lover, and he is thus metamorphosed into "Cupids Statue with a Beard", an ironic contrast to Charis' metamorphosis to Venus in Charis 4 and to the transcendent possibilities of Charis 1. Thus the satiric poet shows how this kind of old lover's response to young beauty might move laughter, while, behind his ridiculous *persona*, the poet is indulging in his own laughter. In Charis 3, "What hee suffered", the lover first claims that he is utterly helpless before the power of his beloved, but then turns to say

> now, all my wreake
> Is, that I have leave to speake,
> . . . .
> To revenge me with my Tongue,
> Which how Dexterously I doe
> Heare and make Example too.

The early Jonsonian belief in the moral value of the virtuous "example" here takes a humorous variation. Thus the poor lover claims to reassert his power and control over women and love by returning to his special role as a poet, though of course the poet Jonson is keeping control throughout the poem on both of his characters, the conventional beloved and the conventional lover, and revenging himself more against the simplicity of usual attitudes about love and of hackneyed kinds of love poetry than against a particular woman.

In Charis 2 and 3 the lover represents himself as at the nadir of devoted subjection to the beloved, while the poet is producing a sophisticated poetry parodic of Petrarchan-Elizabethan love conventions. As the series goes on, values are slowly readjusted; as the lover regains his sight and motion, the beloved assumes a much less imposing role, and the poet returns to a more polished, less slapstick form of wit.

Charis 4, "Her Triumph", is the poet's triumph as well. It shows his utmost skill in creating convincing hyperbolic praise in a lilting lyric stanza. Thus before shifting to the harsher and more ironic appraisals of the later poems in the series, the poet fulfills the promised potential of Charis 1 in illustrating how well he can use language, truth, ardor, and passion in a poem of pure praise under the aegis not of Cupid but of the more impressive love deity of universal harmony. The third stanza of "Her Triumph" appeals to possible human experiences of the reader to validate the perfection of the beloved's beauty. "Have you seene but the bright Lillie grow,/ Before rude hands have touch'd it?" Here the possibility of the sullying reality reasserting itself against the ideal vision provides the transition to the rest of the series.

Charis 5, "His discourse with Cupid", set again in headless iambic tetrameter, returns the series to the humorous deflation of conventional love attitudes through exaggeration and parody. In this poem Charis is the "best/ Of her Sex", but this is ambiguous praise, and the rest of the series slowly clarifies this description by showing its possibilities and its limitations.

Charis 6, "Clayming a second kisse by Desert", follows Charis 5 in stressing the conventional and self-conscious nature of love poetry and the lovers who adhere to its patterns. The love that could affect the course of nature is now reduced to the favors of a "second kisse", and all the speaker's praises compare Charis with other court beauties. If love has become a game, so too has poetry. "Charis guesse" the poet asks "What my Muse and I have done". The speaker assumes a cynical tone about matters of love and marriage. For example, the bride to whom he knowingly compares Charis is "allow'd a Maid". If the conventions of the helpless lover were satirized earlier in the series, the opposite conventions of the cavalier spirit are satirized here and the conventions of the metaphysical lyric in Charis 7. The speaker is no longer feeble and overcome. Instead, he is humorously boisterous in his masculine pride and assertive sexuality.

"Begging another on colour of mending the former", the stanzaic Charis 7, uses favorite Donnean conceits and conventions like the simulation of direct speech and immediate situation. It is a poem of passionate persuasion like Forrest VI or elegy 21, though some of the supposed passion is undercut by the speaker's sly tone, possibly by the image of the weighty lover kissing "lightly as the Bee", and even by the title, which indicates that the speaker will use whatever rhetorical "colour" he feels necessary to achieve his goal. "I long, and should not beg in vaine".

Charis 8, "Urging her of a promise", leaves the kiss motif of poems 6 and 7 and returns to couplets of headless iambic tetrameter. The speaker's tone is neither quivering nor peremptory in the last poem of the series in which he speaks for himself. It is now cooled and controlled, asserting the civility and wit of Charis 1, though without its exaltation, after the extravagances of the intervening poems. The second half of Charis 8 is a humorous curse to keep Charis from typical feminine frivolities if she does not fulfill her promise to "tell/ What a man she could love well".

The poet furthers his "revenge" against the lady and more subtly against himself in Charis 9, "Her man described by her owne Dictamen", where he gives her a voice of 'her own' with which to reveal herself as the reflex of her own ideal lover. The essence of this portrait is in her parenthetical remark, "And a woman God did make me". Even if she is the "best of her sex", (Charis 5), she is not a divinity, not blessed with special magical powers, as a fond lover might at first think. According to 'her' words, she is an ordinary woman in society, not vicious but a bit vain and willful – a woman, as God made them. Charis identifies "Ben" as her taunter and then cheerfully rejects adult male virility – and Ben – as frightening. "Too much beard" would "make *Love* or me afeard". She describes the attractions of her ideal lover's dress and appearance in terms that echo the poet's earlier glorification of her as a Venus, Juno, and Minerva. Her lover must have

"Venus, and Minerva's eyes" and "eye-brows bent like Cupid's bow". In addition, he must be valiant, generous, honest, and, most important, moderate in all things. Her ideal, then, is a compound of romanticized sensual attractions and genuine moral qualities – like his ideal. If she cannot have her ideal lover, she is unwilling to have any.

"Another Ladyes exception present at the hearing", Charis 10, begins "For his Mind I doe not care", indicating by contrast that Charis' brief allusions to her ideal lover's mental and moral qualities do count for something. The second lady is a sheer sensualist who chases the chaster meaning from the *double entendre* in Charis 9. "Tis one good part I'ld lie withall", she says, using the pun of Epigram lxix. Her views do not indicate that she is more 'honest' than Charis or that the author thinks Charis is really no better than this,[11] but the second lady's exception takes Jonson's exposure of the possible characters of women one step farther than Charis 9, though without compromising Charis herself. At their worst, he seems to be saying in Charis 9 and 10, women are mere sluts. At their best, they are what God and the men around them have made them – a little foolish, vain, and overly attentive to externals even when at the same time they are witty, charming, desirable and willing to banter with their poet-admirers on a level of good-natured and equal raillery.

By the end of the series of ten poems, the lover's "storie" promised in Charis 1 is complete, though the Bens and Charises of all the poems of the series are not psychologically consistent dramatic characters. The tale is a balanced one, filled with minor incidents and major reappraisals. In one sense, the poet has accomplished the "revenge" he swore in Charis 3 by exposing the spurious attractions of women's beauty, the vanity, frivolity, and even vice that may exist beneath their apparently pure forms. A beautiful face and form do not necessarily correspond with a beautiful soul beneath, the poet demonstrates for any still-deluded followers of the platonic conventions of Elizabethan love poetry. But obviously the series is not a simple satire on women. Nor

---

[11] Cubeta, "Charis", 180, holds this view. That is, he believes the other woman to be more candid, not more chaste, than Charis.

can it be seen as a typical Renaissance sonnet series moving toward a palinode, the finding of lust beneath the mask of love. The series is a satire on men and on their expectations of women as much as it is about women.

According to Trimpi, Charis represents the realistic mean between the idealistic poet and the sensual lady of Charis 10.[12] One can go farther, however, and see in the entire series the oscillation to a balanced mean in the poet's own attitudes and voices from Neoplatonic praise in the first poem to pseudo-Petrarchan abjection in the second to Ovidian transformation in the fourth to knowing Cavalier cynicism in the sixth to metaphysical masculinity in the seventh to sophisticated raillery in the eighth. The poet's final stage is the most significant. From the high-toned egotism of the opening of "His Excuse for Loving", his "Celebration" of Charis has moved to the point where he withdraws entirely as narrator in the ninth poem. The dramatist then presents her telling "Ben" her excuse for not loving – or at least, not loving him.

The poet makes the lover who speaks in the first eight poems exhibit various kinds of stereotyped thinking: fatuousness, intellectual toying, egotism, and lust that comprise male attitudes to love and lead men into foolishness in life and stupidity in poetry. As the series balances its exposure of the flaws of women by revelation of the flaws of men, so too it balances both against some of the more extravagant claims for the powers of love and beauty and poetry and achieves a just and moderate estimate which indicates some of the genuine possibilities that remain. Thus a woman's beauty and a man's responsive emotions may help him produce poetry which retains its loveliness, its touch with eternal harmony and lasting truths, even though the particular object which started the chain of idealization may prove to be something quite different from the sum of the praise heaped upon it. The speaker, who is also a lover and poet, makes good his claims to language, truth, ardor, and passion, that is, to an honest and realistic poetry, in natural language, that deals with man's pas-

[12] Trimpi, *Jonson's Poems*, 226.

sions and that treats love, woman, and beauty in terms both of
their real social and moral contexts and of their traditional literary
illusions.

Even more important, Jonson demonstrates a new flexibility
in this first set of secular poems in *Under-wood*. Gone is the simple
rhetoric of praise and blame. Here he uses a multiple form and
shifting tones between and within poems. The poet shows a
comic understanding of his characters, who include himself,
rather than an external and one-sided judgment of them. If the
interest of love and women is a new and major concern of the poet
in Jonson's later work, then it is accompanied by an even more
important change of attitude, a vast enlargement of the poet's
scope of empathy and understanding. Again and again in the
Under-wood collection, Jonson creates characters who are mixed
in their vices and virtues, who cannot quickly be labeled and judged
like the static characters of the earlier epigrams, songs, and
epistles. Most important in demonstrating this change is the newly
flexible role of the narrator, who is now more and more often
supposed to be a personal and individual projection of the poet
with all his humorous possibilities and ethical contradictions.

Jonson's love elegies, a genre new in *Under-wood*, repeatedly
consider the question of the relationships between beauty and
love and poetry and the characteristics of lover and beloved that
were presented indirectly and cumulatively in the Charis series.
They explore different aspects of these themes, sometimes as
impersonal laws of nature, sometimes in the context of particular
dramatic situations, which, unlike those in the dramatic songs of
The Forrest, are invented to aid the exploration into love. Furthermore, Jonson's repeated concern in *Under-wood* with lovers and
love is marked by his changing attitude toward the nature of the
poet. Elegy 20, for instance, "Can Beautie that did prompt me
first to write", is a meditation or monologue in which the poet
lover exclaims on the vagaries of love, asks himself questions,
analyzes his feelings, and then answers his own questions.

> Can Beautie that did prompt me first to write,
> Now threaten, with those meanes she did invite:
> Did her perfections call me on to gaze!

Then like, then love; and now would they amaze!
5   Or was she gracious a-farre off? but neere
A terror? or is all this but my feare?
That as the water makes things, put in't, streight,
Crooked appeare; so that doth my conceipt:
I can helpe that with boldnesse; And Love sware,
10   And fortune once, t'assist the spirits that dare.
But which shall leade me on? both these are blind:
Such Guides men use not, who their way would find.
Except the way be errour to those ends:
And then the best are still, the blindest friends!
15   Oh how a lover may mistake! to thinke,
Or love, or fortune blind, when they but winke
To see men feare: or else for truth, and State,
Because they would free Justice imitate,
Vaile their owne eyes, and would impartially
20   Be brought by us to meet our Destinie.
If it be thus, Come love, and fortune goe,
I'le lead you on, or if my fate will so,
That I must send one first, my Choyce assignes,
Love to my heart, and fortune to my lines.

In traditional Renaissance fashion, beauty inspires love and hence
prompts the lover to become a poet, though the Beautie herself
soon adopts the equally traditional role of the cold Petrarchan
lady. Perhaps, he surmises, the apparently near-divine nature of
female beauty is only a reflex of his male emotion, his fears creating
the illusion of her awesomeness.

The competence of his own analysis of his problem provides
the transition in tone from the lover's defensive questioning in the
first eight lines of the poem to the assertive remedy: "I can helpe
that with boldnesse". To the apparently obvious assertion that
boldness will correct fear the poet adds a quasi-mythological
reason through a fable of love and fortune; he uses his typical
tactic of attaining the reader's assent with a truism in order to
lead him on to further propositions. This allegory of love and
fortune shifts the poem's emphasis back from the psychological
state of the speaker to the world of general propositions with which
the poem began. Love creates fear, the argument now seems to
go, but true lovers overcome their fear and so enjoy both love
and good fortune. The focus of attention thus turns from ideal

static forms like those Jonson treated allegorically in the early
"Epode" to a consideration of how things work out in the real
world.

In lines one to eight of the poem the lover is in the power of
love; in lines nine to fourteen he asserts his power over love by
boldness and by a series of allegorical transpositions that make
love seem a delusion anyway. Since love and fortune are both
blind, the deluded lover and the man ruled by fortune are both at
the mercy of forces external to themselves, equally far from the
Jonsonian ideal of self-command, which the speaker of the poem
now re-asserts. Thus if the speaker of the first fourteen lines of the
elegy talks as a lover, the speaker of the rest of the poem criticizes
the follies of all lovers from his residual roles of man and poet.

The end of the poem (11.21-24) is again resolved in familiar
Jonsonian terms of the split between passive resignation to outside
forces and one's own powers of action. Instead of being at the
mercy of these blind abstractions, the speaker is now playfully
disposing of them. He blandly assumes that he can have both,
though perhaps one before another, and that his will controls them.
He is completely altered from the frightened lover of the opening
lines of the poem who was only spurred by the emotional power of
female beauty. He is no longer love's victim; love can remain
in his heart, trusting reason and his "lines" of poetry to win him
acceptance. In this context, love is no longer an all-absorbing
passion. The "fortune" of his "lines", his poetic reputation and
skill, are more important.

This brief elegy, then, moves in a parallel direction with the
Charis series as a whole. In both, a subjected lover overpowered by
female beauty gradually asserts his rational and esthetic control
over himself and his passions, reassesses the importance of love to
himself, and at last awards the palm of his efforts and attentions
not to love but to the poetry which love has inspired and which
lasts even when the illusions of love are outgrown. If the overt
subject of this poem centers on the concepts of love, beauty, and
poetry, we have seen that they are all considerably modified from
more typical love poses by the persistent Jonsonian ideals of manly
self-sufficiency and vigorous action accompanied by knowing

ethical choice. These are the ideals that were praised earlier in the
commendatory epigrams and epistles. Put the other way round,
Jonson has expanded his earlier categorical commendations of
self-sufficiency by an active investigation of passion's assault
upon the integrity of the ego and of the ego's responses. The power
and attractiveness of the passions are not minimized, and the
resulting condition of the ego again in control of the passions is
not taken as fixed or intolerant.

Elegy 24 of the same series similarly begins by praising a woman's
virtue and beauty. It ends, surprisingly, when the conventional
poet-lover supplicates the Beauty not for her own mercies but for
her good influence on a love of his. Even if this fails, he accepts
his less exalted beloved; his final plea is "give me leave t'adore
in you/ What I, in her, am grievd to want". There are thus two
classes of beloved women: virtuous and respected love deities, and
less exalted loves who are desired more presently. One might see this
contrast as one like that between the exalted Charis imaged in
Charis 1 and 4 and the desirable but humanly flawed woman
of Charis 5-9.

These two loves, in various incarnations, can be found throughout Renaissance poetry. Jonson's willingness to praise someone
who he admits is less than perfect indicates his accommodation
to human realities in *Under-wood*, in contrast to the black and white
judgments of the earlier epigrams and epistles. Furthermore, the
line, "what I, in her, am grievd to want", implies the speaker's
equality with the flawed beloved. Similarly, in "The Satyricall
Shrub", a satirical inverted love elegy, the blame is not fixed
exclusively on the censured object as it was in the earlier epigrams
and epistles, but is also humorously directed by the poet at himself for the "foolish deadly sin" of trusting in "a Woman's friendship" (22).

In the elegies of the first group, *Under-wood* poems 20-24, then,
Jonson exhibits a new flexibility of viewpoint toward women
and a new balance in the understanding of the interactions between
men, their illusions, and women. The style of these poems remains
conventionally within the plain and Petrarchan traditions. Jonson's second group of elegies, the series 40, 42, 43, deals with

illusions and confusions between men and women in the manner of
contemporary metaphysical poetry. The speakers of these poems
are introduced in particular dramatic situations.

The crux of elegy 40 is a lover's plea for forgiveness for a committed fault. He pleads that his "weakness" committed the fault,
assuming that this is not an intrinsic part of his character the way
his virtue is. A whole set of analogies proves that the self is not
equal to its faults. In the preceding "Epistle to a Friend" (39), the
poet makes the same distinction, asking the friend to forgive his
harshness "as my frailtie, and not me". So in elegy 40 he says,
"Think it was frailtie, Mistris, thinke me man", and, again, he
speaks of "errour and folly in me" but says "those, not I be lost".
In the epigrams he claimed to be chastising the vices and not the
man, but then he meant that he had types of vicious people, not
particular persons in mind. He did not there allow for the possibility that the man was greater than or different from a specific
flaw; instead, in the satiric epigrams, the vice was the man. Here
in the love elegies the lover as well as the beloved is looked upon as
flawed but not therefore as worthless. Both lover and beloved are
thus cast more humanly, less as positive or negative exemplary
types, and the poet simultaneously changes from being an outside
judge of others' qualities to a participant in the perpetual comedy
of the relations between the sexes.

Elegy 42 contributes to the characterization of the speaker the
idea of the confident and buoyant lover, the "open merrie man".
In contrast, he declares "the grave Lover ever was an Ass" – a
belief for Wittipols and against Lovels, for instance, and in consonance with the free confidence achieved, though only after an
initial period of subjection, by the lovers of Charis and of elegies
20, 21, and 24.

In all these love poems and elegies, then, the defense of the
speaker's sense of identity recurs as a common theme, though
handled with a humorous tolerance of the frailties wrapt up in that
identity. Women and the passions of love are seen in these poems
both as charming and desirable in themselves and as the means
through which men can achieve self-knowledge and breadth of
understanding. In elegy 44 the defense of the speaker's integrity

of character is the dominant theme. The elegy's colloquial opening, "Let me be what I am", is far different from Donne's "for Godsake hold thy tongue and let me love", though the two sound similar in tone and are both addressed to a third person. Unlike Donne, Jonson is not primarily defending the rights of love. He is defending, instead, his own integrity as a poet and as a man and espousing the poet's right to seem to be a lover if he wishes, in order to create moving love poetry, a necessary part of the traditional poet's repertory.[13]

> Let me be what I am, as *Virgil* cold,
> As *Horace* fat; or as *Anacreon* old;
> No Poets verses yet did ever move,
> Whose Readers did not thinke he was in love.

Though stressing his age and improbable physique, then, Jonson does so here in a context of rich allusion. He is not the first immortal poet to bear the infirmities of a man, and he is proud rather than defensive. Like the speaker of Charis 1, he has, and has had, his peers. Here he changes tactics from Charis 1 and other of his poems. When he claims he will be "in Rithme .../ As light, and Active as the youngest hee", he no longer takes the untenable position that he ought to be accepted as a lover because of his poetic talents. He only defends his right to play the role of the lover in poetry and to enjoy certain prerogatives of the poet, like the right to watch all pretty women. He asserts the fact that the poet's experienced energy is in words, not in body. Thus elegy 44 shows a considerable gain in subtlety of discrimination and flexibility in its attitude toward poetic inspiration over the poems of *The Forrest* with their alternate claims for rapt divine inspiration (XII) and sober, unassuming craftsmanship (I, X).

The working poet in "Ivy Garland" uniform sees and loves "all" the beautiful, and he is therefore higher on the ladder of love than the man enslaved by one pretty face, but he is not making

---

[13]   Sir Philip Sidney's "Apologie for Poetrie" is the Renaissance *locus classicus* for the importance of persuasive forcibleness in love poetry, of sounding as though "in truth they feele those passions", in *English Literary Criticism: The Renaissance*, ed. by O. B. Hardison, Jr. (New York: Appleton-Century-Crofts, 1963), 141-42.

transcendent platonic claims. He remains human, humorous, ironic in his transactions with the fair sex. The poet can confer on the ladies he honors the benefit of the poet's supreme power, that of making his subjects immortal, "if they be faire and worth it". No matter that he is cold, fat, old: the poet is superior to other men in his integrity of character, his perception of beauty, his sensitivity in response to it, and his abilities to express these higher perceptions. He retains control of every situation; even in love he knows what he is doing and is not "Wrung on the Withers, by Lord Loves despight".

Thus the love elegies in *Under-wood* follow a pattern that distinguishes them from the songs, epigrams, and epistles written earlier to women and also from the love poems of other contemporary poets. Jonson's elegies begin as considerations of the nature of love and beauty or as set dramatic situations involving lovers. Most of these poems soon shift their focus from the closed world of love and lovers and go on to explore a central concern of Jonson's, the nature of love poetry in terms of its poet and the demands on him, the contradictions and similarities between his roles as man and as poet. Although he occasionally lapses back into his typical earlier role of the harsh judge or moralist, Jonson generally takes a wider view in surveying the frailties of his subjects and himself. Another group of poems uses Jonson's projections of himself as man and as poet more fully and directly than do most of the elegies, and these poems are not always connected with love. Some are poems about friendship, some are about poetry, and some are about the poet's relations with the king and court or with his stage audiences.

As we have seen in Charis and many of the elegies, the poems appeared at times to reflect a covert and good-humored war between the sexes, with the male often trying to shake off the undeniable attractions of female beauty. According to neoplatonic-Elizabethan love theory, the attraction to beauty was natural, since the beautiful form housed a beautiful soul. Throughout his writings, on the other hand, Jonson is concerned with the deceptiveness of appearances, and he questions the equation between apparent beauty and goodness. Thus his frequent use of the myth that love is blind may spring from his concern to probe the appearance of beauty. Another humorous and personal approach for exploring the relations of love and beauty, truth and poetry, is through an emphasis on his own unloveliness, as in the humorous "My Picture Left in Scotland" (11). Love's blindness and the lover's ugliness then play congruent and reciprocal roles in indicating lack of apparent beauty or an inability to perceive anything but the appearance.

The "Picture" begins with the lover's complaint that the lady has been "deafe" to his artfully crafted language. However, in the second half of the poem, the poet drops his pretentious claim to favors he has not received and assumes a defensive position. He turns from his earlier affected style to confess the truth behind his high rationalizations, and he presents himself more honestly and more attractively. Now his problem is not that his beloved could not hear him, but that she could see him only too well. Here his method is not to minimize his deficiencies but to exaggerate them until it seems that the truth must be less negative, and he treats his awkward attributes of gray hair, "mountain belly," and "rockie face" with great and winning good humor.

The lover's command over his medium and over his own expectations is reasserted, and hence also his self-esteem, despite his failure with the fair sex. This failure is shown to be only natural when his own true nature is revealed. The mellowed *persona*, then, maintains his integrity, though not an inflated ego, through the frank and humorous acknowledgment of his limitations and through his willingness and ability to "picture" them in verse that speaks to the understanding eyes and ears.

Like the attitude of the *persona*, Jonson's handling of the technical aspects of the verse shows a new flexibility. In the first ten lines of the poem, where the speaker is attempting various untenable defensive postures, the lines vary in length and rhyme pattern: $a^5b^3b^1b^5a^3c^5c^3c^4a^3a^5$. The next eight lines, in which he relinquishes his pretensions to love and accepts himself as man and poet are more steadily resolved and fall into the symmetrical pattern of five three-foot and three five-foot lines, arranged with interlocking rhyme in the pattern: $d^3e^3e^3d^3e^3f^5f^5e^5$. The last line, a decasyllable, echoes and attains the balance sought in the first decasyllabic line, replacing its negative words "deaf" and "blind" with the more positive and natural "eyes" and "eares". Thus Jonson fits his new flexibility of approach with a flexible stanzaic form invented for the occasion. Trimpi points out the connection between Jonson's presentation of himself as speaker in this poem and the Socrates or Silenus image of the rough and ugly satyr, the old man who is inwardly clean, pure, and chaste.[14] This interesting analogy makes it seem that Jonson presents his outside as at variance with his inner nature, a kind of opposite or disguise. However Jonson does not here treat the matter of appearance so simply. He proceeds in this poem, in Charis, and in *The New Inn* to use the apparent disparities between physical form and the lover's situation or aspirations as an instrument of poetic analysis through which he finds himself. The outside is, ultimately, joined with, not antithetical to, the human character it encases.

By the end of the poem "My Picture Left in Scotland", the speaker has tried false inflation and false deflation of his ego and attained a Jonsonian mean, a balance that represents truth and self-knowledge. The speaker has rejected his own pretense that the old poet is as fine a lover as the young man and has found his own person, if fantastically unsuited for a lady's love, quite satisfactory as an object for poetry and even for a kind of pride in itself. The entire poem may be seen as a "picture" of the poet and his love which is true to him and to the realities of his condition, so that, at last, pride and humility are conflated in just estimation. The role of the poet in these mature love poems is no longer that of simple moralist or gallant; instead it is an adjunct to the role of the wise man, and the writing of poetry becomes a way of defining suitable means for moral action and evaluation, that is, of knowing oneself.

In the same way that Jonson could fit stock exemplary and sententious ideas into any *genre* or adapt a rhetoric based on praise and blame to the most various uses, so, having developed the use of a projected personal image of himself as the speaker in his poems, Jonson then uses it with very wide flexibility to achieve a number of different effects. In "My Picture Left in Scotland", the epistle to Lady Covell, and "The Poet to the Painter", the poet deprecates his ludicrous physical appearance while complimenting his addressee through the Muse unbound by his body. In elegy 39, in contrast, he develops the deeper and less humorous theme of a contrast between his better and worse selves by pleading for the recipient's belief in the dominance of his good self and in his moderation which shuns both the excesses and the defects of friendship.

This confidence in himself despite admitted flaws shows a new tolerance in Jonson's poetry, a new flexibility concerning virtue. In the more unified of his earlier poems, like "To Penshurst" and "To Celia", he restricts the range of contrasts set up in any one poem. Even the beautiful reciprocity of "Inviting a Friend to Supper" rests on the assumption of perfect civility and decorum by both host and guests. Any infraction of taste or morals would violate the spirit of the whole piece. In contrast, the epistle to the friend, Under-wood 39, admits a violation of friendship on the poet's part and then proceeds actively to erase the flaw and revitalize the friendship. In this poem and some of the love elegies the poet uses contrasts in his moral nature directly, while in Charis and other of the love poems he tends to use the incongruities of his physical image as part of a parodic *persona* in order to explore moral matters indirectly. Both these approaches lead away from the stark dichotomies of praise and blame in his earlier poems to a fuller comprehension of human possibilities and limitations, starting with those embodied in himself. In these later poems the speaker attempts to come to terms with himself as man and as poet, and as several different kinds of poet – court laureate, love poet, amuser of ladies, avenger of insults, and learned man of letters in a community of equals. Here he can modulate praise and blame of the same person or thing and can use praise and blame dynamically, as part of an interpersonal process, rather than statically. Thus, for instance, the "Execration upon Vulcan" (45) and the "Fit of Rime against Rime" (31) are not simple satiric invectives. In both poems the poet assumes a familiar teasing tone that takes off the edge of personal bitterness and deflects the reader's attention to the poet not as an isolated priest but as a working craftsman with personal irritations, triumphs, and setbacks in his work. Jonson's more flexible voice in the *Under-wood* collection can theorize about rhyme in rhyme and bewail his losses in a fire as well as poetically mourn the dead or investigate love and beauty.

If much of Jonson's poetry in *Under-wood* divides between a courting man and a court muse, the court voice of Jonson also moves in two directions from his earlier work with its dignified, rather general references to king and country. Much of the more formal and official material to Charles and Henrietta in *Under-wood* is third rate, often dully reworked old material. In contrast to these petrified poems of flattery, many of the poems to the king and his household show considerable freedom and a sense of the poet's right to a hearing. These poems do not praise those at court, but deal instead with the poet's relationships with the court and what it represents. In the poems to Charles and his high officials, Jonson often uses a projected parodic version of himself as speaker to protect himself from the embarrassment of asking for money. The poet often saves his dignity on these occasions by ignoring it, as in the petition to Master John Burges (59). The relationship between man and muse is expressed simply here: "If the 'Chequer be emptie, so will be his Head". The later "Humble Petition of Poore Ben To th' best of Monarchs, Masters, Men, King Charles" (78) combines a similar petition for food with warning of vengeance against the poet's enemies. Yet, the poet does not want to sound as though he is begging. King James granted him a "free Poetique Pension", in just recompense "For done service, and to come". Similarly, the poem titled "An Epigram. To K. Charles for a 100. Pounds He Sent Me in My Sicknesse" (64) does not mention himself or his sickness. Instead the poet praises the king for his bounty in valuing "One *Poet*" more than "other folk ten score", and he thus accepts the gift not as personal charity, but as an appropriate if generous tribute to his office.

In the sad "Epistle Mendicant" (73) to Lord Treasurer Weston in 1631 the poet admits that disease and want "have cast a trench about mee, now five yeares" and that the man is now so ill that "The *Muse* not peepes out, one of hundred dayes/ But lyes block'd up". Here the poet makes no claims of anything due him. The poet and his Muse are sick and humbled, but the poet cuts the appeal to pity in this poem by the tough and traditional imagery of warfare, by the medieval allegory which applies to the body as a walled city besieged by enemies. Moreover, the well-controlled poem gives obvious evidence that Ben's Muse could still write at least on its one day of one hundred.

Thus at various times and in various roles Jonson can represent himself as all man or all Muse, but as he ages, he tends to use the infirmities of the private man, the unlovely lover, the sick and dispossessed courtier, as an ironic or pathetic counterweight to the poetic lover or official laureate and thus as a means of asserting his own complex identity. As he tells the friend wishing to be sealed to the tribe of Ben (49), he knows himself, and he knows those around him. He is self-sufficient as the circle and will "dwell as in my Center as I can".[15] The assertion of self-knowledge and self-sufficiency is familiar to us from the Jonson of the epigrams and earlier moral epistles where it was simply stated as an ideal. Throughout the *Under-wood* collection, in contrast, this self-knowledge is consistently shown being tested by real problems, flaws, passions and awkward situations in the relations between people and within the roles of the single character.

Jonson's two odes to himself show an interesting development in his use of a projected *persona* outside of amorous or official court poetry. Here his 'self' is his subject, and he awards it a careful analysis. In the odes on himself he concentrates directly on the dual nature of his character as 'muse' and as a man, as a public poet with obligations to his craft and as a man with limitations and desires that may run counter to these poetic obligations. The two poems are both representative and both competently crafted. The differences between the two very similar poems indicate some of the problems in Jonson's self-consciously assumed role and

---

[15]   Greene, "Centered Self", 330-31, speaks of the importance of the defense of the central self, self-contained and even isolated, in Jonson's works.

show why he often aroused nearly as much enmity as admiration among his contemporaries and among latter day critics.[16]

The first ode to himself is moderate in tone. In it Jonson manages to score all his points against his critics while still retaining his readers' sympathy. He does this through one of his most typical techniques, that of controlling the kinds of choices and variables, of neatly balanced close alternatives. The result is a poem of convincing unity. On the other hand, the second ode to himself (Uc. 53), appended to *The New Inn*, provoked much hostility against Jonson. This hostility was directed against all the faults usually mentioned in connection with Jonson, chiefly his conceit, arrogance, denigration of rivals, and the 'vulgarity' of his imagery of abuse. Many of the problems typical of Jonson's less successful work appear in some form in this poem. For example, too great extremes in tone and diction and too great variation between tone and content threaten the dignity and unity of the piece and of his pose. His satirical set pieces tend to get out of hand, while his justification of his poetic role blends confusingly with personal claims for himself. The real crux of the matter is that in the *New Inn* ode Jonson regresses from the sympathetic understanding of himself and others that permeates the best poems of *Under-wood* to the old stance of the external moral critic, himself pure and free from all blame, which he can no longer maintain convincingly.

The two odes are similar in many respects. Both poems show extremely skillful handling of a complex stanza form. Each poem is composed of six stanzas. The first ode has stanzas of six lines each, of the rhyme scheme $a^3b^3a^3a^3b^3b^6$. Thus the poem is six times six lines of six syllables plus a six-syllable addition in the last line, a very tight and symmetrical form using only two rhymes per stanza. The second ode is longer and looser. The six stanzas are of ten lines each; the lines are either six or ten syllables long in rhymed couplets, thus giving five rhymes for the stanza in the pattern $a^3a^3b^5b^3c^5c^3d^3d^3e^5e^5$.

---

[16] Contemporary replies to the second ode came from Owen Feltham and Thomas Carew, among others. H & S, 11, 333-46, print seven contemporary poems on *The New Inn*. Robert C. Jones, "The Satirist's Retirement in Jonson's 'Apologetical Dialogue'", *ELH*, 34 (1967), 466-67, discusses the *New Inn* ode as a reflection of Jonson's ambivalence about his role as a poet.

In the first ode "To Himselfe" (25) Jonson commends himself under the guise of criticizing and chastising himself, and he criticizes others as though he is only defending poetry and the criticism is incidental. His eloquent form shows itself off while his use of the second person permits his chastisement of others to seem impersonally free from envy or vengeance. The poem is based on the old rhetoric of praise and blame, but softened and made credible and sympathetic by Jonson's mature multi-faceted presentation of himself.

Where do'st thou carelesse lie
Buried in ease and sloth?
Knowledge, that sleepes, doth die;
And this Securitie,
5   It is the common Moath,
That eats on wits, and Arts, and [oft] destroyes them both.

Are all th'*Aonian* springs
Dri'd up? lyes *Thespia* wast?
Doth *Clarius* Harp want strings,
10   That not a Nymph now sings!
Or droop they as disgrac't,
To see their Seats and Bowers by chattring Pies defac't?

If hence thy silence be,
As 'tis too just a cause;
15   Let this thought quicken thee,
Minds that are great and free,
Should not on fortune pause,
'Tis crowne enough to vertue still, her owne applause.

What though the greedie Frie
20   Be taken with false Baytes
Of worded Balladrie,
And thinke it Poesie?
They die with their conceits,
And only pitious scorne, upon their folly waites.

25   Then take in hand thy Lyre,
Strike in thy proper straine,
With *Japhets* lyne, aspire
Sols Chariot for new fire,
To give the world againe:

30   Who aided him, will thee, the issue of *Joves* braine.

    And since our Daintie age,
    Cannot indure reproofe.
    Make not thy selfe a Page,
    To that strumpet the Stage,
35   But sing high and aloofe,
    Safe from the wolves black jaw, and the dull Asses hoofe.

Like many other Jonson poems, the ode opens with a question. The modifiers "carelesse" and "buried in ease and sloth" provide the answer to the question of where the speaker is, and the implied further question is why the speaker is in this dormant state. All but one of the nouns in this stanza indicate abstract concepts like "sloth" and "security", but these concepts are animated and made concrete by lively verbs and images. It appears that the mind has a life as an independent creature, that it sleeps, lives, and can die. This central figure of the living mind underlies the first stanza and increases the seriousness of the whole poem, since it implies that the poet who is not active in his poetry will die mentally.

In the opening stanza, the poet's attitude to himself is ambivalent. If the poet's address to himself as "thou" is intimate, it is also perhaps somewhat contemptuous. Similarly, his lying "careless" may indicate that he is blissfully without care or that he is behaving recklessly. The word "ease", normally a positive word denoting the good life of pleasures and leisures, is endowed by the addition of "and sloth" with connotations of sinful indolence, smothering and lulling one to sleep and even to death. Assent to the proposition of the death of dormant knowledge comes easily to the reader since everyone knows that unused knowledge tends to be forgotten. Typically, Jonson starts with an obvious fact and then pulls his readers along past it. Similarly, the apparently logical progression from "lie" to "sleep" to "die" develops a variant of the Jonsonian commonplace that to stand still is to go back, that the virtuous man must be continually active. The verbs in this stanza are in the present indicative; the tone is assertive and firm.

The poet has an obligation to himself and others to rouse himself from his lethargy. For his own sake as a craftsman, he must keep in shape through practice and, more generally, since the good life consists of virtuous action, he must continue to act. The image of the "common Moath" Security livens and supports this idea since the moth is traditionally a self-destructive insect as well as one harmful to other things. The staccato iambics of "that eats on wits, and Arts, and [oft] destroyes them both", with the bit-off dental word endings *ts, ts, ts, [ft]*, sound nibbling.[17] The figures of the stanza thus have moved from recounting the dangers of the passive sleep of the mind to warning of active destruction by sloth which operates like an ignoble insect; the damage is only known when it is too late to correct.

The first stanza is focused on the poet, or rather, since he is not yet active in this role, on the idle man of knowledge. The second stanza is focused on the state of poetry, which also turns out to be inactive. A question opens the second stanza, too. The second stanza is entirely allusive and symbolic, not abstract like the first. If the first stanza asked where the poet was, the second asks where poetry is. "Are all th'*Aonian* springs/ Dri'd up? lyes *Thespia* wast?" Thespia "lyes ... wast" as the poet lay "carelesse". Like the inverted stress on "buried" opening line two of stanza one and emphasizing connotations of death, the inverted stress on "dri'd up" in the second line of the second stanza pulls the reader up sharply and negatively after the allusive elegance of "th'*Aonian* springs". This formality of statement serves its own purposes, since it indicates that the poet's skill has not died utterly. The assertion of poetic pride through a display of the poetic craft here is similar to the poet's exercises as poet-lover in several of the amorous elegies and lyrics.

His continuation of the opening question amplifies its allusions into a whole poetic landscape (11. 9-12). These multiple allusions evoke the idea of a poetic world to which the true poet owes a duty. In this ideal poetic landscape, evil "chattring pies" exist. Pies are stealing, raucous, vulgar birds; they are on a higher plane in the scale of creation than the moths of the first stanza, but more odious. Their senseless and artless "chattring" is set against the singing of nymphs as created by poets, and Jonson implies

17   *Oft* is an emendation supported by H & S, 8, 174.

that their noises may block genuine art. The second stanza, like
the first, moves from a passive picture of desolation to an animal
image denoting destruction.

This magic realm of poetry seems to exist eternally even if the
defacing ineptitude of current versers temporarily destroys its
beauty. However, as the "Fit of Rime Against Rime" (31) decries
rhyme while triumphing over its limitation, so these stanzas
raise the possibility of the death of poetry while actively disproving
the hypothesis. In contrast to the conversational and relaxed
first stanza, this second stanza is more obviously poetical with its
heavy alliteration, inversions, allusions, and periphrasis. The mood
is hesitant and questioning. Rhymes point the contrasts in the
stanzas; "wast", "disgrac't", "defac't" present the facts of poetry's
decay, and "springs", "strings", "sings" the possibilities of its
rejuvenation. The stanza makes clear the poet's personal duty
to this immortal tradition and the reciprocal compensation of
poetry's immortality for the mortal poet.

The third stanza returns to the focus on the speaker held in the
first stanza and corrects his judgment against himself outlined
there. Its terms are abstract, like those in stanza one. "If hence thy
silence be,/ As 'tis too just a cause;/ Let this thought quicken
thee". This vague "hence" implies that the entire desolate state of
poetry causes Jonson's silence, which can no longer be attributed
merely to slothful self-indulgence. The parenthetical remark "as
'tis too just a cause" explicitly contradicts the idea of sinful sloth,
though its indirect expression tempers the effect of self-praise.
After the display of official poeticizing in stanza two, the speaker
returns to a natural or conversational voice. The verb "quicken"
indicates the speaker's rejuvenation as he moves from silence to
poetry, from the death of buried knowledge to the active life of
the mind.

The rejuvenating thought is a sententious moral:

> Minds that are great and free,
> Should not on fortune pause,
> 'Tis crowne enough to vertue still, her owne applause.

The line-opening metrical stress on "minds" clearly indicates
the arousal of the sleeping knowledge of the first stanza and

focuses on mind as the essential prerequisite for living and genuine poetry. Through the use of two of his favorite adjectives, "great" and "free", Jonson again stresses that true greatness is a matter of mind, not of birth or title, and that freedom or independence and magnanimity are among the most important characteristics of mental greatness. The connection of the "free" mind and "free will" is close enough that the free mind's freedom from reliance on fortune seems almost tautologically obvious. Therefore the great mind can never be permanently thwarted by the vagaries of fortune, and any hindrance in its activities can only be a temporary "pause", not the burial darkly foreboded in stanza one. The optimism of this sentiment is dramatically appropriate for an exhortation to a languishing poet, while its generalized form avoids the arrogance of the poet directly declaring that his mind is "great and free".

There is no specified relation or subordination between the maxim concluding the stanza (1.18) and the idea immediately preceding it, but the implication of the parallelism between these two clauses is that the virtuous are likely to the synonymous with men of great and free minds. Throughout the poem intellectual power and moral virtue are equated, and both are treated as intimately correlated with poetic skill. The rich word "crowne" exalts this concept of virtue as its own reward, comparing it with kingship, the highest position in the secular social scale. Moreover, as righteousness earns the crown in heaven, so virtue earns the crown of its own applause, which is to be its sufficient reward – and the only possible one, considering the tastes of the audiences Jonson castigates. The high connotations of "crowne" and "vertue" neutralize the less attractive associations of "her own applause". but these associations are still attached to the applause of others, the noisy unimportant approbation of the vulgar. This residual possibility is later activated when the poet censures the contemporary stage and the tastes of its authors, critics, and audiences. Thus stanza three corrects stanza one and responds to the situation described in stanza two, while stanzas three and four together analyze the perilous state of poet and poetry portrayed in stanzas one and two.

Stanza four, like stanza two, turns to the state of poetry, which it discusses in more explicit and less poetic terms than those in the metaphorical stanza two. The subject of stanza four is false taste in poetry. Like stanzas one and two, stanza four begins with a question. The chattering pies of stanza two are replaced by even less dignified animals, the "greedie Frie", voracious as the moth of stanza one. The speaker's tone is contemptuous. It cannot matter, he tells himself, that such vulgar, immature, and tasteless audiences are attracted by false wares. The description of them utterly discounts the fry and their bait through metaphor, as in stanza two, without descending to specific or personal abuse. Though veiled, Jonson's criticism is not softened. The fry will "die with their conceits". The poet need not regard the despicable fry because they are beneath him, and, anyway, they will destroy themselves. Similarly, bad literature dies, in contrast to the human soul and true literature, which are immortal. Thus the kinds of death threatened throughout the poem can only be prevented by the true poet. Though the fry are so inferior as to merit scorn, the speaker implies that one almost pities their self-destructive and deluded folly.

The last two stanzas of the poem maintain the pattern established earlier. Like stanzas one and three, stanza five stresses the poet; like stanzas two and four, stanza six focuses on the world of poetry. Together stanzas five and six form the third and final section of the poem, and they answer all the questions and suppositions raised earlier with firm imperatives. Thus the fifth stanza begins with the poet's instruction to himself, "Then take in hand thy Lyre". Like stanza two, stanza five is phrased in the allusive and formal language of poetry. The poet tells himself to resume his role in the world of poetry, and simultaneously he demonstrably does so. "Then take in hand thy Lyre" is clear and emphatic. The poet should write lyric poetry, yet this action seems simple and physical like a habit resumed after a pause. "Strike in thy proper straine" parallels the first imperative and is even more emphatic with its initial accent on "strike" and binding alliteration. The word "strike" forcefully counters any too-soft connotations of Apollo's lyre. "Straine" has several pertinent meanings: offspring, individual tone or style, melody or passage of poetry, and strong effect. "Thy proper straine", like "thy lyre", implies that Jonson already has a style of his own, that he is a true and original poet who only needs to resume activity to write worthy poetry. This implication is a quiet one, and the rest of the stanza more humbly presents Jonson's solidarity with other poets and the help he receives from sources outside himself.

The third instruction to himself,

> With *Japhets* lyne, aspire
> *Sols* Chariot for new fire,
> To give the world again,

uses a handy double allusion. "*Japhets* lyne" refers to the descendants of the Biblical Japhet, who were supposed to make up the modern European nations, while the children of Iapetus in Greek mythology included Prometheus.[18] The context indicates that the classical reference is intended, but the Biblical form provides a Miltonic corroboration of the consonance of Biblical and classical lineage for the poet. The double reference strengthens the sanction of tradition and legitimacy. As one of Japhet's line, Jonson has changed his primary patron from Apollo to Prometheus, the fire-giver, and he thus portrays the poet as an active benefactor to mankind, not some delicate and irrelevant warbler. "Aspire/ *Sols* Chariot for new fire/ To give the world again" infuses the Jonsonian ideal of didactic poetry with neoplatonic notions of poetry reaching upward to the ideal, finding the highest truths to return to teach to men. These images of energy, courage, and rekindling show that the state of sloth and despair in which the poet reported himself in stanzas one and two is now utterly shaken off. The contrast throughout the poem between the life of the mind and immortal art and the death equated with stupidity and bad art is again tapped by the mention of "new fire" and new life. Jonson's allusions show the poetic tradition operating in action and in health, far above the earth-bound poetic wasteland of stanza two. The immortality of poetry is implicit in these allu-

---

[18] H & S, 11, 61, give only the meaning 'Prometheus' for "*Japhets* line". The *OED* gives only the reference to Noah's son under its listing for 'Japhet'.

sions. "Her own applause" may be "crowne" enough for virtue, but virtuous poetry will presumably win the additional and enduring applause of discerning men of posterity. The last line of stanza five, "Who aided him, will thee, the issue of *Joves* braine", says in terms of classical decorum that God helps those who help themselves. Jonson thus reconciles a humble knowledge of his own flaws and discouragement with the assertion of the permanence of his own integrity as man and poet.

The last stanza turns for the last time to the evil public and age, that is, to the world of practising poetry, but only to dismiss it as irrelevant to the Promethean poet. The stanza picks up from the preceding one as though without a break.

> And since our Daintie age
> Cannot indure reproofe.
> Make not thy self a Page
> To that strumpet the Stage
> But sing high and aloofe,
> Safe from the wolves black jaw, and the dull Asses hoof.

All the terms referring to the "age" and its rhyme word the "stage" are terms of reprehension, but the speaker does not descend to a personal vitriolic tone. His contempt remains superior and sure of itself. The age is dismissed with the euphemistic diminutive "Daintie". The contrast between the dainty contemporary fops and the heroic mythological references of stanza five is striking. As so often in Jonson, the modern is the paltry, vicious, and diminished, while the traditional retains the high values of lost ages.

Because of these flaws in the modern world, the poet tells himself to ignore it. "Make not thyselfe a Page/ To that strumpet the Stage". "Make" is emphatic, as though the poet would have to work hard and consciously to transform himself into a worthless namby-pamby like the current representatives of the "age". "That strumpet the Stage" is strong invective, belted out with heavy alliteration and inverted stress underlining the word "strumpet". The implication is that the only honest role for a playwright is to censure the age. If the age will not tolerate this censure, then there is no longer a place for the honest playwright, and the writer of plays who favors and flatters the age is not a real poet but a tool of the promiscuous immorality of the times.

The honest poet's only choice is to avoid the stage altogether and "sing high and aloofe", and the speaker does regain his dignity to sound "aloofe" from the age for which he feels such contempt. What the poet is staying high above is expressed in the following line, "Safe from the wolves black jaw, and the dull Asses hoofe".[19] The stressed opening word "safe" revises the meaning of "securitie" presented in the first stanza. The poet has rejected slothful security for a true safety, an isolation of the pure self from contaminating surroundings. The true poet must continue on his proper course, keeping his knowledge and skills safe from the internal "moth" of inactivity on the one hand, and, on the other, from the dangerous beasts representing the malice and stupidity of others. Like the "chattring pies" and "greedy frie" of earlier stanzas, the "wolves" and "asses" here are treated as allegorical types rather than as personal or particular butts. The "wolves ... jaw" with its connotations of eating, biting, and destroying is the last and most ominous of the animal-devouring references in the poem. Thus if the poet is contemptuous of the "Daintie age" in which he lives, he also realizes that it can be bestial and dangerous; this perilousness gives dignity to the poet wishing to remain safe from it and from the forces of mental destruction it represents.

As happens often in Jonson's later poems, a formal poetic style replete with allusions, inversions, and devices of sound is balanced in Jonson's first ode to himself against a more conversational style; the poem is unified by its tight structure, pervasive imagery and approach, and fulfillment of the stanzaic requirements of the ode. Only a few words like "greedie", "chattring", "strumpet", and "wolves" hint at the satirical, and these words are surrounded and balanced by the elegant, the abstract, and the sententious. The censures of others are masked in allusion and metaphor, and

---

[19]   Jonson used the same line in the "Apologeticall Dialogue" affixed to the early *Poetaster*. Comparing himself with Seneca, Jonson wrote in *Timber* that he "could, in my youth, have repeated all, that ever I had made; and so continued, till I was past fortie ... but what I trust to [memory] now, ... it layes up more negligently" (*Disc.* 479-507).

the praises of himself are veiled by indirection, supposition, and aspiration. As in many of the picture poems and amorous elegies, a flawed individual regains strength with knowledge of himself and of his proper poetic role. He moves from inaction to proper self-reliant action. The passions he overcomes in the love poems are chiefly desire, fear, and knowledge of his own faults and personal ugliness. In this poem he overcomes hostility against his times, resentment against his critics, and discouragement with his role and profession – that is, the pervasive temptation to withdraw.

Jonson's second ode to himself (Uc. 53), affixed to the unsuccessful play *The New Inn*, displays less internal consistency than the first. Its anger and disgust are less disguised. Jonson opens the poem with the imperative "Come leave the loathed Stage/ And the more loathsome Age", which sounds very much like the end of the earlier ode. The combination of the words "loathed" and "loathsome", in fact, demonstrates one of the tactical flaws of the poem: it is clear what Jonson personally loathes, but the poet does not altogether convince his reader that the objects of his loathing are objectively "loathsome" to anyone else. The characteristics of the loathsome age and stage center for him in its audiences and critics, whose judgment he immediately seeks to discredit by calling them names. The poet's focus in much of the poem is on the bad "taste" of the present age in terms of its plays and playwrights. The poet's chiding of himself in the first ode is gone in the second; all hostile emotions are directed openly against others.

The imagery of stanzas two to five of the second ode to himself is based on the pun on current bad "taste". In stanza two this is represented by coarse food; in stanza three, by garbage; in stanza four, by rags. The idea is repetitious, and the thought is static. The emotional effect is achieved almost entirely from the thickly-piled imagery and derogatory diction.

The mood of the poem shifts sharply in stanza five after its first line, "Leave things so prostitute", which repeats the poem's initial injunction, "Come leave the loathed Stage". The preceding four stanzas of the poem have gone to show that there is no place for an honest playwright. In that state of affairs to write for the polluted stage is to be degraded morally and esthetically. The poet's advice to himself now parallels that in the fifth stanza of the first ode to himself.

... take th' Alcaike Lute;
Or thine owne Horace, or Anacreons Lyre;
Warme thee by Pindars fire. ...

This list of preferences proves the plenitude of good models available to the practitioner of the honorable and true tradition of poetry, that is, the classic lyric tradition. The warmth and encouragement that the poetic tradition offers to the practising poet contrast with the poet's poor physical condition described in the next few lines: his "Nerves" are "shrunke", and his "blood" is "cold". The language here is simple, concrete, and movingly effective. Whereas Jonson at forty or fifty chose to describe himself as "old" in reference to love poetry, he finds the physical debility brought on by a stroke premature at fifty-seven and achieves poignancy with the earnest "ere years have made thee old".

Here he brings up his infirmities not as humble reminders of his limitations but as irrelevant obstacles to be overcome. As in other of his sick-bed poems, Jonson stirs himself from sick impotence and self-pity not so much with thoughts of high lyric poetry as with a desire for vengeance on his enemies. The note is harsh. In the first ode, Jonson found his vigor by reasserting his poetic integrity, telling himself to "Strike" only in his "proper Straine". Here he wishes instead to "strike" his enemies into defeat.

The last stanza of the *New Inn* ode shifts its focus to the poetic subjects worthy of his revived attention. Jonson reasserts his own dignity and saves the poem from simple spitefulness only through this last exaggerated note when he offers to sing "The glories of thy King;/ His zeale to God, and his just awe of men." Hearing Jonson's noble words about the king, his critics "may be blood-shaken, then/ Feele such a flesh-quake to possesse their powers". Jonson's writing here is strong and original, free from the usual clichés of his satire or censure. If their response is to be of the magnitude of an earthquake, the cause must be correspondingly great.

No author writing on a lesser subject "shall truely hit the Starres" as Jonson will, aiming at the traditional end of panegyric, apotheosis. In the final hyperbolic sweep of the last stanza of the ode, the poem is focused firmly on the glorification and triumph of its object the king, not on himself or his quarrels. Thus he does at last, and indirectly, exonerate the still potent abilities of his lyric pen. He does this through his older role of the moral and patriotic poet devoted to straightforward praise and blame rather than through his more mature role of the poet as explorer into the nature of human realities shown in his poems on valor, in the love poems, and on the poems on himself including the first ode. Both of Jonson's odes to himself have as their real subject the nature of his conception of the poet's role and his attempt to fulfill the requirements of that role despite flaws in himself and flaws in his critics, audiences, and society. In the *New Inn* ode, the interplay between the man and the poet tends to fade out, and the poet is either the satirist with a grudge or the flattering panegyrist. In contrast, Jonson's first ode to himself achieves its dignity and sense of detachment through its successful use of the double *persona*, himself as subject and also as speaker of the poem. In this poem, as in the best mature poems, the interrelations between the roles of man and poet are not obscured or simplified.

5. PLAYS, MASQUES, POEMS: FOUR PHASES

The preceding chapters have discussed the differences between Jonson's earlier and later books of verse as defined by the 1616 and 1640 folios. The chapters on *Epigrammes* and *The Forrest* show Jonson's uncomplicated moral stance in most of these poems to be based on a rhetoric of praise and blame. These chapters analyze his typical uses of meter, syntax, and diction, and his preference for rhetorical structures made of contrasted positive and negative patterns in these earlier nondramatic poems. The chapter on *Under-wood* stresses Jonson's handling of the themes of love, valor, and the poet and his more exploratory and flexible attitude to his material. These considerable changes still leave a distinctly unified impression of one man and one work. As we have seen, much in Jonson's nondramatic poetry remains fixed over his lifetime: his Christian humanism, his didactic bent, his ideal of an urbane society of the virtuous few and his contrasting view of the degenerate and greedy present age.

On the other hand, we have detailed considerable variation within each of the three collections. Some of these variations can be accounted for by a study of Jonson's chronological development more precise than the binary division into earlier and later works provided by the two folios. Although there are no sharp or decisive breaks in Jonson's writing style, the four-phase division suggested here allows us to approximate the changing contours of Jonson's work over time and to see analogies between the nondramatic poetry, the plays, and the masques written in the same periods. Our brief survey can perhaps highlight these similarities across *genres* without pretending to provide complete readings of Jonson's great plays and masques. The chronological chart (Table Ten, Appendix) lists datable plays, masques, and poems for the periods 1597-1603, 1603-12, 1613-25, and 1625-37.

I

Ben Jonson appears in dramatic history about 1597 as an actor and a playwright. By that time he had probably been educated at Westminster School under William Camden and served briefly as a bricklayer for his stepfather, then as a soldier in the low countries. In 1597 he was about twenty-five years old and married. He had at least three children, two of whom died by 1603. During a short prison term for killing an actor, he was converted to Roman Catholicism and remained in that faith from 1598 to about 1610.[1]

Jonson chose not to preserve his earliest Elizabethan plays, and only *The Case is Altered* remains of his Elizabethan 'popular' comedies.[2] The Elizabethan plays by which Jonson wanted to be remembered are the four satires or 'humor' plays, *Every Man in His Humor*, 1598; *Every Man Out of His Humor*, 1599; *Cynthia's Revels*, 1600; and *Poetaster*, 1601. In these plays, especially after *Every Man in His Humor*, the nondramatic verse satire of the 1590's finds a comparable embodiment on the stage. Characters in these plays tend to be flat. The plots, reacting against romantic Elizabethan conventions, are static. Various follies, which are sometimes seen as the characters' 'humors' are exposed and ridiculed in discrete episodes. In dramatizing verse satire, these plays also draw on a dramatic background of morality play,

---

[1] H & S use these periods in their introductory life of Jonson. All biographical data is from H & S, 1, 1-118; 11, 571-85, unless otherwise noted. Conjectures about Jonson's conversion are provided by Theodore Stroud, "Ben Jonson and Father Thomas Wright", *ELH*, 14 (1947), 274-82.

[2] 'Popular' here means of the conventional Elizabethan types. H & S, 1, 279ff., and most other critics, regard *A Tale of a Tub* as an early work revised at the end of Jonson's life. However, Joseph A. Bryant, Jr., "*A Tale of a Tub*, Jonson's Comedy of the Human Condition", *Renaissance Papers, 1963* (Published by the Southeastern Renaissance Conference, 1964), 95-105, questions this dating. H & S, 2, 235-45, also discuss references to lost plays by Jonson and dispute the attribution to him of additions to *The Spanish Tragedy*.

tableaux, and masque, and on different strains of classical Greek and Roman precedent.[3]

Fools in these Elizabethan plays include bad poets and neatly ranked representatives of the social classes of court, city, and country. These fools flaunt fancy clothes and borrowed poems as they try to aspire beyond their social and moral worth. The women inspire the uxorious or jealous folly of their husbands and demonstrate their own vanity. In contrast to most Elizabethan popular drama, including *The Case is Altered*, these plays avoid romantic love. The woman-swayed Ovid in *Poetaster*, though sympathetic, is seen as inferior to the high moral poets Horace and Virgil. After *Every Man in His Humor*, no Jonsonian hero marries a good woman until *Bartholomew Fair*. This abstinence is especially surprising in view of the pervasive Elizabethan convention of ending comedies with marriages or betrothals.

The good men of these early plays – Asper, Crites, and Horace – represent idealized figures acting out idealized roles, while the humorous characters usually exemplify folly and ignorance, deluded exaggerations and affectations contrary to reason. In *Cynthia's Revels*, 'self-love' must be turned into 'self-knowledge' for the humors to be cured. In *Cynthia's Revels* the opposition of true to false values evident in Jonson's early works is particularly clear when the vices are masqued as their most-closely-related virtues. This opposition between truth and falsehood often takes the form of an opposition between appearance and reality, and the use of costume or disguise in these early plays is fairly simple.

After *Every Man in His Humor*, the good characters grow less active and more idealized. They tend to stand aloof from the world of folly they observe and chastise. In *Every Man Out of His Humor* moral Asper is the 'public' aspect of the active satirist-

---

[3] Oscar J. Campbell, *Comicall Satyre and Shakespeare's "Troilus and Cressida"* (San Marino: Huntington Library, 1938), developed this thesis, which has been widely accepted. Gibbons, *City Comedy*, 19-24, discusses Jonson's use of earlier traditions. The moralities are described by David Bevington, *From "Mankind" to Marlowe: Growth of Structure in the Popular Drama of Tudor England* (Cambridge, Mass.: Harvard, 1962); the late morality tradition is applied to Jonson by Alan C. Dessen, *Jonson's Moral Comedy* (Evanston: Northwestern, 1971).

malcontent Macilente.[4] "Ile strip the ragged follies of the time,/ Naked, as at their birth" (*EMO* Induction, 17-18), Asper promises, as one "without feare controuling the worlds abuses" (*EMO* Characters, 2). Crites and Horace, idealized and victimized poet-judges, receive their authority and reward from Cynthia and Augustus, monarchs who represent an absolute standard of justice and good order.

Jonson chooses his details in these early plays, as in the poems, for their moral and illustrative value in consonance with literary decorum and with his concept of himself as the didactic poet. Presumably, the plays' exposures of ignorance and affectation suffice for the education of the audiences, and the instantaneous 'cures' of the humors are mere by-products of the comic play structure. The characters in the early plays are thus like the characters of the early epigrams and epistles, statically cast in their respective positive or negative roles.

The poet acts in these plays as satirist, teacher, judge, and lyric singer, and Horace is cast as an idealized Jonson in *Poetaster*. The question of the proper relationship between the poet and his society is a dominant theme of *Poetaster* and *Cynthia's Revels*. The contrast central to *Poetaster* is that between the true poet and the false poetaster who is esthetically and morally inferior. This contrast is not merely a defensive posture adopted for the 'War of the Theaters', for it recurs throughout Jonson's early epigrams and moral epistles. There the true poet is always right in seeing the follies of others and the bad quality of their verses, and for this he receives their 'envy'. Envy and slander are the main weapons hurled by the ignorant against their betters, though, fortunately, they are always ineffective. Horace knows himself and his power, "the strength of his owne *Muse*" (*Po.* prologue, 24), as the poetasters Crispinus and Demetrius and the hypocrite Tucca can not. The caricature of Jonson in Dekker's *Satiromastix* is judged by Jonson's own standards, though Dekker reverses Jonson's evalua-

---

[4]   Kernan, *Cankered Muse*, 138. Jonson's role in the early plays is also discussed by Jones, "Satirist's Retirement"; Kay, "Shaping"; and James Savage, "Ben Jonson in Ben Jonson's Plays", *U. of Mississippi Studies in English, 3* (1962), 1-17.

tion to show "Horace" as an arrogant social upstart who does not live up to his high moral claims.[5]

Jonson is not quite sure of his relation to his audiences in these early works. He seems initially to have harbored illusions about their taste for his kind of learned experimental drama. And if the public theater did not have exactly the right kind of patrons, at first he thought that the children's companies or the court would. The induction to *Every Man Out of His Humor* and the prologue to *Cynthia's Revels* show Jonson taking his "judicious friends" (*EMO*. Induction, 56) into his confidence about his new kind of plays. However, Jonson's prospective faith in his dramatic audiences was quickly and fairly permanently dampened. By the "Apologeticall Dialogue" after *Poetaster*, the "author" withdraws. He refuses to continue comically depicting the follies of a contemporary world that was unable to understand his poetic justice. His own idealized Rome in *Poetaster* mirrored the just understanding of true poetry, and Jonson was to set his next dramatic effort, *Sejanus*, in a learned and literary Rome which provided no straightforward allusions to contemporary English reality.

Jonson wrote no masques in the Elizabethan period, though *Cynthia's Revels* contains a masque and *Poetaster*, the disguising of the love poets as Olympians. Jonson's first few Jacobean masques and entertainments show some resemblances to the Elizabethan poems and plays.

Jonson's earliest datable poems, like his plays, show him moving from conventional Elizabethan to more classical and idiosyncratic forms. Like the early plays, these poems show a confident and simplistic morality that hides some inconsistencies, particularly in its view of the poet's role. The Elizabethan poems include "On My First Daughter" (xxii), "Epitaph on S. P." (cxx), "On Margaret Ratcliffe" (xl), "To True Souldiers" (cviii), the prelude (X) and "Epode" (XI), the epistle to Elizabeth, Countess of Rutland (XII),

---

[5] Dekker, *Satiromastix*, V.ii.

the ode to James, earl of Desmond (27), and uncollected poems
1-13, including the songs from the Elizabethan plays. In the same
style are the "Ode. Allegorike" and "Panegyre" of 1603 (Uc. 14, 15).

These poems include a few classical epigrams and epistles, and
most are resolvable into poems of praise or blame, yet several of
these earliest poems are neither in the plain style *genres* nor based
closely on classical models. *Satiromastix* shows Jonson bragging
about his epigrams, acrostichs, and odes.[6] Epigram xl is an acros-
tich, a form Jonson later ridiculed in "An Execration upon Vulcan"
(45). One of the odes is written in a jogging trimeter with humorous
feminine rhyme (Uc. 10), and several other of these Elizabethan
poems are not in the usual decasyllabic couplets of Jonson's
earlier Jacobean period. Unlike his Jacobean poems, these earlier
poems abound in fulsome adjectives, personification allegory, and
extended conceits. The songs from the plays like "*Queene* and
Huntresse" (Uc. 7) and "Slow, slow fresh fount" (Uc. 4) are the
most successful of these early efforts. In them Jonson exercises
on the accomplished tradition of the Elizabethan lyric his gifts
for selective diction which he later applied more variously.

Several of the early poems touch on Renaissance neoplatonism;
in the "Epode", the discussion of love rapidly becomes a discussion of rational virtue sharply contrasted to pervasive vice. Moreover, as in the epistle to Elizabeth, Countess of Rutland, praise
and blame take up different subjects, violating the unity of the
poem. A discordant note is created in that poem by the sharp
contrast between the Sidneyan ideal of poetry that Jonson invokes,
of "high, and noble matter" springing from "braines entranc'd"
and the actual accomplishments of the verse. For much of the
poem, as at times in the early plays, Jonson seems angry or pom-
pous rather than "rapt with rage divine" (XII).

Jonson's ode to James, Earl of Desmond, in 1600 (27) is typical
of the problems of these earliest poems. Florid and self-conscious
in its imitation of the high pindaric style, the poem is made up of
five elaborate stanzas of thirteen lines each. Jonson urges his
"Invention" to "put on the wings of *Pindars* Muse", and he un-

---

[6] Dekker, *Satiromastix*, I.ii.

convincingly identifies himself as Apollo's "Priest in this strange rapture". The meter is occasionally halting, and the frequent feminine rhyme is used weakly. The overblown invocation is out of proportion to the rest of the poem. Images and allusions like that to "*Brontes*, and black *Steropes*", are grandiose and not immediately relevant, while the poet shows euphuistic confidence in the moral effectiveness of cliché. The poem is uneasily eclectic. A Donnean image, the "Anatomie/ In Surgeons hall" does not contribute functionally to the poem, and loosely used Spenserian diction results in the archaic allegory of "darknesse with her glomie-Sceptred hand". The poem is unlike Jonson's better early verse and mature verse in its large number of padding adjectives. (See Table Eleven, Appendix.)

In short, the ode to Desmond is affected and inarticulate. In addition, its attitude is not consistent. Although the ode is supposed to be commendatory and encouraging, it is overloaded with negative statements.[7] Jonson's technique of balancing positive and negative statements is not handled effectively in this poem: the last stanza ends on a negative note as the poet turns from defending Desmond's innocence to warning him against revolting.

Jonson in the Elizabethan period moves through experiments in the poems and plays toward his own idiosyncratic style. He proudly announces this sense of pioneering in the epistle to the Countess of Rutland, "my strange *poems* ... as yet/ Had not their forme touch'd by an English wit" (XII). In these early poems and plays, he promulgates an exaggerated view of the poet's role as prophet, critic, and leader of society; he regards opposition to this view of the poet's role as truculent envy. Neither his earlier plays nor his earlier poems can always integrate their polarized depictions of reason and of folly. Many of these problems of Jonson's Elizabethan works are absent in the more concentrated and effective productions of his early Jacobean years.

---

[7] There are not quite twice as many positive adjectives as negative in the poem. There are 18 positive, 10 negative, and 4 neutral descriptive adjectives.

II

James' accession brought increased prosperity, success, and influence to Jonson. He was regularly and profitably employed as a writer of court masques for James and Anne, and he wrote his most popular plays in the first half of James' reign. He developed a wide network of patrons and friends, and he apparently lived, not with his wife, but with one patron, Esmé, Lord Aubigny, from about 1602 to 1607. Jonson's troubles with authorities over his plays, starting in 1597, concluded early in James' reign. Jonson was in prison briefly in 1605 for trouble with the Scottish allusions of *Eastward Ho*, his most successful collaborative effort, but he was employed by the government in connection with the Gunpowder Plot shortly thereafter. He rejoined the Anglican communion, enthusiastically, he reported, around 1610. Jonson made his first translation of Horace's "Art of Poetry" around 1605 and completed most of the first folio of his *Workes* before going to France as a tutor for Lord Raleigh's son in 1612-13.

In this early Jacobean period Jonson perfected his most successful and individual technique of integrating his work. He learned to narrow the range of a poem, masque, or play so that most of the contrasts within it occur on a narrow spectrum of the moral scale. This kind of deliberate limitation achieves intensity of effect in Jonson's early Jacobean plays and poems and avoids many of the structural problems of his Elizabethan works.

The plays of 1603-12 include the two Roman tragedies, *Sejanus*, 1603, and *Catiline*, 1611, and three great comedies, *Volpone*, 1606; *Epicene*, 1609; and *The Alchemist*, 1610. Jonson's devotion to classical models in this period is most obvious in the settings and sources for the tragedies, and *Volpone* uses a situation drawn from Roman satire with characters from the beast fable. Jonson's early Jacobean comedies are less closely connected with the *genre* of formal verse satire than were the earlier comedies.

All five of these early Jacobean plays present a world of evil in which the good man has little effect. At best he preserves his own integrity. The darkest of these worlds are Tiberius' Rome and the corrupt Venice of Volpone. In contrast to the Elizabethan plays, the fools are less important in these early Jacobean plays than the knaves, and most of the fools, including the women, are knaves whenever they can be. The class ordering of folly is less prominent than in the earlier dramas. There is no love in these plays, though lust, false friendship, and vanity abound. The misogyny in these plays is even more pronounced than earlier. There are no good women at all in *Epicene*, *The Alchemist*, and *Catiline*; Celia, like many of the aristocratic women commended in the epigrams, seems more divine than human. The worlds of these plays center on ambition, greed, perversion – on vice and crime rather than on folly. The tone of satire is bitter and 'Juvenalian', focused on the object.[8] All the main characters of *Volpone* are motivated, at least in part, by greed. Contrasts are maintained between pridefully overreaching knaves, more simply greedy dupes, and the pallidly virtuous few, but the unifying tone is set by the consistency of the inverted world whose idol is gold.[9] Contributing to this uniformity of satiric effect, the knaves, not the heroes, appear to be in control of these worlds, and, except for Cicero, in control of language. Volpone and Face are master wordsmiths, whereas the gentlemen about town who represent everyday values tend to be much more prosaic in their speech. Truewit at his cleverest assumes the deceptive rattle of the knave.

The good characters like Bonario and Celia are passive or immobilized. Cicero is active and virtuous, but his triumph is ironically undercut by the approaching fall of the Roman republic.[10] The gallants Peregrine, Dauphine, and Lovewit are not much in the dramatic spotlight. The good characters usually work out their plots independently, alone, whereas the knaves form coalitions and combinations. Like the ideal characters of Jonson's Elizabethan plays, the knaves in these early Jacobean plays are ranked. Tiberius is more subtle in evil than Sejanus, as Mosca is than

8   Ronald Paulson, *The Fictions of Satire* (Baltimore: Johns Hopkins, 1967), 21-30, sets up some polarities of the old Horatian/Juvenalian contrast.
9   Partridge, *Broken Compass*, 63, speaks of the worship of gold as the center of *Volpone*.
10   Bryant, "*Catiline* and the Nature of Jonson's Tragic Fable", *PMLA*, 69 (1954), 265-77, reprinted in Barish, *Essays*, 147-59.

Volpone, or Face than Subtle, or Caesar than Catiline. Despite these "venters", conspiracies, and coalitions among the knaves, there is almost no real communication among the characters. Instead, as Barish points out, the language in these plays serves chiefly to expose the vice and folly of these characters, to the point of the "transfigured babble" of Doll's ravings, the alchemists' jargon, or the arguments of *Epicene*.[11]

In these five plays, the characters are much more seriously deluded in their view of the good than in the earlier plays. These vicious delusions are the essence of their characters; there is no finer self for self-knowledge to uncover in Corvino or Morose. Both knaves and fools try to dissimulate through cosmetics, costume, and disguise, and the most successful knaves are the ones who exploit disguises best. Disguises in these plays often symbolize the reality beneath them: Volpone really is sick morally as he pretends to be physically, and the confusion between Doll Common and Dame Pliant, whore and lady, underlines their similarity. The derogatory imagery of the satiric epigrams and epistles often has the same function. Images of animals, disease, and clothing show the objects described by them as bestial, sick and false.

The theme of metamorphosis throughout these plays highlights the prideful presumption of the characters and their inability to change. Sejanus slights the gods and thinks himself their equal; Mosca and Volpone try to transcend human limits and show men as beasts. Several critics see alchemy, the desire to transmute base metal, violating nature by will, as the binding symbol of *The Alchemist*.[12] These characters try to transcend themselves, overreach themselves, and inevitably fail. The knaves are judged in *Sejanus*, *Volpone*, and *Catiline*; but in all five plays the characters ultimately remain as they were, their punishment to remain themselves. The plays move to the revelation of the nature of the evil will.[13]

[11]   Barish, *Language*, 274.
[12]   Partridge, *Broken Compass*, 159; Kernan, *Plot of Satire*, 121ff.
[13]   Gabriele Bernhard Jackson, *Vision and Judgment in Ben Jonson's Drama* (*Yale Studies in English*, 166) (New Haven: Yale, 1968), 1, sees Jonson's work as "drama of revelation".

Many aspects of these five plays, then, give what L. A. Beaurline calls the "illusion of completeness", the sense of a world enclosed in itself, paralleling reality.[14] The sense of completeness in each play comes in part from the multiplication of incidents on one theme which increase in tempo until their plots collapse and the overreachers are brought low. In the first four of these plays, the earlier idealized poet figure disappears to be replaced by evil verbal manipulators like Volpone and the Alchemists. In the Roman tragedies, the sense of completeness is attained partly through Jonson's scholarly historicity. The sense of enclosure in these early Jacobean plays helps them remain funny, sinister as are their themes. The audience may keep its distance and watch evil caricatured into absurdity. The vices portrayed in Jonson's comedies of this period are the Elizabethan follies carried a step further. The earlier jealous merchant becomes Corvino, willing to prostitute his own wife; the "proud mincing Peat" (*EMO.* characters, 58) becomes an androgynous talking machine; the authoritarian old man becomes the mad Morose; the ambitious courtier becomes the universally-grasping Mammon. In *Volpone*, Peregrine and Sir Politic remind their audiences that English follies are at least less depraved than their Venetian exaggerations.

The prologues for all five plays emphasize the separation of audience and author from the world of the plays. None has an induction with the illusion of spontaneity or joke-like personal allusions to the author. Instead, Jonson seeks to establish an ideal relationship with his most select audience. Four of the five plays of this period are dedicated to upper class patrons, the persons praised in the commendatory epigrams, and Jonson sent presentation copies of the quartos of these plays to his patrons and friends.[15]

Jonson's revisions of *Every Man in His Humor* for the 1616

---

[14] Beaurline, "Ben Jonson and the Illusion of Completeness", *PMLA*, 84 (1969), 51-59. Madeleine Doran, *Endeavors of Art: A Study of Form in Eliza-bethan Drama* (Madison: U. of Wisconsin, 1954), 20, speaks of the "exclusion and repetition" through which Jonson solved the problem of dramatic unity.
[15] H & S, 8, 665, give two inscriptions for quartos of *Sejanus* and one for *Volpone*. They also print two inscriptions for *Cynthia's Revels* and one for the 1616 folio.

folio shape the play to fit his early Jacobean artistic views, though the comedy retains its sunny Elizabethan tone. Besides heightening the local color and changing the names in the play, Jonson tightened it structurally. He omitted Lorenzo Senior's defense of poetry – a reminder of Jonson's Elizabethan preoccupations – and he clarified the moral importance of the virtuous exemplar, a key theme of the epigrams and masques of the early Jacobean period (*EMI*. 1616. I.ii.134, II.v.13, 66).

Another set of dramatic worlds, more obviously artificial than those of the plays, is created in Jonson's Jacobean court masques. The masques reflect to the court what it ought to be as a center of virtue and authority. They invite the courtiers' participation in their ideal roles and ideal selves. Orgel sees the development of the Jonsonian masque as an "organic movement" that grows from the artistic conceptions of Jonson and his collaborator, Inigo Jones, independent of the demands of popular taste.[16] None the less, changes in the masques correspond with many of the developments in the poems and plays.

Jonson's first few masques, *The Masque of Blackness* (1605), *Hymenaei* (1606), *The Haddington Masque* (1608), and *The Masque of Beauty* (1608), echo some aspects of his Elizabethan plays and poems. The earliest masques provide the text for a visual emblem or symbol, like the microcosm used in *Hymenaei* and in *The Haddington Masque*. These early masques stress the neoplatonic themes of love and beauty, as some of Jonson's earliest poems do. Despite these reminders of his Elizabethan work, all Jonson's masques of 1605-12 share many features with his early Jacobean poems and plays. They highlight the epigram-ideal themes of fame, truth, and beauty, usually as allegorical personifications. For *Oberon* (1611) Jones devised sliding flats for the scenes, "generalized facades", appropriate to the moral and allegorical character of these masques.

The sharp contrasts between true and false values in Jonson's early Jacobean poems clearly reappear in these masques, where

Orgel, *Complete Masques*, 20, 22, 28-29.

false values dance chaotic antimasques until they are banished by ideals like reason (*Hymenaei*) or fame (*Queens*). In Jonson's more integrated masques, these antimasques are thematically related to the main masques, creating complete imaginary worlds as in the best plays and poems of this period. Not only are the ideals that Jonson praises in the epigrams the same as those he symbolizes in the masques, but also the persons praised in the epigrams often are the court masquers.[17]

Jonson's early Jacobean poems presumably include the bulk of *Epigrammes* and *The Forrest*. Poems of this period include "On My First Sonne" (xlv), dedicatory poems (cx, cxi, cxxx, cxxxi, cxxxii), poems to James (iv, xxxv, xxxvi, li), and to Jacobean dignitaries (xliii, lx, lxiii, lxiv), to the Sidneys (II, XIV), Wroth (III), and Lady Aubigny (XIII), "The New Crie" (xcii), "On the New Motion" (xcvii), "On the Famous Voyage" (cxxxiii) and uncollected poems 14-29, including the songs from *Volpone* and *Epicene*.

In this period Jonson writes most consistently in the *genres* of the Latin plain style, chiefly epigram and epistle, and chiefly in iambic pentameter couplets. He continues to write songs, but "Why I Write Not of Love" (I) is the only other love poem. He invites comparison with the classics during this period through imitation and allusion, as in the epigram "To the Ghost of Martial" (xxxvi). Despite this pervasive classicism, many of his poems rest in a context of Christianity, and, as in *Volpone* and the Roman tragedies, correct values in the satiric epigrams and epistles are often indicated by religious references or images. We do not know what religious questions and moods were connected with Jonson's earlier conversion to Roman Catholicism or his reconversion in this period; perhaps "To Heaven" (XV) reflects a struggle toward religious assurance.[18]

---

[17] Orgel, *Complete Masques*, 18, 33. Studies of allegory in the masques include D. J. Gordon, "*Hymenaei*: Ben Jonson's Masque of Union", *Journal of the Warburg and Courtauld Institutes*, 8 (1945), 107-45; and Earnest W. Talbert, "The Interpretation of Jonson's Courtly Spectacles", *PMLA*, 61 (1946), 454-73.

[18] H & S, 1, 220-22, print the "Citations of Jonson and his wife for recusancy, 1606".

The principal features of Jonson's plain style in the early Jacobean poems are artistically simplified diction; short, easily understandable images; a flexible use of caesura and enjambment in simple metrical forms; and pervasive didacticism. Details of diction, syntax, and rhetoric in these poems follow the pattern of positive values set against negative ones, true against false, indicated by the division of the poems into categories of praise and blame.

As in the plays and masques of the period, the best poems give the "illusion of completeness" through the rigorous selection of details. Praise or blame is captured within a range of close choices; the result is evenness of tone plus intensity of emotional effect. Thus "To Celia" (IX) restricts its range to various complimentary attitudes toward a beloved mistress from appreciation to adoration. On "Inviting a Friend to Supper" (ci) maintains a balance by restricting itself to civilized possibilities of action among urbane equals, and the evils of harsh or pretentious landlords are barely alluded to in the harmonious world of "To Penshurst" (II).

In a very few poems like Jonson's epitaph on his first son (xlv) and "To Heaven" (XV), the carefully controlled and unified poem is expanded by religious and personal emotions bigger than the formal context of the poem allows, and this results in a deepening of the mode. The poem then becomes the instrument for the expression of the conflict between restraint, exemplified by the tightly-structured form, and the overwhelming emotion trying to break through that control.

The primary themes of the works of this period are reasonable virtue, which the poet praises, and irrational vice, which he exposes. The highest affections are the calm love and friendship described in the poems and masques, whereas runaway passions like pride, greed, and lust form the subjects for antimasque and satire in poems and plays. As in the masques of the period, the celebration of virtue in the poems and plays is expressed in general moral terms; vice and folly receive more vivid, more specific treatment. The speakers of the poems are a moral poet like the author of the plays or dramatic characters like Volpone or Lovewit. Neoplatonic love and Platonic conceptions of the author are not stressed in the poems of this period, and women appear chiefly as divinized patrons or as sluts.

Good men are few, ideal, and consistent in the poems of praise of the period. The poet is a good man. As Jonson says in the famous dedication to *Volpone*, wise men "will easily conclude to themselves, the impossibility of any mans being the good Poet, without first being a good man" (11. 21-23). Evil men have various vices, but they, too, are consistent, and the pattern of their follies is easy to discern. It is the poet's duty to find out these follies and hold them up to the ridicule of his audience, who will then be educated to know and so to avoid the same faults, even though the good tend to remain good and the evil are unreclaimable.

The vitality of vice in these works is not intended to lure unwary admiration. Jonson's overt moral intentions are obtrusively clear in these early Jacobean poems and plays. Those who believe Jonson 'really' admired Volpone and the alchemists are, I think, confusing the pleasures of successful representation with an identification with the objects represented.[19] Intelligence and energy are always admirable in Jonson's world, but not when subservient to immoral appetite. Moreover, those who stress the esthetic pleasures of ambiguity often underrate the pleasures of self-righteousness. Jonson's audiences, like modern thriller fans, enjoyed both the titillations of knavery and the satisfactions of feeling themselves firmly on the side of justice and virtue.

As Jonson in this period consistently shows a corrupt world of vice against which the few virtuous stand firm and alone, so a major theme of the Forrest poems is that of withdrawal from a corrupt world and even longing for death. At the same time, the poet withdraws personal references of himself from the corrupt

---

[19] Una Ellis-Fermor, *The Jacobean Drama: An Interpretation* (London: Methuen, 1965, c. 1936), 114, admires Volpone and thinks Jonson did; Empson, "*The Alchemist*", *The Hudson Review*, 22 (1969-70), 595-608, thinks Jonson and his audiences are "half-sympathetic" to the tricksters and that Jonson disliked both Puritans and Cavaliers from a "working class point of view". Judd Arnold, "Lovewit's Triumph and Jonsonian Morality: A Reading of *The Alchemist*", *Criticism*, 11 (1969), 163-66, sees Lovewit as representing Jonson's tolerant, non-censorious satirical attitude.

worlds of his plays during this period. Only in *Epicene* is there
a fleeting mention of "*Jonson* with tother youth" (*SW*.II.ii.118).

Jonson's work of the first two periods in all categories can thus
be seen as the conscious product of 'right reason', of intellectual
judgment guiding esthetic creation to moral ends. Jonson repeatedly says that art's chief enemy is "ignorance";[20] reason and knowledge can guide the good man in all his doings. In the epigram to
Sir Henry Goodyere (lxxxvi), for instance, Jonson states that his
knowledge of Goodyere's moral qualities led to his loving him.

The poet is consistently the moral teacher, not the inspired seer,
in the early Jacobean works. Jonson's satire is still 'Juvenalian';
he places himself outside the world of vice and folly he feels com-
pelled to expose. If this world is corrupt, it is also ridiculous.
Whatever latent attraction Jonson may be supposed to feel for the
spontaneity of the passionate will, the outrageousness of Jonson's
characters keep poet and audience distanced from the comedies
and satiric poems. The virtuous, including the poet, have no moral
flaws, though they are willing to admit that others may be their
social or intellectual superiors. The apparent exception to this
faultlessness of the poet proves the rule. In epigram lxv Jonson
states that he had previously praised an unworthy subject. Instead
of accepting the fact that he has committed a fault against his own
standards, at this stage in his life he rationalizes it away through
the theory of the hortatory benefits of praise. That is, Jonson
reasserts his idea of the didactic function of poetry and the un-
blemished character of the public poet while suppressing the
ambiguities involved in praise or blame that spring from the
mixed moral nature of real men.

When Jonson shifts between praise and blame in the poems of
this period, the integrity of his work sometimes suffers, and, as in
the plays, satiric vigor may overwhelm the conventional descriptions of virtue. However, the bad poems of this period do not suffer
from the floridity of some of the Elizabethan works; quite the

---

[20] Asper says "*Arte* hath an enemy cal'd *Ignorance*" (*EMO*, Induction, 219),
and Jonson writes in *Timber*, "I know no disease of the *Soule*, but *Ignorance*:
not of the Arts, and Sciences, but of it selfe" (*Disc.* 801-802).

reverse. In decorously fitting his own verses (Uc. 27, 28, 29) to
Coryate's Crudities, 1611, Jonson's own style is crude to the
point of slapdash, though "On the Famous Voyage" (cxxxiii)
keeps sewer decorum artistic through mock epic and burlesque
devices. When Jonson tries the plain style in an uncongenial
form, the pindaric ode for William Sidney's birthday (XIV),
the result is arid. The spareness of the writing is not indicated by
the elaborate ten-line stanza form, though it uses rather short lines.
Though the poem starts conventionally with notice of the festivity
that inspires it, Jonson rapidly gets down to his didactic intention.
Classical references are restricted to one mention of the "Thespian
well". There are no complex images or abstruse references. There
are very few adjectives, and positive adjectives outnumber negative
ones by three to one.[21] (See Table Eleven, Appendix.) Normal
speech order is preserved. Diction and rhymes are of stunningly
prosaic simplicity:

> I may tell to *Sydney*, what
> This day
> Doth say,
> And he may thinke on that
> Which I doe tell. ...

The Sidney ode is neither incoherent nor flawed like the earlier
ode to Desmond, but its elaborate stanzaic form seems incon-
gruous with its bald statements, and its persistent didacticism is
not made moving by graces of imagery, example, or figure.

Thus both Jonson's successes and his failures in the early
Jacobean period show concentration and limitation in satire and
eulogy. The earlier problem of the poet's role is resolved through
the firm adoption of the *persona* of the didactic public poet who
remains impersonally behind his plays and masques.

III

The latter half of James' reign saw Jonson increasing in stature
and in girth. He wrote seventeen masques in this period and two

---

[21]   There are 9 positive, 3 negative, no neutral descriptive adjectives in the
poem.

plays. As his appetite and tavern exploits grew, so did his literary influence, and he acquired poetic 'sons' while retaining patrons and friends. He was awarded the honorary degree of Master of Arts, and apparently his scholarly labors increased as well, though many manuscripts and translations were destroyed by fire in 1623. The major external event of his life in this decade was his walking trip to Scotland, 1618-19, and Drummond's *Conversations* present Jonson as storyteller, conversationalist, and oral critic during this period.

The two plays of Jonson's later Jacobean period are *Bartholomew Fair*, 1614, and *The Devil is an Ass*, 1616. Some critics regard *Bartholomew Fair* as a sport in the Jonsonian canon, a unique relaxation of Jonson's stern censure into life-loving acceptance of the world's folly.[22] Although this contrast is overdrawn, it does indicate the direction of some of the changes in Jonson's plays, masques, and poetry in the later Jacobean period.

Instead of claiming to create new forms, the plays of Jonson's later two periods look back to Elizabethan society and drama, which they examine ironically in the light of a new society. The "Stage-keeper" who opens *Bartholomew Fair* preferred "Master Tarletons time" (*BF*. induction, 37), and *The Devil is an Ass* contrasts the simpler esthetics and morals of the old morality play with the new comedy of manners reflecting a more sophisticated, but not better society. Although, as Jackson comments, there are no wholly idealized characters in Jonson's plays after Cicero,[23]

---

[22] Greene, *Centered Self*, 325; and Jackson, *Vision and Judgment*, 164. Freda L. Townsend, *Apologie for Bartholomew Fayre: The Art of Jonson's Comedies* (New York: Modern Language Association, 1947), stresses the *Bartholomew Fair* aspects of all of Jonson's work. Richard Levin, "The Structure of *Bartholomew Fair*", *PMLA*, 80 (1965), 175, sees Jonson's and our attitude to the fair as one of tolerant amusement. Dessen, *Moral Comedy*, 202-204; and Jackson I. Cope, "*Bartholomew Fair* as Blasphemy", *Renaissance Drama*, 8 (1965), 127-52, read *Bartholomew Fair* as Jonson's condemnation of society's folly. Joel H. Kaplan, "Dramatic and Moral Energy in Ben Jonson's *Bartholomew Fair*", *Renaissance Drama*, n.s. 3 (1970), 145, 156, thinks Jonson balances the vitality and the corruption of the fair, "baiting the moralists in us all".

[23] Jackson, *Vision and Judgment*, 164.

the worlds presented by these later plays are not therefore grimmer or more pessimistic than earlier. Jonson's earlier pattern of one good man set against an evil world is replaced by one of decent, active men, often paired, who are able to live and work within a foolish world. They try less hard than their predecessors to control the world they live in, but they often succeed in turning its follies to their advantage. Manly, Wittipol, and Mrs. Fitzdottrell form a kind of "venter tripartite" that works in trust and harmony for a good end, unlike their opponents or the earlier alchemists. Although there is still considerable vitality in the knaves and fools of the Fair and of Meercraft's projections, the focus of interest in these plays shifts away from the knaves' machinations toward the varying responses of the fools and the straight characters.

In *Bartholomew Fair*, the question of how one can know the good man or the good deed is more problematic than in the earlier plays.[24] By *The Devil is an Ass*, a major change has taken place in Jonson's presentation of moral absolutes. Not a villain like Volpone but one of the heroes attempts seduction; even more surprisingly, he is willing to stop and change. Others of the play's virtuous characters are more flexible than earlier, too. In stark contrast to "Author" who believed "good men have a zeale to heare sinne sham'd" (*Po.*, Apol. Dial., 59), Manly says, "It is not manly to take joy, or pride/ In humane errours (wee doe all ill things. ... " (*DA*.V.viii. 169-70). The later Jacobean plays and poems probe beneath the surface of accepted values to explore the nature of integrity of character and the right use of one's talents, mind, and passions. The relationships between value and its reward and between good and evil are more subtle than in the earlier plays. Good men in these plays can use disguise and dissimulation for good purposes, while the evil deceive and disguise less effectively. Moreover, the good characters speak well and persuasively.

A few women in these plays are more reasonable than any of

---

[24] Ray L. Heffner, Jr., "Unifying Symbols in the Comedy of Ben Jonson", in *English Stage Comedy*, ed. by W. K. Wimsatt, Jr. (English Institute Essays) (New York: Columbia, 1954), 74-97; reprinted in Barish, *Essays*, 133-46, believes that the central issue of *Bartholomew Fair* is the problem of authority.

Jonson's previous women and more active than the idealized Celia. Grace exerts herself to escape a foolish marriage, and Mrs. Fitzdottrell's virtue and intelligence help her to escape both her husband's folly and a cavalier seduction. Jonson's presentation of women in this period is less stereotyped than earlier. Manly is surprised at the venality of the projecting ladies, yet more surprised at the virtue of Mrs. Fitzdottrell. Ursula is Jonson's most distinctive female knave, and *Bartholomew Fair* sports a full and differentiated gallery of other women knaves and fools.

In the earlier Jacobean plays, men tried to be gods and showed that they were beasts. In *Bartholomew Fair*, men are more comically seen as madmen, fools, and puppets. In *The Devil is an Ass*, devils burlesque men and men play women – but where Volpone's disguise demonstrates his real sickness, Wittipol's exposes some women's folly rather than his own. Moreover, the characters in these plays can learn from others. So Judge Overdo learns that he is part Adam. Wittipol learns virtue from Mrs. Fitzdottrell and Manly, and in turn he cures Manly by exposing Lady Tailbush. Besides portraying character more flexibly, these later Jacobean plays survey a wider horizon than the three earlier Jacobean comedies. In them there is less concern than earlier with a 'vertical' analysis of a single vice or humor. Instead, society is seen as a Fair or a worse hell. The impression is one of plenitude rather than of concentration.

In Jonson's five last plays, the recurrence of the metaphor of the world as a fair or theater stresses the fact that we are all playing roles. The distinction between playworld and real world is similarly blurred by foolish Fitzdottrell's desire to see a new play, *The Devil is an Ass*. In the induction to *Bartholomew Fair*, Jonson returns to the illusion of spontaneity and the joking personal references to the author last used in *Cynthia's Revels*. The author has opened the enclosed playworld out to the audience.

In the period between 1613-25, Jonson wrote seventeen masques. Like the plays, they reexamine older forms and refer to older authors like Chaucer, Spenser (*The Golden Age Restored*) and Skelton (*The Fortunate Isles*). These later masques are much more various than the principally allegorical earlier Jacobean masques. The later masques include some personification allegory, especially in the main masque (*The Golden Age Restored*), dialect comedy (*The Irish Masque, For the Honor of Wales*), pastoral (*Pan's Anniversary*), city comedy (*Mercury Vindicated from the Alchemists, News from the New World*), and comic revels (*Christmas*).

In these later Jacobean masques, ideal and anti-ideal characters are less firmly opposed than they were earlier. In *A Challenge at Tilt* (1613-14), the two sides are complements to a whole truth, not opposites as in the earlier debate between truth and opinion of 1606 (*Hymenaei*: Barriers). Moreover, the epigrammatic themes of fame and virtue tend to be stressed less frequently in the masques of 1613 to 1625 than earlier. Nature, time, reality, art, and poetry are more frequent themes. As allegory diminishes, the antimasques become more comic and realistic, longer and more obviously the focus of attention. The witches of *The Masque of Queens* of 1609 are personified as aspects of slander, but the gypsies of *The Gypsies Metamorphosed* (1621) are just gypsies. Related to the *Bartholomew Fair* atmosphere in this period is the emphasis on food and revels in the masques of *Christmas, The Vision of Delight, Pleasure Reconciled to Virtue*, and *Neptune's Triumph*.

The relationship of antimasque to masque is also considerably more varied in this later Jacobean period than earlier. As in the plays and poems in which characters are capable of change, several of the antimasque characters of this period are metamorphosed into the ideal rather than being banished by it (*Irish M., Lovers Made Men, Gypsies*). In other masques, the ideal is arrived at by stages, as false fancies yield to true vision in *The Vision of Delight*.[25] The folly of the shepherds delights the main masquers in *Pan's Anniversary*, and the antimasquers talk with the main masquers in *Pleasure Reconciled to Virtue*. Between 1618 and 1625 there are five comic antimasques presented as spontaneous preludes to the masque (*Wales, News from the New World, Augurs,*

---

[25] Harriett Hawkins, "Jonson's Use of Traditional Dream Theory in *The Vision of Delight*", *Modern Philology*, 64 (1967), 285-92. The masques of *Christmas* and *Gypsies Metamorphosed* similarly extend antimasque into revels.

Time Vindicated, Neptune's Triumph), like the inductions to *Cynthia's Revels* and three late plays.

Many of these later masques are social rather than allegorical or ideal, stressing the horizontal axis that Orgel mentions in the stage settings rather than neoplatonic descents of the gods from above.[26] Thus the Welsh and Irish yokels or shepherds or gypsies are subjects to be elevated by the royal presence, but they are not evil. As in the poems of the period, the treatment of love enlarges from simple neoplatonic idealism to the questioning of social and literary roles, as in the two joking Cupids of *A Challenge at Tilt* or the *Lovers Made Men* whose Petrarchan follies are cured by oblivion and wit.

While Jonson restructures the masque form, he also experiments with the mix of its elements – spectacle, song, dance, and poetry. *Lovers Made Men* was "all sung", and James and his court were disappointed by the lack of dancing and spectacle in the masques of 1610-18. Meanwhile, Jonson was collaborating with Jones on new kinds of stage effects. By 1616 *Mercury Vindicated* boasted a naturalistic "full dramatic stage" like the modern, with properties as well as flats. Orgel speaks of the "instantaneous changes of complex perspectives" possible with this new kind of set. These are congruent with the complex perspectives of the period's poems and plays and in contrast to the emblems and general facades of the earlier Jacobean period.[27]

As in the plays, the later Jacobean masques emphasize the variety and ambiguity of the world, not moral clarity and structural tightness. The flexibility of the later Jacobean masques is most clearly highlighted by their references to their author (*News from the New World, Gypsies*) and to the nature of the masque and poetry (*Love Restored, Golden Age, Wales, News, Augurs, Neptune's Triumph, Fortunate Isles*). Indicative of all these tendencies is *The Gypsies Metamorphosed* of 1621. Jonson's decorum admits ribaldry and specific personal references to the king and courtiers only in these later Jacobean masques – perhaps as a result of his

[26]   Orgel, *Complete Masques*, 20.
[27]   Orgel, *Complete Masques*, 22, 33; Orgel, 489, questions whether the entire masque *Lovers Made Men* could really have been sung.

growing familiarity at court, but also in consonance with his increased flexibility in his later Jacobean poems and plays. The courtiers speak along with the professionals, perhaps at Buckingham's wish, and the gypsies joke about stealing the royal seal and make sexual allusions to the courtiers.

The poems of Jonson's later Jacobean period include most of the first sixty items of *Under-wood* and uncollected poems 31-44. Among these poems are the epistle to Selden, 1614 (16); "The Houre-glasse" (10) and "My Picture Left in Scotland" (11), both 1619; the epitaph on Vincent Corbet, 1619 (14); "A Celebration of Charis" (Charis 4, 1616; Charis 7, 1619; Charis 1, ca 1623); "An Execration upon Vulcan", 1623 (45); and dedicatory poems to Raleigh, 1614 (26), Chapman, 1618 (Uc. 38), and Shakespeare, 1623 (Uc. 41, 42). In these poems Jonson moves away from the rigorously selected plain style Latin *genres* to other forms. Poems that are still written in the style of the earlier Jacobean period tend to be longer and more relaxed but less forceful than earlier. As in the masques and plays of the period, Jonson reexamines the English tradition in his later Jacobean poems, writing in the popular metaphysical mode and questioning Petrarchan conventions.

Like the *Bartholomew Fair* puppets, these poems reconsider the Renaissance ideals of love and friendship. The poems of this period are more complex than earlier concerning the relationship between appearance and reality and more specific about the nature of their society. In Jonson's later works the focus tends more often than earlier to be on the interactions between passion and reason. In these poems and in the later plays, Jonson explores valor, the possibilities of love for a reasonable man, and the nature of women. The poems and plays now do not judge from pre-established moral norms so much as they attempt to set up priorities among complicated categories of experience. With this new flexibility of attitude comes new subtlety in the mixture of tones and hence irony.

In these later poems and plays, the elements of praise and blame tend to be modified rather differently than through the

constriction of range of the earlier Jacobean works. One such
change is through the increased emphasis on moderation, the mean
between various extremes, rather than on a set truth set starkly
against a known falsehood. Charis 9 and the song "Oh doe not
wanton" (6) exemplify this faith in moderation.[28] Since the mean
must be carefully found and defined in every new set of circumstances, there is more room for discussion of different points of
view in works seeking a mean than in those exposing a known evil.
The texture of Jonson's later Jacobean verse, too, reflects this
search for a mean. In Charis 1 or elegy 24, for example, clauses are
balanced against other clauses in multiple relations somewhat
more complex than the positive and negative patterning of "Inviting
a Friend to Supper" or "To Celia". Jonson's later Jacobean poems
and plays pay more attention than earlier to the mixtures in
people of truth and falsehood, good and evil. These plays and
poems focus on the vacillations and endeavors of the reasonably
good man of mixed virtues.

   In many of his later poems, Jonson includes references to
himself similar to those in the late masques and plays. In the
later poems, these comedic self-portraits demonstrate the possibilities of different kinds of valuable and ludicrous attributes
coexisting in the same person. The poet now serves less as a judge
of others and more as a guide who joins his reader in the active
and difficult quest for the good life and its moral and esthetic values.
Jonson's earlier poems stress the importance of patterns of reciprocity between king and country, patron and poet, friend and
friend. In his later works, this reciprocity becomes a less exclusive
matter of a virtuous elite and admits a wider mutuality of forgiveness and concern among the author, the subjects of his poems,
and his readers. His satire is thus more 'Horatian' and participatory in this period than earlier. In his later Jacobean poems,
Jonson does take responsibility for faults in his own judgment, as
he did not in epigram lxv. In the later Jacobean epistle to Selden
(16), he admits, "Since being deceiv'd, I turne a sharper eye/
Upon my selfe, and aske to whom? and why?"

[28]   Peter Steese, "Jonson's 'A Song'", *Explicator* 21 (1962), No. 31, points
out the theme of the golden mean in this song.

The Charis series of poems, closely connected with the love elegies, *The Devil is an Ass*, and *The New Inn*, demonstrates many of the attributes of Jonson's later Jacobean period. The series reflects Jonson's interest at this time in different points of view on a single topic, and the chief problem with the understanding of both "Charis" and *The New Inn* seems to be that many critics think Jonson must either be wholly satirical or wholly approving, when the poem and play both present a wide variety of possible relations between love and reality without wholly endorsing any single view.[29] In all of these works a higher, 'Platonic' form of love is set against wrong concepts of love. Wittipol, like Lovel and the speaker of "Charis", tries to win his love through his powers of language during a limited speaking engagement. Instead, he learns to know himself and her through his love. He becomes her friend, protector, and business counsellor, thus taking the typical role of an older man.

The New Inn, like some of Jonson's Caroline poems, goes even farther than *The Devil is an Ass* in leaving ambiguous possibilities open. "The Vision of Ben. Jonson, on the Muses of His Friend M. Drayton" (Uc. 48), for instance, combines praise and overpraise in unclear proportions. Both "Charis" and *The New Inn* are based on the fourth book of Castiglione's *Courtier* with its discussion of the old lover. Like old "Ben" in "Charis", Lovel seeks to win a young woman through his eloquence and passion. His lovetalk is Platonic, moral, and spiritual. The "Vision of Beauty" (Uc. 52) he sings contrasts an ideal beauty with the sullying reality around it, like Charis 4. Lovel, like "Ben", wins kisses from the lady and is cured of the folly of loving by what he thinks is her scorn, though the absurd romance plot later gives Lovel the lady.

---

[29]   Champion, *Ben Jonson's Dotages: A Reconsideration of the Late Plays* (Lexington: U. of Kentucky, 1967), 81ff., believes that *The New Inn* is thoroughly satiric; Cubeta, "Charis", thinks that Charis is all satiric. Knoll, *Jonson's Plays*, 184; and Bamborough, *Ben Jonson*, 133-34, take *The New Inn* as a romance; H & S find the Charis poems passionate to complimentary, 10, 217. Trimpi, *Jonson's Poems*, 209-27, presents a more balanced view of "Charis". Two recent defenses of *The New Inn* try to assess Jonson's accomplishments and intentions in that play: Hawkins, "The Idea of the Theater in Jonson's *The New Inn*", *Renaissance Drama*, 9 (1966), 205-26; Douglas Duncan, "A Guide to *The New Inn*", *Essays in Criticism*, 20 (1970), 311-26.

The narrator of Charis has many of Lovel's attributes, though, since he is deprived of the ironic context of dramatic action, he is more ironic, many-faced, and detached in himself. He is old and therefore ridiculous as a lover, but he defends his right to love. Many of his arguments are hyperbolic and Platonic; others are as sensual as Beaufort's or the unreformed Wittipol's. Ultimately, he loses the lady but cures himself. "Another lady", the speaker of Charis 10, represents the wholly sensual attitude that confuses love with lust, like Beaufort in *The New Inn*. Lovel's melancholy and Ben's stupefaction are excessive, too, but their ideals are not therefore erroneous. Charis, like Mrs. Fitzdottrell and Pru, is self-determined, reasonable, and articulate. Thus Charis, many of the Under-wood elegies, *The Devil is an Ass*, and *The New Inn* show a progression from love to knowledge, not, as in the earlier Goodyere epigram (lxxxvi), from knowledge to love.

IV

Charles' reign saw Jonson fall from court patronage, from financial prosperity, from good health, and from theatrical success. Charles did not employ Jonson regularly as a writer of masques, although the King sometimes responded to Jonson's begging poems. Jonson's Caroline 'sons', including many of the young cavalier literary sparks, joined him at the Apollo in the early years of the reign. In 1628 the poet suffered from a partially-paralyzing stroke, and he became increasingly disabled thereafter. Jonson died, much elegized, in 1637. Caroline aristocrats and officials were among his last patrons; Sir Kenelm Digby edited the posthumous second folio of Jonson's works, which appeared in 1640.

We have seen that *The New Inn*, 1629, is closely related to several of the late Jacobean works. Jonson's other two new Caroline plays, *The Staple of News*, 1626, and *The Magnetic Lady*, 1632, also continue the examination of multiple points of view and the ironic return to old forms of the preceding period, though with less flexibility and energy. *The Staple of News* tries to combine personification, allegory and contemporary city satire; *The New Inn* surrounds romantic comedy with irony, and *The Magnetic Lady* conflates old humors with new comedy of manners. Jonson also revised *A Tale of a Tub* for production in 1633 and apparently worked on the unfinished *Sad Shepherd* in his latest years.[30] Appropriately, death and resurrection themes appear in these final plays. *The Staple of News* has a prodigal son and a father returned from death; *The New Inn* ends with the reunion of an entire 'dead' family; and a baby and wife vanish and reappear in *The Magnetic Lady*.

Indicating Jonson's shifting values in these Caroline plays are the new ironic-idealized characters, unlike the earlier gallants or moralists – the good but ludicrous Pennyboy Canter and Lovel. Jonson's later Jacobean emphasis on his 'straight' characters and women continues in these plays as well. His Caroline heroes can manipulate language and circumstances, and they can change. The prodigal Pennyboy, Jr., genuinely reforms, and Compass resolves conflict and orders apparent chaos. Pecunia and the Magnetic Lady are symbolic centers of their plays. Talkative Polish and midwife Chair act as knaves in *The Magnetic Lady*, and that late play is the only one in which women's deceptions originate the comic action. In *The New Inn*, Prudence's judgment and reason balance the excesses of the other characters. Prudence the maid is Jonson's only attractive lower-class woman, and her name reflects a combination of female virtue and the intellect usually reserved to men like Wittipol and Truewit. Pru assumes the upperclass and male role of 'sovereign' of the day's sports, but, instead of being punished for her presumption, she is rewarded. At the end of the play she wins wealth and status through marriage as Jonson's gallants so often do – to the play's most rational male, Lord Latimer.

As in Jonson's later Jacobean period, motives and vices become less important than the ends and means of actions in these Caroline plays. *The Alchemist* and *The Forrest* epistles reveal greed in its many forms, whereas *The Staple of News* and the later epistles and

---

30 Gerald E. Bentley, *The Jacobean and Caroline Stage*, 4 (Oxford: Clarendon, 1956), 627, 634, believes that both *The Sad Shepherd* and *A Tale of a Tub* are Caroline writings.

begging poems emphasize the proper use of money. The meaning of costume and disguise, too, depends on their use more than their appearance. Thus the same expensive dress in *The New Inn* that shows Snuff's fetishism and Pinnacia's ambition – both taking the appearance for the reality like the obscene groom of elegy 44 – demonstrates that Prudence deserves to marry the young lord who has watched her virtuous and rational gaiety.

As in the later Jacobean works, the prologues of *The Staple of News* and *The Magnetic Lady*, with their personal references to Jonson, operate like the metaphor of the world as theater in these plays to break down the differences between audience and playworld. In these last plays Jonson returns to his much earlier role of correcting, rather than identifying with, his audience, though at times he appeals to their favor. That is, audience and playworld join, but the author separates himself from both. The 'audiences' that he incorporates as choruses in the last plays are more critical and foolish than idealized, though they are given information on the author's concerns and constructive skill. In J. B. Bamborough's term, there is a "take-it-or-leave-it" attitude to his audience in Jonson's Caroline plays.[31]

Jonson's last four masques and entertainments, *Love's Triumph through Callipolis* and *Chloridia*, 1631, and *The King's Entertainment at Welbeck*, 1633, and *Love's Welcome at Bolsover*, 1634, dabble in fashionable neoplatonism. Like Jonson's Caroline court poetry, their eulogies seem tired. The masque form which Jonson had expanded in his later Jacobean period here collapses into the formless spectacle that gives *Chloridia* eight antimasque entries and exploded the antagonism between Jonson and Jones.[32]

The poems of Jonson's Caroline period include *Under-Wood* 60-86 and uncollected poems 45-64. These poems include a dedication to Drayton, 1627 (Uc. 48); an epithalamion for Jerome Weston, 1632 (77); elegies on the deaths of Jane and Katherine Ogle,

---

[31]   Bamborough, *Ben Jonson*, 130, thinks that all of Jonson's plays have this quality, though it increases in his later plays.
[32]   Orgel, *Complete Masques*, 37-39, discusses the Jones-Jonson controversy.

1625, 1629 (Uc. 45, 49), Jane Pawlet, 1631 (85), and Venetia Digby, 1633 (86); the Cary-Morison (72) and New Inn (Uc. 53) odes, 1629; various court poems; and the expostulations with Inigo Jones, 1631 (Uc. 56, 57). These poems follow Jonson's later Jacobean ones in moving from classical to contemporary forms and from the general and moral to the specific and social. There are fewer love poems than in the late Jacobean period, but Jonson's late Jacobean tendency toward extended and expanded forms continues, especially in the elaborate pindarics of 1629 and the many funeral elegies that replace the earlier epitaphs. The over-extended structure of the Caroline masques is repeated in some of the Caroline poems. The most ambitious undertaking in the late poems is the incomplete series elegizing Lady Venetia Digby.

If the theme of love is less prominent in Jonson's Caroline than in his later Jacobean period, that of valor continues and is reassessed. Jonson in some of his late sick poems and funeral elegies defines true valor, like Lovel in *The New Inn*, as the endurance of "poverty, restraint, captivity,/ Banishment, losse of children, long disease" (*NI*. IV. iv. 106-107). Death and the consolations of Christianity are prominent themes. In the Caroline plays the satiric knaves and fools are often stupid and boring. In the late poems, Jonson shows his changed interests by omission: satiric epigrams and epistles directed against social types simply do not appear. Instead, the Caroline poems include personal invectives that replace generalized satire, petitions for money that exalt the poet's function, and generally hackneyed court poetry for occasions like the King's birthday and the Queen's lying-in. A kind of artistic nadir is reached with the 1630 epigram on Charles II's birth: "And art thou borne, brave Babe? Blest be thy birth" (67), while Jonson's Panglossian "Epigram Consolatorie" of 1629 (65) is an insensitive opposite to his earlier epitaph on his own son. In the "Epigram Consolatorie" Jonson instructs the bereaved royal parents that God "can, he will, and with large int'rest pay,/ What (at his liking) he will take away." In the worst of these poems there is a return to Jonson's earliest problems of padding, incoherence, and uncongenial conceits.

The attitudes of the Caroline poems, too, show some regression to the exclusive morality of Jonson's first two periods and to the withdrawal of the solitary self.[33] Sometimes Jonson in these last poems sympathetically shows the vicissitudes of his wine-inspired, disease-beleaguered Muse, though he insists on the prerogatives due the public poet and he wants to take verbal vengeance on an unappreciative world.

If Jonson's last poems, plays, and masques are often marred by structural unwieldiness, perhaps the best poem of his Caroline period is saved by his adoption of a very strict and elaborate form in the pindaric Cary-Morison ode. Here his aged petulance and moral impatience, too, disappear in the consideration of his lifelong themes of true friendship, art, and death.

Compared to the rhetorical fat of the Desmond ode (27) and the didactic lean of the Sidney ode (XIV), Jonson's last and greatest pindaric ode, "To the Immortall Memorie, and Friendship of That Noble Paire, Sir Lucius Cary, and Sir H. Morison" (72) achieves a balance by successfully embodying its didactic meaning in appropriate images and symbols in a functional stanzaic form. In several attributes of style, the poem falls between the other two odes. There are proportionally more adjectives and fewer verbs than in the Sidney ode, and the reverse for the Desmond one. (See Table Eleven, Appendix.) The ratio between positive and negative adjectives, too, falls between that of the other two odes.[34] More important, the poem shows a development over the earlier odes in the breadth and sympathy of its content and in the varied role that the poet takes within the poem.

The opening allusion, to the "Brave Infant of *Saguntum*" shows the extravagance of Jonson's earliest and latest periods, but it is thematically justified as the first of a series of examples of the complete short life. The poem then oscillates to the negative

---

[33] Greene, "Centered Self", 329-30, discusses only Jonson's early Jacobean and his Caroline works and thus sees this regression as continuous.

[34] There are about two and one half positive adjectives to each negative one: 38 positive, 17 negative, and 2 neutral descriptive adjectives. The 128-line poem is artfully patterned after its pindaric model: Carol Maddison, *Apollo and the Nine: A History of the Ode* (London: Routledge & Kegan Paul, 1960), 296-303; and Robert Shafer, *The English Ode to 1660: An Essay in Literary History* (New York: Haskell, 1966), 97-108.

example of the old lord's long, useless life before introducing Morison in the second Counterturn as the authentic contemporary example of the virtuous short life. Morison "stood" and fulfilled all his public and private roles perfectly. (Jonson's highest word of praise, "perfect", denoting both the complete and the ideal, is used three times in this poem; "imperfect", once.) Jonson describes Morison's moral perfection in esthetic terms, so that his rationally-controlled life is seen as a work of art, a perfect poem reflected in this poem about him. "All Offices were done/ By him, so amply, full, and round,/ In weight, in measure, number, sound" that "His life was of Humanitie the Spheare".

After praising Morison, Jonson turns, as he so often does in his later works, to himself and the corrupt age whose "masse of miseries" is shown on the stage. His own "age", too, is swollen with miseries, and the poem thereby identifies the corruption induced by living too long in an evil society with the "age" of history. In contrast, the great life is shown by actions "done and wrought/ In season, and so brought/ To light". This line combines recurrent images of natural cycle in the poem with one of light, which, like the circle, is a symbol of absolute goodness and purity abstracted from surrounding conditions. Jonson caps these two images with the central analogy of the poem, that of life as poetry:

> ... her measure's are, how well
> Each syllab'e answer'd, and was form'd, how faire;
> These make the lines of life, and that's her ayre.

Living the good life is like writing harmonious lyric poetry; living uselessly is like writing topical satiric plays.

The stanza summing this set of comparisons between the good short life and the long, useless one is the functional center of the poem:

> It is not growing like a tree
> In bulke, doth make man better bee;
> Or standing long an Oake, three hundred yeare,
> To fall a logge, at last, dry, bald, and seare:
> A Lillie of a Day,
> Is fairer farre, in May,
> Although it fall, and die that night;

> It was the Plant, and flowre of light.
> In small proportions, we just beauties see:
> And in short measures, life may perfect bee.

In this stanza positives are carefully balanced against negatives. The images of plants, light, and poetry adumbrated in the previous few stanzas are combined so that the conclusion stresses the congruence of the moral and the esthetic, the natural and the artificial. Behind these images, as in many of the later poems, is a Christian reference to the source of all value. The lily hints at a proper reliance on God's love, while light, proportion, and measure indicate the supreme order and artistry of Creation.[35]

Alliteration and assonance bind this striking stanza, as in the best of Jonson's poetry at all periods, while the adjectives control the reader's responses, revaluing "small" into "just", "short" into "perfect". The line lengths enforce the idea that the brief "Lillie of a Day" in the short line is superior to the oak "standing long" in the long line. The overweening, then toppling growth of the tree is indicated in the verse by the run-on first line, while the line "To fáll a logge, at lást, drý, báld, and seáre", is slowed by its five pauses and six stresses. In contrast, the "Lillie of a Day" is poised in the short central fifth line, and the last four lines of the stanza, on measure and proportion, are all neatly bisected by the caesura.

The most significant fact about this stanza, however, lies outside the poem itself. This stanza is based on a brave, humorous, and somewhat pathetic personal allusion to the poet. Writing to a young friend who knew him well, Jonson could rely, I think, on a reference to something growing "in bulke", "old, withered, bald, and seare" being identified with himself. Persistently in the poems of his last years Jonson refers to his prodigious bulk and to his doddering age. The references in the previous stanza to the stage, too, would direct the reader's attention to the author

---

[35] Many anthologists have divorced this stanza from its context. Swinburne, *Jonson*, 75, thought the stanza showed up particularly well alone since the rest of the poem was so bad. George Held, "Jonson's Pindaric on Friendship", *Concerning Poetry*, 3 (1970), 41, suggests that Jonson may intend a pun on Cary's first name 'Lucius' and the Latin 'lux'.

at this point. Thus behind the natural imagery, artistically convincing in itself as it is, there is another version of the contrast between the long lonely life and the short lovely one.

However, Jonson's very nearness to death allows him to project himself as a member of the heavenly choir who can justly play the poet-priest, revealing the truths of the next world and celebrating the purest relationship of this one. He shows Morison as active in death as in life, and the "bright eternall Day" Morison enjoys fulfils and replaces the transcience of the "Lillie of a Day". Jonson's poem, earlier a "garland" of nature turned to art, is now seen as the "*Asterisme*" of natural and heavenly light.

In the final turn and counterturn, Jonson returns to his role as didactic teacher to exalt the perfect friendship of this double star, and he leads the poem back from the exalted mysteries of the next world to the moral duties of this one. As in his earlier poems and masques, the praised friends are shown as effective exemplars of virtue, and their names epitomize every ideal.

Some main themes of the early epigrams, the moral efficacy of the virtuous exemplar, for instance, and the joys of ideal friendship, receive their fullest expression in this late poem. Instead of the presumptuous priest of Apollo in the Desmond ode, unable to justify his high claims for himself, or the straight-forward moral teacher in the Sidney birthday ode, in the Cary-Morison ode Jonson creates and fulfils his own role at its widest breadth of inclusiveness. As in many of the later Jacobean poems, he is a friend and participant in the friendship, loss, and consolation he writes about as well as the priest of poetry and the didactic teacher.

We have seen Jonson's poems, plays, and masques changing and developing throughout his life. In each period Jonson sometimes can mobilize all his resources to produce a few perfect and many competent works. His Elizabethan poems and plays show him sifting through the available conventions, moving toward his own adaptation of classical forms and toward his own idiosyncratic style. His best earlier Jacobean works are like the bright lilies of May: in them, total control of form illuminates firmness of moral conviction with esthetic radiance. In respect to the balance of

thetic means and moral ends, "Inviting a Friend to Supper" is
s much a paeon to order as "To Penshurst", and "To Penshurst"
works through the same verbal means of balance, give and take,
as "To Celia", despite the decorously different range of choices
involved.

The particular contribution of Jonson's later Jacobean works
is that in them he learns to be more various, more pluralistic, more
understanding in tone, to mediate between praise and blame, and
to hold more than one attitude at the same time, particularly
through the ironic use of a projected *persona* of himself, the fat
boisterous poet, ludicrous lover, and flawed and forgetful friend,
who remains, none the less, as a real character, always greater
than the sum of his parts. Through his essential role, that of
the conscious craftsmanly poet, he presents this vision of total
human experience through a compassionate and participatory
irony.

It remains to be asked why the increased sophistication and
complexity of attitude that Jonson shows in his later works seems
to have produced fine poems but inferior plays. The first answer
given here has been through attention to Jonson's total chronology.
In his later Jacobean years, Jonson produced strong poems,
masques, and, I think, two good plays. Then the Caroline plays,
masques, and poems show decline. In Jonson's Caroline verse,
individual poems are abysmal, while other poems of the same dates
remain in control of their subjects. In the Caroline plays, the
unevenness of quality is clearly seen within the plays. Moreover,
though Jonson stopped writing satiric epigrams, he continued to
create satiric characters in his Caroline comedies – often badly.
For his early Jacobean *Volpone*, *Silent Woman*, and *The Alchemist*,
Jonson devised a structural formula that showed off his dramatic
powers at their best. He bounded his dramatic worlds tightly so
that comic turbulence was displayed through the transparent
structural shell. Similarly, much of the power of his early Jacobean
poems derives from the emotions suppressed under strict restraint.
In the later poems, moral ambivalence is allowed to surface. Thus
the powerful earlier indirection of "Yet dare I not complaine, or
wish for death" (XV) is replaced by the overt, sophisticated, and

much less powerful indirection of "Farre I was from being stupid,/ For I ran and call'd on *Cupid*" (4.2). With *Bartholomew Fair* and the later Jacobean poems, Jonson moves away from the 'illusion of completeness' toward more open and complex structural forms and toward more irony in attitude, but his structural endoskeletons could not always bear as much weight as the older shells. In Jonson's later plays, no clearly authorial characters sort values for the audience; the viewers are left bewildered as fools speak wise doctrine and worthy characters shrink into bathos. In *The New Inn*, at the extreme of this tendency, there are no clues to disentangle literary parody from genuine sentiment.

Jonson's Caroline works are thus still writings of experiment and expansion in form, though they evidence a constriction of energy and attitude – like the circles cast by a stone in a pond that gradually expand, break, and disappear.

6. CONCLUSION

This study places Ben Jonson's nondramatic poetry first in the context of his three published collections of poetry, then in comparison with his plays and masques. Events in Jonson's biography have been indicated, too, in connection with his writings throughout the four phases outlined in the preceding chapter. Jonson's Elizabethan writings set peerless poetry against envy and ignorance as Jonson seeks to establish the authority of the poet and the relationship between the poet and other authorities. In Jonson's earlier Jacobean writing, learning and virtue expose ambition and vice, and the separate works of art become self-enclosed forms. Then Jonson's later Jacobean work opens out again to consider the nature of society and the complex interactions of social relationships; rational moderation and tolerance strive to balance human folly and fallibility. Finally, Jonson's Caroline work tries to face scorn and death with fortitude and equanimity. The writings of this last period again turn inward, to the poet himself and to his canon as a comprehensive literary unit.

Like Jonson's Caroline writing, this study refers Jonson's accomplishments chiefly to each other and to himself. However, confusing as sometimes is the picture, Jonson benefits from being seen in the broadest possible context. These concluding brief remarks are intended only to sketch some of the connections between Jonson's development and the literary and social currents of his age. These issues deserve far more comprehensive treatment, and beyond the borders of this study wait still other questions, relating Jonson's work, for example, to continental models, to neoclassicism, and to the varied histories of the *genres* in which he wrote.

Jonson is often described as typically Jacobean, the man of his age.[1] This designation is somewhat misleading, but it has two venerable sources. One is the contrast with the universal Shakespeare, who, we are told, transcended his time as Jonson did not. Second, Jonson tells us himself that his comedies mirror the times, especially their follies. Yet Jonson in exasperation wanted to quit both the "loathed stage" and "the more loathsome Age" (Uc. 53), and his relationship to the trends of his times is complex. At moments during his life he seems to represent his age in terms of its prevailing philosophies, social attitudes, and literary taste; often he is ahead of, behind, or different from contemporary tendencies.

Everyone who knew Jonson reported him as a unique and charismatic personality, and also a baffling and difficult one. Whereas Shakespeare has come down to us epitheted as "gentle", Jonson is labeled either "honest" or "arrogant". Both the positive and the negative forms bear witness to his lifelong defense of his personal and artistic integrity. He was an outsider to formal education and to high society who redefined himself as one of the only true insiders. He was an Arcadian social conservative, looking back to a mythical patriarchal past. Most important, Jonson was a literary leader who influenced the following generations of writers, but whose comprehensive literary program was not carried forward. A popular writer, he sought to dominate his age and to establish a new position for his plays as literature and for himself as poet, and part of Jonson's reputation for arrogance was derived from his startling innovation in publishing his plays as "works" in full folio.

Although Jonson's literary taste seems to have been formed by the interaction between his classical reading and the needs of his

---

[1] Wedgwood, *17th-Century*, 59-60; H & S, 1, 121, after discussing Jonson's "rarity", summarize, "in some aspects he was the most completely 'of his age' among them all". L. C. Knights, *Drama and Society in the Age of Jonson* (London: Chatto & Windus, 1937), 198, describes Jonson's tone as that of a man who has "seen many civilizations, and is at home in one".

personality, his standards for his contemporaries were set by the great Elizabethans. Throughout his life, Jonson's highest praise, despite some reservations, went to Shakespeare, Donne, and Bacon, all of whom had literary reputations by 1600. Of the preceding generation, he alludes to Sidney, Spenser, and Southwell. Jonson frequently ridicules the conventions of Shakespearean comedy and Shakespeare's fluency, and he does not praise any single Shakespeare play, though he seems to have genuinely admired Shakespeare's power and poetry. Jonson told Drummond that John Donne's best work was written before 1600, and Drummond reports Jonson quoting from Donne's earliest elegies and verse letters (*Cv.* 118-22). However, while admiring Shakespeare and Donne, in 1600 Jonson is already well launched on a very different kind of literary program, writing poetry different from both of theirs. He is already the well-known, self-conscious young "Horace" who also writes for the popular stage. From 1598 through the first half of James' reign, Jonson is a dramatic leader, creating and shaping satirical or humor comedy, city comedy, court masque, and correct historical tragedy.

In the midst of seventeenth-century English dramatic plenitude, these earlier Jonson plays usually satisfied both popular and critical applause, even though the same audiences also delighted in romantic drama. In the first half of his career, then, Jonson's plays formed or coincided with his audiences' tastes, though there is scattered evidence for audience displeasure even with the early Jacobean comedies. As the popular base of Elizabethan drama eroded, Jonson's audiences changed over the late Jacobean and Caroline years, and their tastes also changed. Jonson's later plays were more often box-office failures than earlier, despite the fact that Jonson's social prejudices favored the learned and landed classes who formed this more sophisticated later audience. But 'velvet' proved as insensitive as 'rug' to the poet. When his audiences did not seem to understand what he was doing, Jonson incorporated caricatures of them into the texts of his late plays and continued to write as he thought fit. I do not think that Jonson ever wrote a work merely to exploit contemporary taste, nor did he materially change his course to meet it. Jonson in his early years experimented, set new directions, and was followed and applauded. In his later years, he continued to experiment, even though his former followers and their audiences were diverging from him, often in paths set down by his own earlier works.

Related to the question of audience taste, though more difficult to assess, is the question of audience moral standards. The 'morality' of Jonson's plays is a recurrent issue in modern Jonson studies that benefits from analysis in the perspective of the conventions of the Stuart drama. Critical anxieties about whether Jonson is too moral to be funny – as in *Volpone* – or too lax to be moral – as in *Bartholomew Fair* – receive some light from contemporary opinion and practice.[2] In the dedication to *Volpone*, Jonson indicates that the punishments ending that play were contrary to his understanding of the "strict rigour of comick law" (1. 110); they were deliberate demonstrations to the moral critics of the drama. Less reputable attackers were answered more comically by the puppet's replies to Rabbi Busy in *Bartholomew Fair*. Throughout Jonson's comedies, the good are recognized and rewarded, and the evil or ridiculous exposed. Allowing the witty to keep sometimes ill-gotten spoils is quite common in Jacobean comedy, as is the happy ending of marriage with an heiress, even an imperfect one. If a Jacobean tragedy usually ends with the evil characters destroyed, and also many of the good, Jacobean comedies end with the good rejoicing, and also many of the vicious. Dryden felt that Restoration standards of dramatic justice in this respect were more refined than Jacobean ones. Ignoring Jonson's appeal to comic decorum in the epilogue, he cited *The Alchemist* as an example of how even the best earlier dramatists had failed.[3] However, I do

---

[2] Jonson's 'morality' is frequently discussed by his critics. The subject is extensively treated by Jackson, *Vision and Judgment*; Dessen, *Moral Comedy*; and Helen W. Baum, *The Satiric and the Didactic in Ben Jonson's Comedies* (Chapel Hill: U. of North Carolina, 1947). Also see the citations in notes 19 and 22 to chapter five, above.

[3] Dryden, "Preface" to *An Evening's Love* in *Works*, 10 (1970), 208. William V. Spanos, "The Real Toad in the Jonsonian Garden: Resonance in the Nondramatic Poetry", *Journal of English and Germanic Philology*, 68 (1969), 6, 17, sees the endings of *Volpone* and *The Alchemist* as examples of Jonson's "deliberate inclusion" of "apparently incompatible elements" which gives Jonson's poetry its "resonance".

not think that the ending of a Jonson comedy sums its moral meaning in the way that we sometimes assume. Jonson always defended his work in all *genres* as both moral and delightful, even though this sometimes meant that his audiences ought to be pleased and instructed whether they were or not.

Compared to the "coterie" dramatists with whom Jonson is often connected because of his satirical tone and social attitudes, Jonson is more consistent in a Christian stance that is morally conventional.[4] Although modern critics may hunt bawdy puns in Jonson's writings, his plays and poems are never salacious.[5] None of his plays sport honest whores or sympathetic incest. All of Jonson's characters adhere to Sir Thomas Browne's boast of avoiding vices without names.[6]

A leader of one kind of drama in his early Jacobean period, Jonson diverged from contemporary dramatic standards and practice in his later Jacobean and Caroline years. His 'dotage' should be set against a weakening drama in need of new direction and experimentation, even if Jonson's attempts were confusing, impracticable, against current taste, and sometimes badly executed. Jonson's attempts to combine contemporary with earlier traditions in his later poems, masques, and plays can be seen as part of a program to provide alternate models for later Jacobean and Caroline tastes. Allegory, morality play, Elizabethan pastoral, folk tale, and Skeltonic doggerel are all enlisted in this effort.

As Stuart poetry and drama became more introspective and psychological, so did Jonson's work. But there is a significant difference. Whereas his contemporaries become increasingly interested in abnormal psychology, sentiment, and sensational spectacle, Jonson shifts from describing the grotesques of his humor plays to

---

[4] Harbage, *Rival Traditions*, identifies Jonson with antimiddle class "coterie" social values, though he sees Jonson's "integrity" keeping him from adopting the "coterie" morality.

[5] Coburn Gum, *The Aristophanic Comedies of Ben Jonson: A Comparative Study of Jonson and Aristophanes* (*Studies in English Literature*, 40) (The Hague: Mouton, 1969), 46ff.

[6] Sir Thomas Browne, *Religio Medici*, in *The Prose of Sir Thomas Browne*, ed. by Norman Endicott (Garden City: Doubleday, 1967), 77, "I thanke the goodnesse of God I have no sinnes that want a name; I am not singular in offences".

examining normal psychology and his own character in his later poems and plays. Jonson's later villains become less fantastic than earlier, and Jonson also avoids the extravagant virtues of the Fletcherian tradition. He has no martyrs to eternal virginity or heroic loyalty in his comedies, though he treats tender passions sympathetically in the distanced pastoral of *The Sad Shepherd.* In *The New Inn,* Jonson parodies Caroline neoplatonic fashions while upholding their ethical substrate. In that play and throughout his Caroline masques and poetry, Jonson glances toward the Restoration concepts of love and honor, but he always redefines them in terms of his humanist psychology, and he never glorifies them beyond Renaissance reason.

In nondramatic poetry, as in the drama, Jonson's early Jacobean work set precedents for the next generations; then his later Jacobean and Caroline writings varied from the trends he had helped establish, often by returning to earlier forms. The sometimes patronizing friend of Shakespeare and Donne in his later days became the 'father' of Brome and Herrick and the sometimes patronized companion of Caroline wits like Carew and Suckling. Jonson's early Jacobean work is his more Augustan and Neo-classical; he moved away from the style as his age moved toward it. Jonson took up metaphysical love elegy and funeral elegy long after Donne had laid them down. Although he told Drummond of his preference for end-stopped couplets in 1619, his later non-dramatic poetry includes a higher percentage of run-on lines than earlier (See Table Nine, Appendix), and he moved from habitual iambic pentameter couplets to more elaborate stanzaic forms in his later poetry.

Jonson's 'sons' in nondramatic poetry, like those of many a self-made man, exceeded their father in grace and sophistication and often did not realize how much they lacked of the old man's strength and force. They sometimes took his inheritance for granted, made fun of his foibles, were embarrassed by his drinking and his criticism of others. They discounted him a little too soon. When he died, they piled up sincere and mostly banal eulogies to him.[7] Jonson's powers of poetry reappeared, scattered but stronger,

7   H & S, 11, 362-494, print a selection of such comments on Jonson in his

in the disparate generation of his literary grandchildren. Despite their opposing political orientations, Jonson's successor as a dedicated defender of poetry is John Milton, and the poet who develops Jonson's controlled classicism most fruitfully is another ornery puritan, Andrew Marvell. In *Timber* and in his later plays, Jonson shows an increasing use of continental dramatic criticism and the beginnings of a critical synthesis that will be developed in the Restoration. Similarly, Jonson's sense of dramatic construction and his satirical wit look forward to Dryden and Pope.

Jonson's social attitudes were always conservative, even reactionary, but, like his esthetics, they were strongly marked by his individual character. He identified with the values of the country house aristocrats, but he often ridiculed representatives of legal authority.[8] A Roman Catholic for many years, Jonson bore a Restoration distaste for Puritan faction and enthusiasm and a Latitudinarian appreciation for sensible common doctrine. He always disliked and distrusted the 'vulgar' with whom he had perhaps been too closely associated for his comfort as a bricklayer's stepson and apprentice. Throughout his life, he is a defender of divine right monarchy and of a paternal model of secular authority. His early panegyrics and masques to James stress the importance of James' example to the nation; they suggest that the King can learn from the poet, from the virtuous and the learned. Jonson praises James' popularity. Jonson's last works show a vehement and unreflecting defense of Charles and of unpopular ministers like Lord High Treasurer Weston. The earlier admonitory note to James is missing in these late poems for

---

lifetime and eulogies from *Jonsonus Virbius* and other elegies. A good recent treatment of the nondramatic "heirs" is Joseph H. Summers, *The Heirs of Donne and Jonson* (London: Chatto & Windus, 1970); Geoffrey Walton, *Metaphysical to Augustan: Studies in Tone and Sensibility in the Seventeenth Century* (London: Bowes & Bowes, 1955) follows the transition from Jonson to the Augustans. The later dramatic heirs are discussed by Joe Lee Davis, *The Sons of Ben: Jonsonian Comedy in Caroline England* (Detroit: Wayne State, 1967).

[8] Bevington, *Tudor Drama and Politics: A Critical Approach to Topical Meaning* (Cambridge, Mass.: Harvard, 1968), 275-87, speaks of Jonson's artistic and social elitism with regard to secular authority.

Charles, and Jonson's Caroline court writings often retreat to celebration of Charles and Henrietta Maria as paragons of married love. Jonson treated Charles' unpopularity, like that of his own late plays, as an example of the people's ignorance. Even in his last entertainments presented for the King, Jonson concentrates on lauding the benefits of a peaceful succession. He thus returns to an important political motif of 1603 while ignoring the political realities of the 1630's.

Throughout his life, Jonson remains firmly against almost all innovations in his society. He treated newspapers, amateur scientific investigation, capitalist manufacture, and parliamentary and religious reform with equal ridicule. Paradoxically, one of the few areas in which Jonson appeared to favor contemporary social trends was in relation to the rights of women. In two of his later works he approved social changes conducive to the improvement of women's lot; Grace Wellborn defends her right to exercise veto power over an unsatisfactory marriage, and Frances Fitz-dottrell asserts control over her own property when married to a foolish spendthrift. Altogether, women appear as more reasonable beings in Jonson's later works than they do earlier, and these works even hint at the possibilities of marriages of companionship.[9]

Thus Jonson notices some contemporary developments and ignores others, endorses few innovations in society and makes many in literature. His last writings reflect a social as well as a literary nostalgia: A Tale of a Tub is set in the late Queen's countryside,[10] and The Sad Shepherd combines Spenser's fairyland, Sidney's Arcadia, and Robin Hood's forest. The emphasis on feasting, revelry, and 'Merry Old England' in Jonson's latest plays and entertainments is congruent with his cavalier politics. The play of the past and of the countryside was associated with the

---

[9] Lawrence Stone, The Crisis of the Aristocracy, 1558-1641 (Oxford: Clarendon, 1965), 596ff., lists the marriage of companionship, the acceptance of the individual's veto over his or her unacceptable marriage, and the wife's control over her own property as seventeenth-century advances in attitudes to women and marriage.

[10] Bentley, Stage, 4, 634, believes that A Tale of a Tub is set in Queen Mary's time.

glorification of the old, hierarchical order against urban Puritan prudery, hypocrisy, and revolution. Jonson's isolation as a sick old man recalls the desire for withdrawal expressed in some of his earlier Jacobean works. Withdrawal to the past, to art, to the self, are also the typical responses of the Caroline poet to his troubling times.[11]

It is pleasant to consider Jonson's work as a whole and in the round – to borrow Ben's favorite circular metaphors. We may even decide that Jonson deliberately grew into "one great blot" like the Heidelberg Tun (54) to remind us of the difficulties of squaring his circle. A limited figure, Jonson and his work continually challenge our definitions of his limits. Hopefully, in broadening our knowledge to the full circumference of his writings, we will still be 'understanders' rather than 'overreachers', ready to embrace the "mountain belly" and "rockie face" of the complete fat corpus of Jonson's works.

[11]   Miner, *Cavalier Mode*, 179, sees the common Cavalier response to the times, after Jonson, as "retreat". The relationship between Cavalier politics and country revelry is discussed by Leah Sinanoglou, "The Politics of Playfulness", unpublished essay, 1973.

APPENDIX

TABLE ONE

Jonson's Most Commonly Used Words

Major nouns, verbs, and adjectives repeated ten times or more in 1000 lines of the *Epigrammes* (l-lxvi, c-cxxii) compared with Miles' count of words repeated ten times or more in the first 1000 lines of *Under-wood*, with numbers of occurrence rounded off to the nearest five.[a]

Word	Epigrammes	Under-wood
good	40	25
great	40	10
poor	—	10
sweet	—	10
true	10	10
age	10	—
book	10	—
day	10	10
eye	—	15
face	—	10
fame	15	—
fate	10	—
fire	—	10
friend	10	—
God	15	10
grace	10	10
hand	—	10
heaven	10	—
heart	—	10
life	15	10
love (n. & v.)	20	55
man	50	45
muse	10	—·

[a] Miles, *Continuity*, 32-36, 524.

Word	*Epigrammes*	*Under-wood*
name	35	10
nature	—	10
sun	—	10
state	10	—
time	15	—
virtue	15	—
wit	20	—
world	15	10
call	10	10
came	—	10
cry	10	—
dare	10	—
find	10	10
give	15	15
go	—	15
hear	—	10
judge	10	—
keep	10	—
know	30	25
leave	10	—
live	10	—
make	50	45
pay	20	—
praise	15	—
read	10	—
rise	—	10
say	10	—
see	—	25
take	15	20
tell	10	15
think	20	15
write	10	—

TABLE TWO

Relationships Between Line and Syntax in Epigram ci

Section	Sentence	Lines	Coord. Clauses	Subord. Clauses	Sentence Length in Lines
I Introduction	1	1-6	1	5	6
	2	7-8	1	1	2
II Food	3	9-16	3	3	8
	4	17-20	1	3	3½
III Reading	5	20-26	3	3	6½
IV Wine	6	27-32	2	6	6
	7	33-34	1	1	2
V Conclusion	8	35-39	4	1	4½
	9	39-42	1	2	3½

TABLE THREE

Distribution of Epigrams of Praise and Blame
by Social Class of Subject (Both Sexes)

Poems to	Praise	Blame	Total
Social superiors	39	17	56
Equals	19	13	32
Inferiors	1	29	30
Total	59	59	118

TABLE FOUR

*Distribution of Epigrams of Praise and Blame
by Social Class of Subject (Women Only)*

Poems to	Praise	Blame	Total
Social superiors	10	1	11
Equals	1	0	1
Inferiors	0	4	4
Total	11	5	16

TABLE FIVE

List of Attributes and the Number of Times They are Praised in
Fifty-eight Commendatory Epigrams on Particular Persons

Virtue and piety	24
Mind and learning	17
Poetry and literature	12
Public deeds, office	11
Family, "bloud"	10
Self-sufficiency	9
Beauty	9 (2 to men)
Friendship	7
Valor	7
Favors to Jonson	4
The King's favor	3
Reference to a Golden Age	11
Mythological reference	7

TABLE SIX

Poems of The Forrest

Poems in the two major groups with their line length in number of syllables, rhyme schemes, and total length.

Group One. Songs. Light and Humorous Poems.	Stanza form	Total Lines
I. Why I Write Not of Love	8 aa	12
V. Song. To Celia. "Come my *Celia*."	7 aa	18
VI. To the Same. "Kisse me, Sweet."	7 aa	22
IX. Song. To Celia. "Drinke to me, onely."	8/6 abcbabcb	16
VII. Song. That Women are But Mens Shaddowes.	9a 8b 9a 8b 8c 8c	12
VIII. To Sicknesse.	7 aa	48

Group Two. Moral and Religious Poems.	Stanza form	Total Lines
II. To Penshurst	10 aa	102
III. To Sir Robert Wroth	10/8 aa	106
X. "And must I sing?" (Prelude)	10 aaa	30
XI. Epode	10/6 aa	116
XII. Epistle. To Elizabeth Countesse of Rutland	10 aa	100
XIII. Epistle. To Katherine, Lady Aubigny	10 aa	124
XIV. Ode. To Sir William Sydney, on His Birth-day	10a 8b 2c 2c 6b 4a 4d 4d 4e 10e	60
IV. To the World, a Farewell for a Gentlewoman, Vertuous and Noble	8 abab	68
XV. To Heaven	10 aa	26

TABLE SEVEN

Comparative Line Counts for "To Sir Robert Wroth"
and "To Penshurst"

Type of Passage	"To Sir Robert Wroth"		"To Penshurst"	
	Lines	Number of Lines	Lines	Number of Lines
Negative contrast	1-12 67-90	12 } 24 } 36	1-6 45-50	6 } 6 } 12
Idyllic description				
Natural	13-46	34 } 54	7-44	38 } 76
Social	47-66	20 }	51-88	38 }
Moral-religious	91-106	16	89-102	14
Total		106		102

TABLE EIGHT

"To Penshurst" and "To Sir Robert Wroth"

The ratio of verbs to descriptive adjectives to nouns in three parallel ten-line passages of the two poems.[a]

To Penshurst (JI)		Verbs	Descriptive Adjectives	Nouns
11. 21-30	Ideal description	11	7	23
11. 45-54	Partly negative description	13	5	17
11. 93-102	Moral conclusion	11	6	19
To Sir Robert Wroth (III)				
11. 35-44	Ideal description	6	9	18
11. 67-76	Partly negative description	13	2	19
11. 97-106	Moral conclusion	12	8	17

[a] There are some ambiguities and problems of classification using these standard terms, in comparison, for instance, with the linguistic categories of Louis Milic, *A Quantitative Approach to the Style of Jonathan Swift* (The Hague: Mouton, 1967). However, the older terms seem preferable here in simplicity and in ease of comparison with the work of earlier critics like Miles.

TABLE NINE

Percentage of Run-on Lines in Some Representative
Jonson Poems in Pentameter Couplets

	Date	Poem	Approximate Percentage of Run-on Lines	Total Number of Lines in Poem
I	1599	Dedication to Thomas Palmer (Uc.1)	50	31
	1599	Epistle. To Elizabeth, Countesse of Rutland (XII)	20	92
	1603	Panegyre (Uc.15)	33	162
II	1603	Epigram xlv	15	12
Before	1612	Epigram ci	20	42
"		Epigram cxxxiii	20	196
"		To Penshurst (II)	20	102
"		To Heaven (XV)	15	26
III				
After	1612	To Sacvile (15)	45	164
"		Elegie (40)	25	122
?		Elegie (41) (Donne)	35	70
After	1612	Elegie (42)	40	50
"		Elegie (43)	20	22
"		Elegie (44)	45	88
	1623	Execration upon Vulcan (45)	20	216
IV	1625	Elegie on Katherine Ogle (Uc.49)	35	40
	1631	An Expostulation with Inigo Jones (Uc.56)	30	104
	1633	Elegie on my Muse. Eupheme (86.9)	30	228

TABLE TEN

Dates of Jonson's Works[a]

	Date	Plays	Masques	Poems	*Other*
I	1597	Isle Dogs			Bacon *Essays*
	1598	Case Alt.		Uc.1	BJ jailed, RC
		EMI			
	1599	EMO		xl, XII, 27	Globe opens
	1600	CR		Uc.2-7	
	1601	Po.		cviii, X, XI	*Hamlet*
				Uc.8-13	
	1602			cxx, pre-xxii	
II	1603	Sej.	E. Althorp	xlv, Uc.14-15	James I
				post-iv,	
				lxvii, lxxiv, II	
	1604			v, xxxv, xxxvi,	*Malcontent*
				Uc.16	
	1605	E.Ho	Blackness	xliii, lx, lxiii	K. *Lear*
				lxvi, cxxxii,	Gunpowder
					Plot
				post-xcii, civ	post-*Art Po.*
	1606	Volp.	Hymenaei	xxvii, xxxii, xxxiii,	
				li, post-xci, xcvii,	
				III, V,	
	1607			post-cxxxiii,	
				approx. lxxxv, lxxxvi	
	1608		Beauty	lxiv	Milton b.
			Hadd. M.		
	1609	SW	Queens	cx, cxi, cxxx,	*Faithful Shep.*
				Uc.26, post-XIII	
	1610	Alch.	P. Hen. Bar.		
	1611	Cat.	Oberon	cxxix, XIV,	A. V. Bible
			Love Freed	Uc.27, 28, 29	Donne, *Anniv.*
					Tempest
	1612		Love Rest.	approx-I	BJ in France
III	1613		Ch. Tilt	Uc.31, 32,	*Duchess Malfi*
			Irish M.	post-48	
	1614	BF		16, 26, Uc.34, 36	
	1615		Gold. Age		
	1616	D.isA.	Merc. Vind.	33, 34, pre-	BJ's 1st folio
			Christmas	Charis 4, Uc.37	Shakespeare d.
					BJ's pension
	1617		Vis. Del.		
			Lov. M. Men		
	1618		Pleas. Virt.	pre- 5, 90, Charis	BJ trip to Scot.
			Wales	7, Uc.38	Drummond, *Cv.*

1619			10, 11, 14, Uc.39	
1620		*News*	22	
		Pan's An.		
1621		*Gypsies*	21, 30, 53	*Anat. Mel.*
1622		*Augurs*	Uc.40	*New Way..Old Debts*
1623		*Time Vin.*	45, 50, approx-Charis 1, Uc.41, 42	fire of BJ mss.
1624		*Nep. Tri.*	49, Uc. 44	Apollo rm.
		Owls	pre-15	
1625		*Fort. Isles*	Uc.45	

IV				Charles I
1626	*SN*			
1627			37, Uc.47, 48	
1628			62, post-61	BJ stroke
1629	*NI*		17, 64, 65, 66, 72 Uc.49, 50, 51, 53	
1630			67, 68, 69, 70, Uc.54	
1631		*Lov. Tri.*	60, 73, 79, 85	Dryden b.
		Chlor.	Uc.56, 57, 58	
1632	*ML*		74, 75, 76, 77, Uc.60	*Love's Sacri.*
1633	*TT*	*E. Welb.*	84, 86, pre-80	
1634		*E. Bols.*	Uc.61	*Comus*
1635			81, Uc 63.	*Lady Pleasure*
1636			Uc.64	
1637				BJ dies

---

a Dates for this table are compiled from H & S; Bentley, *Stage*; Orgel, *Complete Masques*; and E. K. Chambers, *The Elizabethan Stage*, 4 vols (Oxford: Clarendon, 1923).

TABLE ELEVEN

Verbal Ratios in Three Jonson Odes

Desmond Ode (27)	Verbs	Descriptive Adjectives	Nouns
Stanza One	11	8	22
(13 lines, 45 feet)			
Stanza Five	10	9	14
Sidney Ode (XIV)			
Stanza One	9	2	6
(10 lines, 27 feet)			
Stanza Five	10	0	7
Stanza Six	6	1	11
Cary-Morison Ode (72)			
Stanza One	10	6	15
(10 lines, 32 feet)			
Stanza Eleven	10	2	13
Stanza Six	19	1	18
(12 lines, 4. feet)			
Stanza Twelve	12	4	18

BIBLIOGRAPHY

Arnold, Judd
    1969   "Lovewit's Triumph and Jonsonian Morality: A Reading of *The Alchemist*", *Criticism*, 11, 151-66.
Babb, Lawrence
    1951   *The Elizabethan Malady: A Study of Melancholia in English Literature from 1580 to 1642* (East Lansing: Michigan State).
Bamborough, J. B.
    1970   *Ben Jonson* (London: Hutchinson).
Barish, Jonas A.
    1960   *Ben Jonson and the Language of Prose Comedy* (Cambridge, Mass.: Harvard).
    1963   *Ben Jonson: A Collection of Critical Essays (Twentieth Century Views)* (Englewood Cliffs: Prentice-Hall).
Baum, Helen W.
    1947   *The Satiric and the Didactic in Ben Jonson's Comedies* (Chapel Hill: University of North Carolina).
Beaurline, Lester
    1966   "The Selective Principle in Jonson's Shorter Poems", *Criticism*, 8, 64-74.
    1969   "Ben Jonson and the Illusion of Completeness", *PMLA*, 84, 51-59.
Bentley, Gerald E.
    1941-68   *The Jacobean and Caroline Stage*. 7 vols. (Oxford: Clarendon).
Bevington, David
    1962   *From "Mankind" to Marlowe: Growth of Structure in the Popular Drama of Tudor England* (Cambridge, Mass.: Harvard)
    1968   *Tudor Drama and Politics: A Critical Approach to Topical Meaning* (Cambridge, Mass.: Harvard)
Bredvold, Louis I.
    1950   "The Rise of English Classicism: A Study in Methodology", *Comparative Literature*, 2, 235-68.
Browne, Sir Thomas
    1967   *Religio Medici* in *The Prose of Sir Thomas Browne*, ed. by Norman Endicott (Garden City: Doubleday).
Bryant, Joseph A., Jr.
    1954   "*Catiline* and the Nature of Jonson's Tragic Fable", *PMLA*, 69, 265-77.

1964   *"A Tale of a Tub:* Jonson's Comedy of the Human Condition",
        Renaissance Papers, 1963 (Southeast Renaissance Conference),
        95-105.

Bullett, Gerald
1956   "Drinke to Me Only", *Times Literary Supplement*, June 1, 329.

Bush, Douglas
1962   *English Literature in the Earlier Seventeenth Century, 1600-1660.* 2nd
        ed. (*Oxford History of English Literature,* 5) (Oxford: Clarendon).

Campbell, Oscar J.
1938   *Comicall Satyre and Shakespeare's "Troilus and Cressida"* (San
        Marino: Huntington Library).

Chambers, Sir Edmund K.
1923   *The Elizabethan Stage,* 4 vols. (Oxford: Clarendon).

Champion, Larry S.
1964   "The Comic Intention of Jonson's *The New Inn*", *Western Humanities
        Review,* 18, 66-74.
1967   *Ben Jonson's Dotages: A Reconsideration of the Late Plays* (Lexing-
        ton: University of Kentucky).

Cope, Jackson I.
1965   "*Bartholomew Fair* as Blasphemy", *Renaissance Drama,* 8, 127-52.

Craig, Martha
1967   "The Secret Wit of Spenser's Language", in *Elizabethan Poetry:
        Modern Essays in Criticism,* ed. by Paul J. Alpers (New York:
        Oxford), 447-72.

Croll, Morris
1966   *Style, Rhetoric and Rhythm: Essays,* ed. by J. Max Patrick *et. al.*
        (Princeton: Princeton).

Cubeta, Paul M.
1958   "' A Celebration of Charis': An Evaluation of Jonsonian Poetic
        Strategy", *ELH,* 25, 163-80.
1963   "A Jonsonian Ideal: 'To Penshurst'", *Philological Quarterly,* 42, 14-
        24.

Curtius, Ernst
1963   *European Literature and the Latin Middle Ages,* translated by W. R.
        Trask (New York: Harper & Row).

Danby, John F.
1949   "Poets on Fortune's Hill: Literature and Society, 1580-1610", *The
        Cambridge Journal,* 2, 195-211.

Davenant, William
1908   "Preface to *Gondibert* (1650)", in *Critical Essays of the Seventeenth
        Century,* ed. by Joel E. Spingarn (Oxford: Clarendon), 2, 1-53.

Davis, Joe Lee
1967   *The Sons of Ben: Jonsonian Comedy in Caroline England* (Detroit:
        Wayne State).

Dekker, Thomas
1953   *Satiromastix* in *Dramatic Works,* ed. by Fredson Bowers (Cambridge:
        Cambridge), 1, 299-395.

Dessen, Alan C.
1971   *Jonson's Moral Comedy* (Evanston: Northwestern).

Doran, Madeleine
　　1954　*Endeavors of Art: A Study of Form in Elizabethan Drama* (Madison: University of Wisconsin).
Drummond of Hawthornden, William
　　1619　"Ben Jonson's Conversations with William Drummond of Hawthornden", in Herford and Simpson, 1, 128-77.
Dryden, John
　　1956-71　*The Works of John Dryden*, ed. by H. T. Swedenberg, *et. al.* 17 vols. (Berkeley: University of California).
Duncan, Douglas
　　1970　"A Guide to *The New Inn*", *Essays in Criticism*, 20, 311-26.
Eliot, T. S.
　　1956　"Ben Jonson", in *Essays on Elizabethan Drama* (New York: Harcourt Brace), 65-82, c. 1932.
Elliott, Robert C.
　　1960　*The Power of Satire: Magic, Ritual, Art* (Princeton: Princeton).
Ellis-Fermor, Una
　　1965　*The Jacobean Drama: An Interpretation*, 5th ed. (London: Methuen), c. 1936.
Empson, William
　　1953　*Seven Types of Ambiguity*, 3rd ed. (Norfolk, Conn.: New Directions), c. 1930.
　　1969-70　"*The Alchemist*", *The Hudson Review*, 22, 595-608.
Enck, John J.
　　1957　*Jonson and the Comic Truth* (Madison: University of Wisconsin).
English, Hubert M., Jr.
　　1955　"Prosody and Meaning in Ben Jonson's Poems", Unpublished dissertation, Yale University.
Evans, Willa M.
　　1965　*Ben Jonson and Elizabethan Music* (New York: Da Capo), c. 1929.
Fike, Francis
　　1969　"Ben Jonson's 'On My First Sonne'", *Gordon Review*, 2, 205-20.
French, John T.
　　1968　"Ben Jonson: His Aesthetic of Relief", *Texas Studies in Literature and Language*, 10, 161-75.
Furniss, W. Todd
　　1958　*Ben Jonson's Masques* in *Three Studies in the Renaissance*, ed. by B. C. Nangle (*Yale Studies in English*, 138) (New Haven: Yale), 97-179.
Gibbons, Brian
　　1968　*Jacobean City Comedy: A Study of Satiric Plays by Jonson, Marston, and Middleton* (London: Hart-Davis).
Gordon, D. J.
　　1945　"*Hymenaei*: Ben Jonson's Masque of Union", *Journal of the Warburg and Courtauld Institutes*, 8, 107-45.
Greene, Thomas M.
　　1970　"Ben Jonson and the Centered Self", *Studies in English Literature*, 10, 325-48.

Gum, Coburn
1969 *The Aristophanic Comedies of Ben Jonson: A Comparative Study of Jonson and Aristophanes* (*Studies in English Literature*, 40) (The Hague: Mouton).
Harbage, Alfred
1941 *Shakespeare's Audience* (New York: Columbia)
1952 *Shakespeare and the Rival Traditions* (New York: Macmillan).
Hardison, O. B., Jr.
1962 *The Enduring Monument: A Study of the Idea of Praise in Renaissance Literary Theory and Practice* (Chapel Hill: University of North Carolina).
Hart, Jeffrey
1962-63 "Ben Jonson's Good Society", *Modern Age*, 7, 61-68.
Hawkins, Harriett
1966 "The Idea of the Theater in Jonson's *The New Inn*", *Renaissance Drama*, 9, 205-26.
1967 "Jonson's Use of Traditional Dream Theory in *The Vision of Delight*", *Modern Philology*, 64, 285-92.
Heffner, Ray L, Jr.
1954 "Unifying Symbols in the Comedy of Ben Jonson", in *English Stage Comedy*, ed. by W. K. Wimsatt, Jr. (*English Institute Essays*) (New York: Columbia), 74-97.
Held, George
1970 "Jonson's Pindaric on Friendship", *Concerning Poetry*, 3, 29-41.
Herford, C. H. and Simpson, Percy and Evelyn, eds.
1925-52 *Ben Jonson*, 11 vols. (Oxford: Clarendon).
Hibbard, G. R.
1956 "The Country House Poem in the Seventeenth Century", *Journal of the Warburg and Courtauld Institutes*, 19, 159-74.
Hollander, John
1961 "Introduction", *Ben Jonson* (New York: Dell), 9-26.
Horsman, E. A.
1956 "Drinke to Me Only", *Times Literary Supplement*, June 8, 345.
Hudson, Hoyt H.
1947 *The Epigram in the English Renaissance* (Princeton: Princeton).
Hunter, William B., Jr., ed.
1968 *The Complete Poetry of Ben Jonson* (New York: W. W. Norton).
Jackson, Gabriele Bernhard
1968 *Vision and Judgment in Ben Jonson's Drama* (*Yale Studies in English*, 166) (New Haven: Yale).
Johnston, George B.
1945 *Ben Jonson: Poet* (New York: Columbia).
Jones, Robert C.
1967 "The Satirist's Retirement in Jonson's 'Apologetical Dialogue'", *ELH*, 34, 447-67.
Jonson, Benjamin. See editions of Herford and Simpson and of Hunter.
Kaplan, Joel H.
1970 "Dramatic and Moral Energy in Ben Jonson's *Bartholomew Fair*", *Renaissance Drama*, n.s. 3, 137-56.

Kay, W. David
  1970 "The Shaping of Ben Jonson's Career: A Reexamination of Facts and Problems", *Modern Philology*, 67, 224-37.
  1971 "The Christian Wisdom of Ben Jonson's 'On My First Sonne'", *Studies in English Literature*, 11, 125-36.
Kernan, Alvin
  1959 *The Cankered Muse: Satire of the English Renaissance (Yale Studies in English*, 142) (New Haven: Yale).
  1965 *The Plot of Satire* (New Haven: Yale).
Kerrigan, William
  1973 "Ben Jonson Full of Shame and Scorn", *Studies in the Literary Imagination*, 6, 199-217.
Knights, L. C.
  1937 *Drama and Society in the Age of Jonson* (London: Chatto & Windus).
Knoll, Robert E.
  1964 *Ben Jonson's Plays: An Introduction* (Lincoln: University of Nebraska).
Leavis, F. R.
  1963 "The Line of Wit", *Revaluation: Tradition and Development in English Poetry* (New York: W. W. Norton), 10-36, c. 1947.
Levin, Richard
  1965 "The Structure of *Bartholomew Fair* ", *PMLA*, 80, 172-79.
MacLean, Hugh
  1964 "Ben Jonson's Poems: Notes on the Ordered Society", in *Essays in English Literature from the Renaissance to the Victorian Age Presented to A. S. P. Woodhouse*, ed. by M. MacLure and F. W. Watt (Toronto: University of Toronto), 43-68.
Maddison, Carol
  1960 *Apollo and the Nine: A History of the Ode* (London: Routledge & Kegan Paul).
Marotti, Arthur F.
  1972 "All about Jonson's Poetry", *ELH*, 39, 208-37.
Martz, Louis L.
  1954 *The Poetry of Meditation (Yale Studies in English*, 125) (New Haven: Yale).
Meagher, John C.
  1966 *Method and Meaning in Jonson's Masques* (Notre Dame: University of Notre Dame).
Miles, Josephine
  1951 *The Continuity of Poetic Language: Studies in English Poetry from the 1540's to the 1940's* (Berkeley: University of California).
  1957 *Eras and Modes in English Poetry* (Berkeley: University of California).
Milic, Louis
  1967 *A Quantitative Approach to the Style of Jonathan Swift* (The Hague: Mouton).
Miner, Earl
  1971 *The Cavalier Mode from Jonson to Cotton* (Princeton: Princeton).

Nichols, J. G.
1969   *The Poetry of Ben Jonson* (London: Routledge & Kegan Paul).
Orgel, Stephen
1965   *The Jonsonian Masque* (Cambridge, Mass.: Harvard).
1968   "To Make Boards Speak: Inigo Jones' Stage and the Jonsonian Masque", *Renaissance Drama*, n. s. 1, 121-52.
1969   *Ben Jonson: The Complete Masques* (New Haven: Yale).
Parfitt, George A. E.
1968   "The Poetry of Ben Jonson", *Essays in Criticism*, 18, 18-31.
1969   "Ethical Thought and Ben Jonson's Poetry", *Studies in English Literature*, 9, 123-34.
1971   "Compromise Classicism: Language and Rhythm in Ben Jonson's Poetry", *Studies in English Literature*, 11, 109-23.
Partridge, Edward B.
1958   *The Broken Compass: A Study of the Major Comedies of Ben Jonson* (London: Chatto & Windus).
Paulson, Ronald
1967   *The Fictions of Satire* (Baltimore: Johns Hopkins).
Putney, Rufus D.
1966   "This So Subtile Sport: Some Aspects of Jonson's Epigrams", *University of Colorado Studies* (*Series in Language and Literature*, 10), 37-56.
Sackton, Alexander H.
1948   *Rhetoric as a Dramatic Language in Ben Jonson* (New York: Columbia).
Savage, James E.
1962   "Ben Jonson in Ben Jonson's Plays", *University of Mississippi Studies in English*, 3, 1-17.
Schelling, Felix
1898   *Ben Jonson and the Classical School* (Baltimore: Modern Language Publications).
Shafer, Robert
1966   *The English Ode to 1660: An Essay in Literary History* (New York: Haskell House).
Sidney, Sir Philip
1963   "An Apologie for Poetrie" in *English Literary Criticism: The Renaissance*, ed. by O. B. Hardison, Jr. (New York: Appleton-Century-Crofts), 99-146.
Sinanoglou, Leah
1973   "The Politics of Playfulness", unpublished essay.
Spanos, William V.
1969   "The Real Toad in the Jonsonian Garden: Resonance in the Non-dramatic Poetry", *Journal of English and Germanic Philology*, 68, 1-23.
Steese, Peter
1962   "Jonson's 'A Song'", *Explicator*, 21, No. 31.
Stone, Lawrence
1965   *The Crisis of the Aristocracy, 1558-1641* (Oxford: Clarendon).

Stroud, Theodore
1947 "Ben Jonson and Father Thomas Wright", *ELH*, 14, 274-82.
Summers, Joseph H.
1970 *The Heirs of Donne and Jonson* (London: Chatto & Windus).
Swinburne, Algernon
1889 *Ben Jonson* (London: Chatto & Windus).
Talbert, Earnest W.
1946 "The Interpretation of Jonson's Courtly Spectacles", *PMLA*, 61, 454-73.
Thomson, Patricia
1952 "The Literature of Patronage, 1580-1630", *Essays in Criticism*, 2, 267-84.
Townsend, Freda L.
1947 *Apologie for Bartholomew Fayre: The Art of Jonson's Comedies* (New York: Modern Language Association).
Trimpi, Wesley
1962 *Ben Jonson's Poems: A Study of the Plain Style* (Palo Alto: Stanford).
Van Deusen, Marshall
1957 "Criticism and Ben Jonson's 'To Celia'", *Essays in Criticism*, 7, 95-103.
Walker, Ralph S.
1933-34 "Ben Jonson's Lyric Poetry", *Criterion*, 13, 430-48.
Wallerstein, Ruth
1950 "The Laureate Hearse: The Funeral Elegy and Seventeenth-Century Aesthetic", *Studies in Seventeenth-Century Poetic* (Madison: University of Wisconsin), 1-150.
Walton, Geoffrey
1955 *Metaphysical to Augustan: Studies in Tone and Sensibility in the Seventeenth Century* (London: Bowes & Bowes).
Wedgwood, C. V.
1950 *Seventeenth Century English Literature* (Home University Library) (London: Oxford).
Whipple, T. K.
1925 *Martial and the English Epigram from Sir Thomas Wyatt to Ben Jonson* (*University of California Publications in Modern Philology*, 10) (Berkeley: University of California), 279-414.
Williams, Raymond
1968 "Pastoral and Counter-Pastoral", *Critical Quarterly*, 10, 277-90.
Wilson, Gayle Edward
1968 "Jonson's Use of the Bible and the Great Chain of Being in 'To Penshurst'", *Studies in English Literature*, 8, 77-90.
Wilson, Edmund
1948 "Morose Ben Jonson", *The Triple Thinkers* (New York: Oxford), 213-32.
Winters, Yvor
1939 "The Sixteenth-Century Lyric in England: A Critical and Historical Reinterpretation", *Poetry*, 53, 258-72, 320-35; 54, 35-51; reprinted in *Elizabethan Poetry: Modern Essays in Criticism*, ed. by Paul J. Alpers (New York: Oxford, 1967), 93-125.

1959   "Poetic Styles, Old and New", in *Four Poets on Poetry*, ed. by D. C.
        Allen (Baltimore: Johns Hopkins), 44-75.

Wykes, David
1969   "Ben Jonson's 'Chast Booke' – The *Epigrammes*", *Renaissance and
        Modern Studies*, 13, 76-87.

INDEX

Jonson's poems are listed separately in alphabetical order by the first word of the poem's title. Poem titles are in italics. Jonson's plays and masques are listed under the general heading for "Jonson, Ben."